The Short Story after Apartheid
Thinking with Form in
South African Literature

English Association Monographs: English at the Interface

Series Editors
Claire Jowitt, University of East Anglia
Jennifer Richards, Newcastle University

Editorial Board
Martin Eve, Birkbeck, University of London
Clare Lees, King's College, London
Gail Marshall, University of Reading
Anshuman Mondal, University of East Anglia
Sinead Morrissey, Newcastle University
Rick Rylance, Director, School of Advanced Studies, University of London
Lyndsey Stonebridge, University of Birmingham
Greg Walker, University of Edinburgh

Established in 1906, The English Association is the oldest established association in the UK for all those interested in English at all levels, from primary to higher education. Its aim is to further knowledge, understanding and enjoyment of the English language and its literatures and to foster good practice in its teaching and learning at all levels. In 2006, the English Association launched a new series – *English Association Monographs*, which is now published by Liverpool University Press.

English Association Monographs invites submissions that explore or represent English Studies at the interface with other languages, cultures, professions and disciplines from the medieval period to the present day. It also welcomes submissions that reflect on or contribute to interdisciplinary conversations, or which are the product of thinking across disciplines or across sectors, or which explore the intersections between English Studies, Digital Humanities, and the new technologies of any period. The General Editors and the Editorial Board will work with authors to produce books that are written clearly and eloquently, and represent the best and most exciting new work in English Language and Literature.

Also in this series:
Decolonising the Conrad Canon by Alice M. Kelly

Keeping the Ancient Way: Aspects of the Life and Work of Henry Vaughan (1621–1695) by Robert Wilcher

John Keats' Medical Notebook: Text, Context, and Poems by Hrileena Ghosh

Tyranny and Usurpation: The New Prince and Lawmaking Violence in Early Modern Drama by Doyeeta Majumder

Reimagining Urban Nature: Literary Imaginaries for Posthuman Cities by Chantelle Bayes

GRAHAM K. RIACH

The Short Story after Apartheid

Thinking with Form in
South African Literature

LIVERPOOL UNIVERSITY PRESS
THE ENGLISH ASSOCIATION

First published 2023 by
Liverpool University Press
4 Cambridge Street
Liverpool
L69 7ZU

Copyright © 2023 Graham K. Riach

Graham K. Riach has asserted the right to be identified as the author of this book in accordance with the Copyright, Designs and Patents Act 1988.

All rights reserved. No part of this book may be reproduced, stored in a retrieval system, or transmitted, in any form or by any means, electronic, mechanical, photocopying, recording, or otherwise, without the prior written permission of the publisher.

British Library Cataloguing-in-Publication data
A British Library CIP record is available

ISBN 978-1-83764-470-4

Typeset by Carnegie Book Production, Lancaster
Printed and bound by CPI Group (UK) Ltd, Croydon CR0 4YY

Contents

Acknowledgements vii
List of Illustrations ix

Introduction: Long Story Short 1
1 Nadine Gordimer: Past, Present, and Future 47
2 A Moment's Monument: Counter-Monuments in Ivan Vladislavić 75
3 Zoë Wicomb and the 'Problem of Class' 103
4 Phaswane Mpe's Aesthetics of Brooding 137
5 Spatial Form in Henrietta Rose-Innes 161
Conclusion: Small Medium at Large 203

Bibliography 213
Index 237

Acknowledgements

My heartfelt thanks to Chris Warnes, whose clarity of thought, generosity of spirit, and good sense gave this project its best possible start. Drew Milne, Priyamvada Gopal, Malachi Macintosh, and Tim Cribb have all sharpened my thinking and broadened my horizons. Without the support of the Department of English Literature at Glasgow University I would never have met Willy Maley and Vassiliki Kolocotroni, whose critical acuity and friendship I value greatly. I acknowledge financial assistance from the Arts & Humanities Research Council, Emmanuel College, the Cambridge University Faculty of English, and the Smuts fund.

Ivan Vladislavić and Henrietta Rose-Innes were both extremely generous with their time in meeting me and responding to emails. Ed Charlton has been a great friend and collaborator throughout this project as well as a sharp, perceptive reader. Dennis Walder lent his experience and warm support to my work at a time when it was much needed, and I am very grateful. Peter D. McDonald has been a model of intellectual integrity and a source of great conversation at the (other) Cape of Good Hope. David Attwell has shared with me his deep knowledge of South African literature and in so doing greatly improved this book. Elleke Boehmer has offered astute scholarly insight and sound advice. Rob Turner has been both a brilliant interlocutor and a generous reader of my work. My time at Oxford was greatly enriched by Michelle Kelly, a great mind and an ideal colleague. Ben Higgins brought both moral support and much-needed practical help. Helen Small gave sage counsel and granted walks with Titus. At the University of Amsterdam, Carrol Clarkson was a wonderful colleague and friend, and I thank her for bringing me into a department where I met the incomparable Nick Carr, Rudolph Glitz, Joyce Goggin, Kristine Johanson, Ben Moore, and many others. Christabel Scaife and the anonymous reviewers at Liverpool

University Press were wonderful to work with and improved this book in ways that may not be apparent from its current form. For help reading drafts, discussing aspects of this project, and tracking down source materials, I would like to thank Alexander D'Angelo, Alice Bamford, Rita Barnard, Santanu Das, Michael Gardiner, Nick Gaskill, Rob Gaylard, Josie Gill, Lucy Graham, Patrick Hayes, Imke van Heerden, Diana Leca, Robert Macfarlane, Kate McLoughlin, Ankhi Mukherjee, Tinashe Mushakavanhu, the staff at NELM, Thando Njovane, Josie O'Donoghue, Eleni Phillipou, Katie Reid, Corinna Russell, Hedley Twidle, Jennifer Upton, Andrew van der Vlies, Claire Wilkinson, and Andy Wimbush.

The librarians and administrative staff at the Cambridge English Faculty, Emmanuel College, and the Oxford Faculty of English Language and Literature made it possible for me to focus on writing this book, and more than that, have been extremely helpful and kind.

Thanks to graduate students Ali Hazel, Gavin Herbertson, Martha Swift, Caitlin Talbot, and Eileen Ying, whose work I supervised but who in turn shaped my thinking and methods.

If I were to start listing the friends whose company has made writing this book the pleasure it has been I would never be done, but thank you all in Brussels, Cambridge, Glasgow, London, Oxford, and further afield.

All my love to Rhoda, Fraser, Calum, Amy, Olly, Hamish & Eilidh, and Astrid.

Illustrations

1. Cover of *Landfall: A New Zealand Quarterly*, 176. Reproduced by kind permission of *Landfall*. Photo of graffiti in the Cape Town area by Rene Weideman.   115
2. Cover of *The End of a Regime? An Anthology: Scottish–South African Writing Against Apartheid*, edited by Brian Filling and Susan Stuart, 1991. Cover art by Bhekisani Manyoni.   116
3. Cover of *The One That Got Away* by Zoë Wicomb, 2008 © UMUZI, an imprint of Penguin Random House South Africa.   117
4. The Doulton Fountain and Templeton carpet factory, Glasgow © MSeses / Wikimedia Commons / CC BY-SA 4.0.   128
5. The South Africa panel of the Doulton Fountain, author's photograph.   130
6. Statue of a miner at the Clocktower Mall, Cape Town, author's photograph.   182

Introduction
Long Story Short

The trick is to find a tiny way into a huge subject.[1]

Amy Hempel

The history of South African literature is, in most accounts, largely that of the novel. Guides to the country's literary production, whether in the form of university syllabuses or online listicles, often feature the same titles: Alan Paton's *Cry, the Beloved Country*, Nadine Gordimer's *The Conservationist*, J.M. Coetzee's *Disgrace*, Phaswane Mpe's *Welcome to Our Hillbrow*, or any number of other canonical – which is not to say universally appreciated – suggestions.[2] What you probably won't find, however, are short stories. And yet the South African short story is one of the country's most extraordinary literary achievements. In 2010 Craig MacKenzie claimed that it is 'in the genre of short fiction that South African literature has most consistently excelled', even suggesting that 'the form is destined to play a major role in bodying forth South Africa's future in imaginative terms'.[3] This book is, in

---

1 Michael Schumacher and Amy Hempel, 'Amy Hempel', in *Reasons to Believe: New Voices in American Fiction*, ed. Michael Schumacher (New York: St Martins, 1988), pp. 28–45 (p. 31).
2 See, for example, Imraan Coovadia and Eve Gerber, 'The Best South African Fiction', *Five Books*, 2011 <https://fivebooks.com/best-books/south-african-fiction-imraan-coovadia/> (accessed 6 September 2022). Even *The Cambridge History of South African Literature* devotes only 22 of 877 pages to the topic.
3 Gareth Cornwell, Dirk Klopper, and Craig MacKenzie (eds), *The Columbia*

the first instance, an attempt to expand on these claims by arguing that the form occupies an important, if largely uncharted, place in post-apartheid literature. By bringing these diminutive texts into clearer view, I further hope to make the case that greater attention to form is essential to understanding the social purchase of writing after apartheid. The short story, I suggest, offers writers and readers a new way to think about the restless pull between formal and extra-formal concerns in a changed political present.

The contours of the present moment, and so what it means to write 'after' apartheid, are worth looking at more closely, particularly as it is unclear what exactly has changed and when that change occurred. The most obvious answer to 'when?' would be 1994, the year of the first democratic elections. However, the transition from apartheid to what has followed has been one of gradual change that in hindsight looks more like an analogue shift than a digital one. Contact between the South African government and Nelson Mandela began during the 1980s, with the pace of change quickening in 1990 through the unbanning of the African National Congress (ANC), the Pan African Congress (PAC), the South African Communist Party (SACP), and various other political organisations. The Convention for a Democratic South Africa (CODESA) talks in the early 1990s – which included drafting the new constitution – and the Multiparty Negotiating Forum that followed were both important steps towards the formation of a post-apartheid state. Even 1994 did not mark a clean break, though, with many of the oppressive structures, societal ills, and government officials of the apartheid period remaining in place. The intervening years have seen great societal shifts – Christopher Warnes draws particular attention to 'the Truth and Reconciliation Commission, the Land Reforms Commission, the Commission on Gender Equality, the Human Rights Commission, the Employment Equity Bill, and the Reconstruction and Development Plan' – but the long-awaited societal transformation has, for many, been too slow and too partial.[4] Perhaps in response to dissatisfaction with the rate of change, after nearly thirty years of ANC rule, the results of elections

---

Guide to South African Literature in English since 1945 (New York: Columbia University Press, 2010), pp. 176, 181.

4 Christopher Warnes, 'The Making and Unmaking of History in Ivan Vladislavić's *Propaganda by Monuments and Other Stories*', *MFS: Modern Fiction Studies*, 46.1 (2000), 67–89 (pp. 71–72).

in South Africa from 2016 to 2021 raise questions about their performances in 2024 and future elections, suggesting that a new political reality may be on the horizon.[5]

The difficulty of marking a clean historical break between the apartheid and post-apartheid eras is matched by the challenge of separating the country's literature into neat periods. Harry Garuba describes the fraught process of literary periodisation:

> Even at the most propitious of times, when a convergence of historical events and a creative ferment of the imagination appear to announce their evidence, literary periodisation remains a messy business [...] As boundaries demarcating neat categorisations, therefore, literary periods and schools are as porous as they come. As markers of general trends, however, they retain some usefulness, more like provisional maps, open-ended rather than closed, always inviting revision [...][6]

The shift from apartheid to what came after offers one such coming together of literary endeavour and historical circumstance, but it would be wise to heed Garuba's warning that literary periodisation is a compromised and tentative process. As much as a strong caesura between apartheid-era and post-apartheid literature would be critically convenient, such a distinction is, in practice, untenable. As will become apparent in the chapters that follow, although the authors I analyse write after apartheid, to do so often means to write in full knowledge of the past. One explanation for why the concerns of apartheid-era writing remain so immediate to these authors is given in an interview by Ivan Vladislavić: when asked if he was a post-apartheid writer, he replied: 'I might be in the sense that I write after apartheid, or the beginnings of the end of it, but I'm not a post-apartheid person – not in terms of my history.'[7] Each of the writers to whom I devote a chapter in this book spent a considerable period of their early lives under apartheid:

---

5 For example, in the 2021 local elections, the ANC vote dipped to 46%, the first time it had fallen below 50% in South Africa's democratic history.
6 Harry Garuba, 'The Unbearable Lightness of Being: Re-Figuring Trends in Recent Nigerian Poetry', *English in Africa*, 32.1 (2005), 51–72 (p. 51).
7 Christopher Thurman, 'Places Elsewhere, Then and Now: Allegory "Before" and "After" South Africa's Transition?', *English Studies in Africa*, 53.1 (2010), 91–103 (p. 91).

Vladislavić was born in 1957, Zoë Wicomb in 1948, Phaswane Mpe in 1970, and Henrietta Rose-Innes in 1971. Nadine Gordimer, with whose work I begin this study, lived from 1923, well before apartheid began, until 2014, quite some time after it ended. Given the overlap between these authors' lives and the apartheid years, it is unsurprising that their writing would be influenced by their experience during that period, and, as writing is as much a response to existing modes of writing as it is to historical events, by the kinds of literary response those years provoked.

However, even writers of the 'born free' generation live with the daily reality that although apartheid as a system of government has been weeded out, its roots are long, maintaining a tenacious grip on contemporary life. To show the continuities of literary concern between the apartheid and post-apartheid periods, while identifying developing trends, in four of my five chapters I begin with a story first published before 1990. The decision to analyse stories from the late 1980s onwards, albeit with a weighting towards more recent texts, is an attempt to represent the trajectories of individual authors while showing their contribution to, and embeddedness within, the gradually evolving post-apartheid present. This issue is further complicated in that a story's date of composition sometimes differs from that of its publication, and multiple variants of the same story are often in circulation in different magazines, collections, and anthologies, accreting paratextual cues and lures across multiple printings, something I address across the following chapters. While including some stories that are not uncomplicatedly post-apartheid texts introduces a degree of historical untidiness, this is at least representative of the messy character of post-apartheid change. Further, the temporal complexity of the post-apartheid period, in which the past inhabits the present, has become one of post-apartheid literature's most important concerns, and is one that the authors I analyse all engage through the short story form.

In bringing a greater generic and formal concern to criticism of post-apartheid literature, *The Short Story after Apartheid* hopes to further understanding of the relationship between texts, readers, and the social world. This relationship is particularly at issue in South Africa, where the question of literature's perceived political agency (or lack of it) has strongly shaped both writerly practice and critical reception. As David Attwell and Derek Attridge observe, it was often a 'counterhegemonic, didactic version of literary studies that prevailed in the English-language academy during the apartheid period', and while criticism's political coordinates have somewhat shifted since then, it remains the case that the relationship between literary form and its material outsides is still central to many analyses of the country's literature.[8]

How the relationship between word and world should be conceived, however, remains at issue both in South Africa and in postcolonial analyses more broadly. Often, a deterministic or indexical understanding of form's relation to the social is put forward; that is, formal features are taken to be caused by social or political matters, and so can be read as indices or symptoms of them. For example, a fractured structure results from a fractured society, or a hybrid poetics is taken as the marker of societal mixity. Certainly, the conditions in which a text is composed will be one of a network of forces influencing its aesthetic characteristics, but an indexical model gives at best a partial picture of literature's role in the world. This book proposes that rather than indexing the world, form acts as a nimble interlocutor to social thought, offering readers an invitation to think with the text. Forms, in Jonathan Loesberg's words, are 'ways of arranging details so that we can see new significance', and short narratives bring with them horizons of generic expectation and formal arrangements that novels, poems, and plays rarely do.[9] This is not to say that short stories are somehow more formal than these other forms, but rather that they arrange details differently from them, and this allows for different modes of thought. As Terence Cave argues in *Thinking with Literature: Towards a Cognitive Criticism*, 'literary works make you think differently', as they have the 'capacity [...] to alter the cognitive environment of the reader in ways that are powerful, potentially disturbing, and not at all self-evident'.[10] I do not pursue the consequences of his position in a hard cognitivist direction, but rather

---

8 David Attwell and Derek Attridge, 'Introduction', in *The Cambridge History of South African Literature*, ed. David Attwell and Derek Attridge (Cambridge: Cambridge University Press, 2012), pp. 1–13 (p. 8). In terms of how the country's literary production remains shaped by the political urgency of the apartheid years, Michael Chapman notes as late as 2011 that 'books tangential to heavy politics, or even to local interest, have begun to receive national recognition'. Michael Chapman, *SA Lit: Beyond 2000* (Scottsville: University of KwaZulu-Natal Press, 2011), p. 1.

9 Jonathan Loesberg, *A Return to Aesthetics: Autonomy, Indifference, and Postmodernism* (Stanford, CA: Stanford University Press, 2005), p. 9.

10 Terence Cave, *Thinking with Literature: Towards a Cognitive Criticism* (Oxford: Oxford University Press, 2016), p. 5.

in the more general sense that the texts we read change us, and so gain some purchase on the world of which they are a part. I.A. Richards famously suggested that 'a book is a machine to think with', but what kind of device is a short story, and how it might catalyse our thinking about the world in which it circulates?[11]

Recognising literary form's capacity to shape our understanding of the world does not entail that each reader will come to the same conclusions. Rather, the experience of form is, at least in part, a mental projection in response to experiencing the work, a dynamic, evolving structure which can serve as a heuristic tool for conceptual or use-oriented thought, all while remaining irreducible to it. Form can, as Robert Kaufman suggests, serve as a

> mould or frame for the construction of conceptual thought [...] the formal and imaginative engine for new, experimental (because previously nonexistent) concepts: concepts that may bring obscured aspects of substantive social reality to light, or at least may provide the formal ability to do so.[12]

Kaufman's persuasive argument is quite closely focused on lyric poetry's capacity to make available the 'intellectual-emotional apparatus for accessing, and to that extent the social material of, the new'.[13] In exploring the heuristic potential of short stories, I want to suggest that they offer formal experiences that differ from those of the lyric poems Kaufman analyses, and so might hold the kernel of new modes of social thought. It must be stressed that I am not arguing that this is what these texts are *for*; they are far too slippery to be pinned to any single function. Rather, one of their 'affordances', to borrow a term from Caroline Levine, is to allow readers to think differently about the social world.[14] Neither is this to suggest a strong argument for art's political force. Whatever we might wish of art, it is only on rare occasions that

---

11 I.A. Richards, *Principles of Literary Criticism* (London: Kegan Paul, Trench, Tubner, 1924), p. 1.
12 Robert Kaufman, 'Everybody Hates Kant: Blakean Formalism and the Symmetries of Laura Moriarty', *MLQ: Modern Language Quarterly*, 61.1 (2000), 131–55 (p. 148).
13 Ibid., p. 148.
14 Caroline Levine, *Forms: Whole, Rhythm, Hierarchy, Network* (Princeton, NJ: Princeton University Press, 2015), p. 6

aesthetic experiences have direct and large-scale consequences for how the world works in practice. But if reading literature can effect any social change, it is surely through art's role in offering new ways to think, new understandings of the world, and perhaps even a spur to act differently. This is unlikely to lead to dramatic worldly consequences, but I hope that the readings I offer in the following chapters can suggest to others some of the ways short stories have allowed me to think differently, and so might serve as an example, or counter-example, for others.

One of the difficulties in turning to literature to gain such understanding is that the process offers no guarantees and rarely produces consistent results. Not only will different readers come to different kinds of insight in their encounters with texts, even the same reader may find a text's meaning changing on different encounters. Literature's role in co-producing knowledge cannot therefore be to provide consistently reproducible examples. Rather, it is one of literature's great assets as a heuristic device to offer a restless and dynamic foil to test our preconceptions against the experiences it offers. As a result it can cause us to explore our beliefs and assumptions, and perhaps revise them. In Michael Basseler's words, the kind of knowledge that literature gives us is 'tentative knowledge contingent on historical contexts, the author's belief system, and the reader as interpreter and co-constructor of meaning'.[15] The affordances of short stories are in part a product of texts but they are also informed by acts of reading, and the kinds of insight that can be gained are the result of the mutual shaping resistances of these two forces. Literature pushes back, just as we push back at it, and in this process we explore our conception of the world. The experience is not like that of a franking machine impressing the same details and design onto the blank surface of the reader, but is rather something harder to grasp in metaphor. Perhaps a recurrent neural network in which recursive, iterative operations occur between readers and texts, with inputs and outputs informing one another in a temporally dynamic manner. This interaction is processual and to some extent unpredictable. To draw again from Kaufman, form is 'a fashioning that is occurring now [...] an ongoing and foundational practice calling forth constant (re)projection of form, thereby contributing to the possibilities of critical thought and agency'.[16] Let us say that the outcomes of the meetings between texts and readers

---

15 Michael Basseler, *An Organon of Life Knowledge: Genres and Functions of the Short Story in North America* (Bielefeld: Transcript, 2019), p. 64.
16 Kaufman, 'Everybody Hates Kant', p. 155.

are in some way probabilistic: there will likely be trends or similarities in the readings that emerge, but there are also surprising deviations from the mean, original readings that realise an unthought aspect of a text, and in so doing can shape the possibilities of interpretation more broadly. Short stories in South Africa since apartheid's end, their formal properties, their recurring preoccupations, the horizon of generic expectation readers bring to them, and the singular reading experiences they allow, together offer a resource with which to think through the changes and continuities of this turbulent period.

Any mention of readers in the context of South African literature requires some critical reflection. Writing, as I do, from within the Western academy risks portraying my readings as somehow normative. I hope to make clear throughout that I do not assume my own position to be that of the general reader. Each reader will bring with them plural domains of experience, ideological orientations, and so on, which will surely influence – although not determine – how they will read. My aim is not, however, to decide what these texts *are* or *mean* in any absolute sense, but rather to explore some of what they *might allow*. This entails that the short stories I analyse would maintain their productive energies through different critical analyses, and I hope that my readings will encourage others to expand on what these texts can offer.

Foregrounding form and genre in such a highly politicised context as post-apartheid South Africa might risk accusations of quietism and abstraction when compared with the historicist orientation of much criticism in this field. However, the formalism I hope to model in this book is one that offers readings of texts that are sensitive to questions of form, genre, and style; that recognises the interoperation of form and content; that explores how formalist readings might draw on the conditions of a text's production and reception; and that considers how literary texts can influence our understanding of the world in which they circulate. Rather than constituting a retreat from historical questions, I hope this approach will offer a greater understanding of how the formal and generic aspects of literature might intersect with an analysis of the social, and moreover, that it will make clear that this kind of analysis does not exhaust or explain the works it analyses. It is one of literature's great assets, and great frustrations, that it is irreducible to propositional information about the world, even though it may well offer us ways of thinking about it.

However, before expanding on how the short story might catalyse social thought, it might be helpful to outline the broader backdrop against which this study finds its place. To do this, in the sections that follow I establish the relative dearth of criticism on the short story in comparison to the novel in postcolonial contexts, and in South Africa in particular. This leads me to the role that formal and generic analysis have played in postcolonial criticism, and how this can be supplemented – albeit with some caveats – with thinking from the cluster of approaches described as new formalism. This introduction ends with a brief history of the short story in South Africa, considering its waxing and waning prominence, before offering an outline of the book's structure.

A Novel Approach

The postcolonial world abounds with genres and forms – epics, ghazals, trickster tales, radio plays, telenovelas – but postcolonial studies has in the main focused on the novel, meaning that critics analyse quite a limited range of the texts available to them.[17] This generic bias has led to an accrual of critical practices around how to read texts from formerly colonised countries. Postcolonial literary studies has foregrounded questions of nationhood, with the nation often tied to the novel form. As Shital Pravinchandra notes, this trend has been present since 'the early days of postcolonial studies, when Fredric Jameson laid down his infamous dictum regarding Third World texts'.[18] This dictum, that 'Third-World texts, even those which are seemingly private [...] necessarily project a political dimension in the form of national allegory', established nationhood as a central concern of postcolonial criticism.[19] Nationhood and nation-building are seen to be best explored through

---

17 Two influential counter-examples to this tendency can be found in Timothy Brennan, *At Home in the World: Cosmopolitanism Now* (Cambridge, MA: Harvard University Press, 1997); Jahan Ramazani, *The Hybrid Muse: Postcolonial Poetry in English* (Chicago: University of Chicago Press, 2001). See also Ed Charlton, *Improvising Reconciliation: Confession After the Truth Commission* (Liverpool: Liverpool University Press, 2021); Lucy Evans, *Communities in Contemporary Anglophone Caribbean Short Stories* (Liverpool: Liverpool University Press, 2014).
18 Shital Pravinchandra, 'Not Just Prose', *Interventions*, 16.3 (2014), 424–44 (p. 432).
19 Fredric Jameson, 'Third-World Literature in the Era of Multinational Capitalism', *Social Text*, 15 (1986), 65–88 (p. 69).

the novel form, and the novel, in Leela Gandhi's words, becomes 'a sort of proxy for the nation'.[20]

The novel has certainly been important for postcolonial cultural production, but to focus on it to the exclusion of other forms results in a picture that is inevitably partial, both in its corpus and in its modes of reading. The examples critics use imply a judgement on cultural value, and moreover, they are not simply descriptive of knowledge, but rather participate in its production and reproduction. The choice of the novel has strongly influenced the kinds of analysis produced and the forms of knowledge created. As Ben Etherington and Sean Pryor argue, models are often 'determined by the example's specific contours', and postcolonial studies' preference for the novel has strongly informed its practices of reading.[21] If narrative is a way of knowing the world, as Jameson among others suggests, it follows that short narratives are likely to help us know the world in different ways than long ones, and this can open up new possibilities for postcolonial analysis.

The interest in taking up the South African short story is, then, twofold. First, to do so brings into critical view a body of works that often receive limited attention. This is not, to my mind, a form of special pleading for works that might not merit it, but is rather to point out South African writing's achievements in the short story form, and to argue that in ignoring them we miss an important facet of the country's literature. Secondly, the short story offers a change of focus both in and from the aesthetic articulation of nationhood, augmenting the national with different scales, and different modalities of being. In Michael Chapman's words, while

> the novel is equated with big ideas, big events, the story favours flexibility, ellipses, surprise, emotion, implication. With large, singular plots discredited (the narrative of nationalism or socialism), the story permits us smaller, various, often unconventional insights. These find consonance in a country in the complexity of its transition from an authoritarian order to a civil imaginary.[22]

20 Leela Gandhi, *Postcolonial Theory: A Critical Introduction* (New York: Columbia University Press, 1998), p. 151.
21 Ben Etherington and Sean Pryor, 'Historical Poetics and the Problem of Exemplarity', *Critical Quarterly*, 61.1 (2019), 3–17 (p. 4).
22 Michael Chapman, 'A Case of Story: Coetzee, Gordimer, Bosman…!', *Current Writing*, 16.1 (2004), 1–14 (p. 3).

Characterisations of this kind always risk eliding the specifics of actually existing texts, and Chapman rightly foregrounds that the novel is 'equated with' large-scale narratives rather than being reducible to them, while the short story 'permits us', but is not limited to, more 'unconventional insights'. It might nevertheless be allowed that we can talk about general tendencies towards these two poles even if the model will not hold true in every case. Short stories could then hold the promise of a different perspective on the country's 'civil imaginary'. Given this, it is surprising that short stories have received so little sustained attention, particularly in studies of post-apartheid literature, but also in work on African literature more broadly.

There is a growing body of criticism on the short story as a form, usually dealing with American or European texts, yet there are few book-length studies available on the African short story, and fewer still on the short story in South Africa.[23] William Feuser noted in 1981 that '[a]lthough it is bursting with life, the short story in Africa is a neglected genre'.[24] 'Critics', he held, 'have paid scant attention to the short story and have treated it as a footnote to the novel. And yet short story writers were deeply involved in the genesis of African writing in European languages.'[25] In 1991, ten years after Feuser's observation, F. Odun Balogun published *Tradition and Modernity in the African Short Story*, the first book-length study on the form.[26] The dearth of available critical material was evident in his subtitle: *An Introduction to a Literature in Search of Critics*. In his introduction, Balogun notes with heavy heart that '[t]he most significant study of African short stories as a body

---

23 For some useful books on other regions, see Bruce Bennett, *Australian Short Fiction: A History* (St Lucia, Australia: University of Queensland Press, 2002); Jeremy H.C.S. Davidson and Helen Cordell, *The Short Story in South East Asia: Aspects of a Genre* (London: School of Oriental and African Studies, University of London, 1982); Reingard M. Nischik, *The Canadian Short Story: Interpretations* (Rochester, NY: Camden House, 2007); Evans, *Communities*; Lucy Evans, Mark McWatt, and Emma Smith (eds), *The Caribbean Short Story: Critical Perspectives* (Leeds: Peepal Tree, 2011); Maggie Awadalla and Paul March-Russell (eds), *The Postcolonial Short Story: Contemporary Essays* (Basingstoke: Palgrave Macmillan, 2013).
24 Willfried Feuser, *Jazz and Palm Wine, and Other Stories* (Harlow: Longman, 1981), p. 1.
25 Ibid., p. 1
26 F. Odun Balogun, *Tradition and Modernity in the African Short Story: An Introduction to a Literature in Search of Critics* (New York: Greenwood, 1991).

until now has been a 1978 conference paper by Helen O. Chukwuma, appropriately titled "The Prose of Neglect".[27] Balogun's study makes useful headway in laying the foundations of African short story criticism, but since then there has been very little extended commentary on the short story in Africa as a whole, save a collected edition titled *Writing Africa in the Short Story* (2013), which helpfully draws attention to the importance of the Caine Prize for African Writing in furthering the short story's visibility, while lamenting an 'abysmal lack of interest' among critics.[28]

In South Africa, short story criticism has been sparse. There is to date only one published single-author volume – Craig MacKenzie's *The Oral-Style South African Short Story in English* (1999) – and one special issue of the *Journal of Commonwealth Literature* that was later published as a collected volume titled *The Short Story in South Africa: Contemporary Trends and Perspectives* (2022). These books are joined by a handful of doctoral theses: Martin Trump's 'South African Short Fiction in English and Afrikaans Since 1948' (1985); Rob Gaylard's 'Writing Black: The South African Short Story by Black Writers' (2008); Sopelekae Maithufi's 'The South African Short Story and its Mediation of the Hegemonic Tendencies of Nationalism' (2009); and Sue Marais's '(Re-)Inventing Our Selves/Ourselves: Identity and Community in Contemporary South African Short Fiction Cycles' (2014). The slight intensification of publication since the turn of the millennium perhaps suggests a growing interest in the form, but in absolute terms the number of studies remains small.

MacKenzie's *The Oral-Style South African Short Story in English* focuses on stories marked by oral expression, and most often featuring a frame narrator. He concentrates on the period 1860–1950, which was 'dominated by the oral-style tale', before a 'steady and irreversible progression' occurred among post-war, particularly white, writers, 'from fireside tale [...] to modern short story'.[29] In contrast to this progression among white authors, MacKenzie's assessment of the short story by black authors describes a partial reversal of this trend, with more authors adopting aspects of oral expression. The extent to which

---

27 Ibid., p. 3.
28 Ernest N. Emenyonu (ed.), *Writing Africa in the Short Story: African Literature Today* (Woodbridge, Suffolk: James Currey, 2013), p. 1.
29 Craig MacKenzie, *The Oral-Style South African Short Story in English: A. W. Drayson to H. C. Bosman* (Amsterdam: Rodopi, 1999), p. 9.

this turn to orality took place is moot,[30] although collections such as Zachariah Rapola's *Beginnings of Dream* (2007) and Niq Mhlongo's *Affluenza* (2016), *Soweto, Under the Apricot Tree* (2018), and *For You, I'd Steal a Goat* (2022) suggest that there is a lively writing tradition influenced by orality that continues.[31] MacKenzie's study offers an admirable reach into the past, but his focus on oral-style works up till the mid-1980s means that he engages quite a different corpus of texts from that explored in this book.

Rebecca Fasselt, Corinne Sandwith, and Khulukazi Soldati-Kahimbaara's editorial introduction to *The Short Story in South Africa* gives a useful overview of emerging trends in recent South African short fiction, such as the shifting terrain of anthologisation and the rise of flash fiction, genre fiction short stories, and an increasing exploration of marginalised perspectives. The editors emphasise the growth of popular short story forms in opposition to those with a more 'modernist aesthetic', and so offer a useful counterpoint to the more formally experimental texts on which I concentrate.[32] Given its format as an edited collection, *The Short Story in South Africa* does not advance a sustained argument about the short story as a form. Rather, its strength lies in its breadth of reference, and what *The Short Story after Apartheid* might sacrifice in breadth I hope is compensated for in its depth of engagement with the generic and formal characteristics of the texts I examine.

Martin Trump's thesis is useful for drawing short fiction by black and white authors writing in English and Afrikaans together under a

---

30 For an insightful critique of oral storytelling Njabulo Ndebele's *Fools*, see Michael Vaughan, 'Storytelling and Politics in Fiction', in *Rendering Things Visible: Essays on South African Literary Culture*, ed. Martin Trump (Johannesburg: Ravan, 1990), pp. 186–204.

31 Mhlongo states in an interview that 'I prefer writing stories in the way I speak [...] my stories will remain written the way I talk'. Niq Mhlongo, Rebecca Fasselt, and Corinne Sandwith, '"My Stories Will Remain Written the Way I Talk": A Conversation with Niq Mhlongo', in *The Short Story in South Africa: Contemporary Trends and Perspectives*, ed. Rebecca Fasselt and Corinne Sandwith (Abingdon: Routledge, 2022), pp. 242–55 (p. 251).

32 Rebecca Fasselt, Corinne Sandwith, and Khulukazi Soldati-Kahimbaara, 'Introduction: The Short Story in South Africa – New Trends and Perspectives', in *The Short Story in South Africa: Contemporary Trends and Perspectives*, ed. Rebecca Fasselt and Corinne Sandwith (Abingdon: Routledge, 2022), pp. 1–27 (p. 3).

single banner, a position that was at odds with much literary criticism in the 1980s and before. He draws out the common themes of the stories he analyses and shows points of overlap between languages and writers from different apartheid-era racial categories that give the lie to the idea that these are wholly separate traditions. Rob Gaylard's study offers a close reading of short stories by black authors from the 1950s to the 1980s, with some material on earlier authors. He aims to tease out the 'singularity of particular texts [...] as well as their embeddedness in their particular place and time'.[33] In so doing, he provides a welcome corrective to homogeneous depictions of so-called protest fiction. The depth of his exploration into this period is admirable but it means he can only gesture towards the 'imaginative challenges that lie ahead in the post-apartheid period'.[34] Maithufi's thesis draws on Njabulo Ndebele's theorisation of the spectacular and the ordinary to offer readings of stories by black South African writers published between 1970 and 1990. It offers welcome analysis of critically neglected authors such as Bheki Maseko, Mandla Langa, Farida Karodia, and Sindiwe Magona, as well as chapters on the better-known Ndebele and Wicomb. Marais, like MacKenzie, concentrates on a generic category within the short story – the short story cycle – and covers mainly texts from the 1980s and 1990s, except Wicomb's *The One That Got Away* (2008). In so doing, she highlights the centrifugal and centripetal dynamics of national and aesthetic grouping.

These studies all have much to offer, but none focuses at length on more recent short texts. There are various individual articles on short stories and longer studies which analyse short stories as part of a larger project, such as Andrew van der Vlies's *Present Imperfect: Contemporary South African Writing* (2017), Rita Barnard's *Apartheid and Beyond: South African Writers and the Politics of Place* (2007), and Barnard and van der Vlies's co-edited volume *South African Literature in Transition* (2019). However, while each of these contains material *on* short stories – Barnard on Gordimer and van der Vlies on Wicomb in particular – a consideration of these texts *as* short stories is not their focus, and so the short story's formal and generic features are for the most part de-emphasised.

33 Rob Gaylard, 'Writing Black: The South African Short Story by Black Writers' (unpublished DLitt thesis, University of Stellenbosch, 2008), p. iii <http://hdl.handle.net/10019.1/1202> (accessed 12 October 2022).
34 Ibid., p. 306.

In short story criticism more broadly, much recent work has pursued a historicist approach, in contrast with the formalist approaches that dominated criticism in the 1980s and 1990s.[35] In the words of Paul Delaney and Adrian Hunter, the editors of the *Edinburgh Companion to the Short Story in English*, '[w]here for these earlier critics questions of formal and generic definition were central, today it is the cultural, historical and ideological functions of the short story that predominate'.[36] However, there are some signs of the tide turning: Kasia Boddy's *The American Short Story Since 1950* (2010) argues convincingly for the moment of crisis as a formal device that is central to the workings of American short fiction in the late twentieth and early twenty-first centuries. Michael Basseler's *An Organon of Life Knowledge: Genres and Functions of the Short Story in North America* (2019) takes up the question of genre and form explicitly, and his idea that the short story can be an 'instrument of thought or knowledge' confirms my own estimation of the short story's heuristic potential.[37] To explore how this formal renaissance in short story criticism might be brought into dialogue with South African literature, it is worth turning to the question of how form's uneasy relationship with the world outside the text has been understood in postcolonial studies, and how some ideas from the politicised end of new formalism might helpfully be adapted to think about the short story's political affordances. In so doing, new

---

35 For some of the most interesting recent work on the short story, see Adrian Hunter, *The Cambridge Introduction to the Short Story in English* (Cambridge: Cambridge University Press, 2007); Martin Scofield, *The Cambridge Introduction to the American Short Story* (Cambridge: Cambridge University Press, 2006); Alfred Bendixen and James Nagel (eds), *A Companion to the American Short Story* (Oxford: Blackwell, 2010); Paul Delaney and Adrian Hunter (eds), *The Edinburgh Companion to the Short Story in English* (Edinburgh: Edinburgh University Press, 2019); Jose R. Ibanez, Jose Francisco Fernandez, and Carmen M. Bretones (eds), *Contemporary Debates on the Short Story* (Bern: Peter Lang, 2007); Paul March-Russell, *The Short Story: An Introduction* (Edinburgh: Edinburgh University Press, 2009); Kasia Boddy, *The American Short Story Since 1950* (Edinburgh: Edinburgh University Press, 2010); Ailsa Cox (ed.), *The Short Story* (Newcastle: Cambridge Scholars Publishing, 2008); Evans, *Communities*; Erin Fallon and others (eds), *A Reader's Companion to the Short Story in English* (Westport, CT: Greenwood, 2001).

36 Delaney and Hunter (eds), *Edinburgh Companion to the Short Story*, p. 1.

37 Basseler, *An Organon of Life Knowledge*, p. 17.

formalism might bring something new to postcolonial criticism, and postcolonial literature may well cast new formalism in a new light.

Thinking with Form

Amid the renewed attention to form in some recent studies of the short story, it is important to remember that the word 'form' means different things to different people. For some critics, the word is almost synonymous with genre, and indeed it is often difficult to distinguish between these concepts. For some critics, reading for form means something close to narratological analysis, and so concentrates on the thematic and modal dimensions of how stories are constructed. For others, in might entail the analysis of style, grammar, syntax, and so on, leading Tom Eyers to define form as the 'aspects of literary texts that, in themselves, are indifferent to theme, character, or what is conventionally known as "content"'.[38] Aaron Kunin, by contrast, argues for character *as* form.[39] These various, indeed sometimes contradictory, notions of what form is and does attest to Angela Leighton's observation that '[f]orm, which seems self-sufficient and self-defining, is restless, tendentious, a noun lying in wait for its object'.[40] Faced with the risk of form's collapse into meaninglessness, Jonathan Kramnick and Anahid Nersessian adopt a pluralist position, in which form is 'not a word without content but a notion bound pragmatically to its instances', which is to say that the meaning of 'form' needs to be understood in terms of what it is supposed to do in a particular analysis.[41]

My use of the terms 'form' and 'genre' allows a certain flexibility, but I mainly use 'genre' when considering how reading is informed by a genre's 'horizon of expectation', which for the contemporary short story

---

38 Tom Eyers, *Speculative Formalism: Literature, Theory, and the Critical Present* (Evanston, IL: Northwestern University Press, 2017), p. 8. For more on the different interpretations of what constitutes form, see Sandra MacPherson, 'A Little Formalism', *ELH*, 82.2 (2015), 385–405; Catherine Gallagher, 'Formalism and Time', *MLQ: Modern Language Quarterly*, 61.1 (2000), 229–51.

39 Aaron Kunin, *Character as Form* (London: Bloomsbury, 2019).

40 Angela Leighton, *On Form: Poetry, Aestheticism, and the Legacy of a Word* (Oxford: Oxford University Press, 2007), p. 1.

41 Jonathan Kramnick and Anahid Nersessian, 'Form and Explanation', *Critical Inquiry*, 43.3 (2017), 650–69 (p. 661).

might include features such as an expectation of (relative) shortness, modest scope, epiphanic moments (whether ironised or otherwise), and reliance on inference as part of its narrative mode.[42] 'Form' I use for more localised aspects of narrative organisation: length as it operates in a single story (both overall and in paragraphs and sentences), as well as details of syntax, rhythm, sound, figures of speech, and so on. These features contribute to the total meaning event of a story, and this is often in conjunction with the content of the text. While some analyses separate form from content (or at least claim to) my analysis sees the two as tightly intertwined. What happens in a work of literature can only be understood through its shaping by genre and form, and likewise, we can only properly understand form through its alignments with content. Material in art is only comprehensible as material through its framing, and form becomes formal only through a provisional alignment with its materials. In thinking through this recursive dynamic, I hope to move away from the idea that form is best analysed as if it were void of content. Forms, like genres, offer what Rosalie Colie calls 'a set of interpretations, of "frames" or "fixes" on the world', and particularly in genres that do not have fixed formal qualities – unlike villanelles, rondeaux and so on – our experience of form happens through the text's materials, just as those materials only take on their meaning through formal arrangement.[43]

The claim that there is insufficient attention to genre, form, or more broadly aesthetics in postcolonial studies has become one of the hallmarks of a long-standing formalist turn in the field. In 2014 Ato Quayson, Debjani Ganguly, and Neil ten Kortenaar launched the *Cambridge Journal of Postcolonial Literary Enquiry*, with the stated goal of 'bringing back the term *literary* to the idea of postcolonial inquiry' in order to 'signal the centrality of a paradigm of reading that we feel has been somewhat eclipsed in recent decades by the field's voracious extratextual and interdisciplinary perambulations'.[44] In the same year, a special issue of the *Journal of Commonwealth Literature*

---

42 Hans Robert Jauss, *Towards an Aesthetic of Reception*, trans. Timothy Bahti (Minneapolis: University of Minnesota Press, 1982), p. x n., 22–23, 88–89.
43 Rosalie L. Colie, *The Resources of Kind: Genre-Theory in the Renaissance* (Berkeley: University of California Press, 1973), p. 8.
44 Ato Quayson, Debjani Ganguly, and Neil ten Kortenaar, 'Editorial: New Topographies', *Cambridge Journal of Postcolonial Literary Inquiry*, 1.1 (2014), 1–10 (p. 6).

edited by Jarad Zimbler, Ben Etherington, and Rachel Bower sought to establish 'craft and technique [...] [as] the fundamental grounds for critical interpretation rather than subsidiary concerns for cultural critique and "textual analysis"', in postcolonial studies.[45] Going back a little further, Eli Park Sorensen's *Postcolonial Studies and the Literary: Theory, Interpretation and the Novel* (2010) argues that 'postcolonial studies needs to return to a discussion of the literary'.[46] Gayatri Chakravorty Spivak's *Death of a Discipline* (2003) bemoans an approach that 'bypasses the literary and the linguistic', and calls for an increased 'attention to language and idiom'.[47] As much as I support these critics' calls for attention to the 'the literary', however they conceive it, I am less convinced that postcolonial studies as a whole has sidelined questions of aesthetics in favour of cultural identity, content, or ideology critique. While there are certainly postcolonial analyses that have paid less attention to aesthetic questions, many studies have fully integrated such concerns, including convincing arguments that the entwined histories of context, content, and form have always been central to postcolonial literature and criticism.[48] This considerable number of studies, dating

---

45 Jarad Zimbler, Ben Etherington, and Rachel Bower, 'Crafts of World Literature: Field, Material and Translation', *The Journal of Commonwealth Literature*, 49.3 (2014), 273–78 (p. 273).

46 Eli Park Sorensen, *Postcolonial Studies and the Literary: Theory, Interpretation and the Novel* (Basingstoke: Palgrave Macmillan, 2010), p. x.

47 Gayatri Chakravorty Spivak, *Death of a Discipline* (New York: Columbia University Press, 2003), pp. 4, 70.

48 A selective chronological list would include titles such as Peter Hallward, *Absolutely Postcolonial: Writing Between the Singular and the Specific* (Manchester: Manchester University Press, 2001); Ramazani, *The Hybrid Muse*; Deepika Bahri, *Native Intelligence: Aesthetics, Politics, and Postcolonial Literature* (Minneapolis: University of Minnesota Press, 2003); Nicholas Harrison, *Postcolonial Criticism: History, Theory and the Work of Fiction* (Cambridge: Polity, 2003); Derek Attridge, *J.M. Coetzee & the Ethics of Reading: Literature in the Event* (Chicago: University of Chicago Press, 2004); Nicholas Brown, *Utopian Generations: The Political Horizon of Twentieth-Century Literature* (Princeton, NJ: Princeton University Press, 2005); Natalie Melas, *All the Difference in the World: Postcoloniality and the Ends of Comparison* (Stanford, CA: Stanford University Press, 2006); Chris Bongie, *Friends and Enemies: The Scribal Politics of Post/Colonial Literature* (Liverpool: Liverpool University Press, 2008); Neil Lazarus, *The Postcolonial Unconscious* (Cambridge: Cambridge University Press, 2011);

back to at least the early 2000s, suggests that there has been a sustained interest in how questions of form and aesthetics might inform postcolonial analyses, and this lineage could easily be traced back further, for example to Edward Said's consideration of the novel's formal properties in *Culture and Imperialism*.⁴⁹

It is surprising, given this attention to literature's particular ways of addressing the social, that none of these studies engages with the more politically driven versions of new formalism that also rose to prominence around the turn of the millennium. Emerging against a backdrop of several decades of dominant historicisms, since around 2000 there has been a resurgence of studies addressing formal questions. Some critics have called for a heightened awareness of aesthetic experience, often wary of the idea that a critic's role is primarily to unveil hidden ideological structures, while others seek to reinvigorate politicised criticism with greater formal attention. In the first of these groups – bearing in mind that there is considerable overlap and cross-pollination between them – are texts which argue, in Rita Felski and Elizabeth S. Anker's words, that 'the intellectual or political payoff of interrogating, demystifying, and defamiliarizing is no longer quite so self-evident'.⁵⁰ These works have shaped my thinking in various

---

Akinwumi Adesokan, *Postcolonial Artists and Global Aesthetics* (Bloomington: Indiana University Press, 2011); Patrick Crowley and Jane Hiddleston (eds) *Postcolonial Poetics: Genre and Form* (Liverpool: Liverpool University Press, 2011); Philip Dickinson, *Romanticism and Aesthetic Life in Postcolonial Writing* (Basingstoke: Palgrave Macmillan, 2018); Elleke Boehmer, *Postcolonial Poetics: 21st-Century Critical Readings* (Basingstoke: Palgrave Macmillan, 2018); Sourit Bhattacharya, *Postcolonial Modernity and the Indian Novel: On Catastrophic Realism* (Basingstoke: Palgrave Macmillan, 2020).

49 For more on the long history of form's place in postcolonial thought, see William Ghosh, 'The Formalist Genesis of "Postcolonial" Reading: Brathwaite, Bhabha, and *A House for Mr Biswas*', *ELH*, 84.3 (2017), 765–89.

50 Elizabeth S. Anker and Rita Felski (eds), *Critique and Postcritique* (Durham, NC: Duke University Press, 2017), pp. 3, 2. See also Eve Kosofsky Sedgwick, *Touching Feeling: Affect, Pedagogy, Performativity* (Durham, NC: Duke University Press, 2003); Stephen Best and Sharon Marcus, 'Surface Reading: An Introduction', *Representations*, 108.1 (2009), 1–21; Rita Felski, *The Limits of Critique* (Chicago: University of Chicago Press, 2015); Rita Felski, *Hooked: Art and Attachment* (Chicago: University of Chicago Press, 2020); Peter de Bolla, *Art Matters* (Cambridge, MA: Harvard University Press, 2001); Derek Attridge, *The Singularity of Literature* (London: Routledge, 2004).

ways, not least for their vivid articulations of what attention to form and aesthetic experience can offer literary studies. By expanding and enriching the critical vocabulary around how we experience artworks, these studies offer an essential resource for this project, which seeks to give a fuller account of how form, aesthetic experience, and social thinking might be read together.

The Short Story after Apartheid, however, is more immediately in dialogue with studies that have combined formalist approaches with projects of critique, sometimes described as 'political formalism'. Studies by Caroline Levine, Anna Kornbluh, and Tom Eyers offer three prominent examples of such projects, and below their work is engaged in some detail. The pressure point in combining formal and social analysis is nearly always the model of reference that is offered between text and world, and in what follows I consider how each of these studies conceives of that relationship, and where my study differs from them. These differences fall under two main rubrics: 1) the role of readers in realising a form's worldly purchase, and 2) the likely efficacy of literary critics in effecting societal change. I expand on each of these below, but in short, I find that some account of how texts might influence readers is essential, and that the role of literary critics in analysing and changing societal structures is often overstated.

There are a few obvious ways in which my study differs from Levine's, Kornbluh's, and Eyers's. First, *The Short Story after Apartheid* considers how recent formalist criticism might be usefully brought into dialogue with postcolonial approaches, and secondly, it focuses on the short story. The books I discuss below argue, respectively, that artistic form affords thinking about social forms, that literary form contains a speculative component that is irreducible to its historical determination, and that form constructs exportable schematic alternatives to the actually existing world. Whichever of these models one adopts, it is apparent that both the social context and the forms analysed will be of great importance. The examples offered by these three authors – novels and a TV series for Levine, nineteenth-century English novels for Kornbluh, and twentieth-century European poetry for Eyers – lead to perceptive readings, but if forms do the things these critics claim, then South African short stories will surely do things differently. While postcolonial studies can benefit from new formalism's attention to how work and world collide, then new formalism might equally benefit from expanding the range of forms and cultural contexts it engages.

Levine's *Forms: Whole, Rhythm, Hierarchy, Network* argues that aesthetic objects and societal structures have a property in common: their formal arrangement. The book's most influential idea has been to bring the concept of an 'affordance' into literary criticism from design theory. In her words, an '*Affordance* is a term used to describe the potential uses or actions latent in materials and designs', which is to say that a chair might be used as intended, for sitting on, but 'imaginative users' might also think to stand on it or use it to prop open a door.[51] For Levine, literary forms also have affordances, and these can be adapted for societal analyses. This way of thinking about forms, in which meta-structures are exportable into discrete domains, allows for transfer between art and other spheres due to their shared formal characteristics. Although it is not Levine's main focus, the aspect which interests me most is the role of 'imaginative users'. Levine, unlike the design theorists on which she draws, is less concerned with 'the relations between an object and its users' and more in 'what actions or thoughts are made possible or impossible by the fact of a form'.[52] However, in my understanding, 'actions or thoughts' come about relationally between readers and forms, and a form is not an immovable fact so much as a co-constituted entity that arises when texts and readers come together. Literary forms are, like Roman Ingarden's understanding of artworks, 'ontically heteronomous', that is, they depend on acts of consciousness towards them to be realised.[53] Forms are not things that texts and objects unproblematically have, but rather they emerge when texts and readers, objects and users, come together.[54] Given this, it is important to foreground that the short stories I analyse offer quite different formal experiences from the large-scale works that Levine prioritises, and so the kinds of insight they allow will also differ. Moreover, the point of transfer between aesthetic and worldly form needs to allow for the shaping – although not determining – force of the imaginative user in establishing the kind of fact a form might be.

51 Levine, *Forms*, p. 6.
52 Ibid., p. 16, n. 15.
53 Roman Ingarden, *The Literary Work of Art: An Investigation on the Borderlines of Ontology, Logic, and Theory of Literature*, trans. George G. Grabowicz (Evanston, IL: Northwestern University Press, 1973), p. 126.
54 This is excepting, perhaps, strongly determined forms such as the haiku, although even such forms only come to take on meaning in a context of the genre's historical development and through readerly engagements with them.

In *The Order of Forms*, Anna Kornbluh describes a project of 'political formalism', which covers 'the order of forms, the order made by forms and the forms made by order'.[55] Contrary to the distrust of form she perceives in 'anarcho-vitalist' theories,[56] Kornbluh argues that 'formed, mediated relations are the truth of our social being', and so are essential to building a more just society.[57] One of the book's central claims – that literary forms, like mathematical forms, can be used as abstract frameworks through which thought can move – is a useful extension of Levine's affordances, as it offers a stronger sense of making rather than recognising forms. Kornbluh goes further than Levine in de-emphasising the act of reading in claiming that a 'rigorous formalism without recourse to phenomenology' is necessary, as a work of literature has

> a structurality that is agential and essential to its form independent of its apprehension. Outside the time of reading, it remains possible to access that structurality, to apprehend and appreciate it, in a register that consolidates the paraconceptuality at stake in the work. It may take a hundred hours to read *Bleak House*, but it does not take a hundred hours to cinch the synthetic thought that *Bleak House* thinks.[58]

It is certainly the case that some phenomenological accounts overemphasise the moment of reading over (also embodied) retrospection, but it is a different matter to say that this is not part of a phenomenology of reading, which should include how past readings help structure current thought. Texts stay with us, and to overlook the concentric aftershocks of a reading would be to miss an important aspect of how texts work on and with us. Rather than bracketing phenomenology from 'rigorous formalism', I would rather emphasise how phenomenological experience in both its immediate and remembered forms might

---

55 Anna Kornbluh, *The Order of Forms: Realism, Formalism, and Social Space* (Chicago: University of Chicago Press, 2019), p. 27.
56 This various group includes 'neo-Deleuzianisms and neo-Spinozisms such as those of Hardt and Negri, messianisms such as Agamben's, antistatism in Foucauldian and Marxist flavors, antinomianism in queer theory, assemblage theory'. Ibid., p. 19.
57 Ibid., p. 27.
58 Ibid., p. 40.

usefully be understood as integral to the generative capacity of form that Kornbluh so usefully examines. This emphasis allows, on the one hand, for an understanding of literary works that is irreducible to a single 'synthetic thought'. On the other, it suggests that the extended experience of reading doorstopper novels, so often interwoven with that of daily life, cannot easily be mapped onto that of the curtailed temporal experience of the short story, which is often bracketed from worldly intrusions and so orients the reader differently towards their 'social being'. The question of how formal experience relates to social thought has important consequences when we remember that analyses of postcolonial literature, and more immediately South African literature, also privilege novelistic scale. If novels are read as the means through which national registers of social being are best explored, it follows that short stories should allow for different scales and modes of social thought.

A further nuancing of the relationship between word and world is offered by Tom Eyers in *Speculative Formalism: Literature, Theory, and the Critical Present*. His book offers a subtly argued Althusserian account of how literary form – in practice, poetic form – is neither mimetic of nor wholly determined by its 'outsides – materiality, history, politics, nature'.[59] Rather, literature is relatively autonomous, and through its 'formal speculative capacity' can ward off its 'final absorption or neutralization by those prior conditions'.[60] For Eyers, the term 'speculative' entails a 'speculative link or reference between the two ['literary language and its apparent outsides'], one irreducible to mimetic or historicist accounts of literature's successes'.[61] In this model, 'literary history and politics are especially vivid folds in literary form', and the 'outsides' of a text both 'determine and are determined by the textual or conceptual-scientific structures'.[62] Eyers addresses the role of readers explicitly, putting useful pressure on both 'the notion of the self-contained text as uniquely causative, and its mirror image of the reader as sovereign creator of literary sense'.[63] My own position is, like his, keen to 'trouble the very self-sufficiency of these categories – text, context, reader, author, history', and so falls somewhere in the muddy

---

59 Eyers, *Speculative Formalism*, p. 1.
60 Ibid., p. 1.
61 Ibid., p. 3.
62 Ibid., p. 10.
63 Ibid., p. 177.

middle ground, with neither the text nor the reader offering the sole key to interpretation or the only route to political possibility. It is nevertheless important to clarify that whatever process might allow texts to refigure their outsides in concrete terms would require a real reader's involvement. If, through the experience of a form, a reader is either given a different way of experiencing or parsing the world, this would offer at least a chance of change coming about, even if it is never realised in practice.

If the question of how reading figures in accounts of political formalism is one issue, then another is the likely range and efficacy of its interventions. The question of form's political purchase has been important to analyses of postcolonial cultural production, and at times has been overstated. Anne McClintock warns of what she calls the 'fetishism of form', that is, 'the projection of historical agency onto formal abstractions that are anthropomorphized and given a life of their own' so that 'messier questions of historical change and social activism' are elided.[64] The accounts of form's political agency offered by Levine and Kornbluh at times run this risk, and at others are too quick to grant the literary critic a privileged interpretative role in other fields. In making parallels between the forms of aesthetic and extra-aesthetic objects, Levine argues that literary critics should '*export* those practices [of formal analysis], to take our traditional skills to new objects – the social structures and institutions that are among the most crucial sites of political efficacy'.[65] A central aim of this formal analysis is, then, 'radical political change'.[66] For Kornbluh, literary formalists are experts in how 'language furnishes a medium for composing sustained repetitions, delimited contours, performative conjurings, and synthetic abstractions', and this equips them to 'understand and even engineer parallel formations in the phenomenal realm of everyday life'.[67]

If these parallel formations were also linguistic, there might be some truth to this, but this is a long way from saying that literary formalists have a 'unique worldly purchase'.[68] As much as literary critics may want to be at the forefront of making 'new forms, new arrangements,

---

64 Anne McClintock, *Imperial Leather: Race, Gender, and Sexuality in the Colonial Contest* (New York: Routledge, 1995), p. 66.
65 Levine, *Forms*, p. 23.
66 Ibid., p. 18.
67 Kornbluh, *The Order of Forms*, pp. 4–5, 29.
68 Ibid., p. 4.

new institutions, new relations', their sphere of influence is in reality too small and their interests too marginal for this to be likely, or even helpful, when there are people more directly dedicated to the transformation of such structures.[69] Again, Eyers's account is the most convincing in this regard, as he allows that the extent to which history and politics can be determined – even influenced – by literary form is quite small. In his words, 'ideological, empirical, and conceptual forces' are 'refigured [...] often ineffectually or incompletely by the text's own internal resources of speculative possibility', resulting more often in 'stasis or immobility rather than, say, contestation or critique'.[70] This position, while less ambitious in its aims, is much closer to my sense of the likely political efficacy of literary formalism. *The Short Story after Apartheid*'s claims about the political purchase gained from the formal analysis of literature are, like the forms I analyse, rather modest. While radical political change is unlikely to come about in any immediately causal way from artworks and their analysis, it might be allowed that by offering unique arrangements of materials, artworks might help us to understand the world differently. The role of the text can perhaps be considered as something like a catalyst, accelerating the speed at which new ways of conceiving the world might be attained, and without being exhausted in the process.

The question of how reading short stories might lead to different ways of thinking is one that I pursue throughout this book, but let me offer a first account of how the formal and generic inclinations of short stories might prompt different kinds of thought, or offer a 'machine to think with'.[71] Narrative is one of the ways through which we understand the world, and short stories can help give us access to states of mind, moments of realisation, and experiences of duration, embodiment, and finitude that shape our understanding of the materials they describe and the world in which they circulate. Take, for example, the short story's most explicit generic marker and formal property: its length. The experience of brevity or scale in an artwork affects the way we think and feel about it, and so the links we forge between it and the world of which it is a part. One thing to clarify immediately is the difference between length and duration. A text can be short in terms of the number of words that make it up, but this does not always give a reliable guide to

---

69 Ibid., p. 29.
70 Eyers, *Speculative Formalism*, pp. 49, 1.
71 Richards, *Principles*, p. 1.

the length of time it will take to read it, never mind understand it. For Paul Zumthor, 'the length of a text in terms of its linguistic materiality does not necessarily give the measure of its duration', and moreover, 'brevity is never random but constitutes a structuring model'.[72] That is to say, brevity is not just a volumetric calculation, but is rather a property of a text that gives it particular characteristics and that allows it to do particular things.

Much like genres such as the parable, the shortness of the short story often makes it feel like the condensation of an ethical complex, which can be realised or understood in multiple ways. For Michael Bassler, drawing on the work of Renate Brosch, it is precisely the short story's shortness that makes us more likely to read universal significance into it: 'the shorter, the more compressed a narrative becomes, the more it tends toward [...] [the] implication of general, trans-individual, and exemplary issues'.[73] For Brosch, because short stories 'do not have room to elaborate on the determining factors of the fictional world and its values', the reader's 'own perspective is constantly co-present with, projected onto and interactive with those of the fiction'.[74] This leads readers to understand short stories as meaning something other than what they seem to be about. And yet short stories are often so specific that they would seem not to refer to anything other than themselves. We are then faced with a dilemma: we tend to read them – as with parables – as symbolising or gesturing towards other situations, but to do so is in some way to traduce the short story's detailed attention and specificity. What this requires of us as readers is an ability to uphold particularity while, paradoxically, extrapolating from it.

If shortness, in part, creates a tension between the general and the particular, it further creates a sense that there is more going on than is made explicit in the text. This differs from allegory or parable in that it is not a question of one thing meaning another, but rather that there is missing information even at the level of the world of the text. Ernest Hemingway's 'Iceberg Theory' is perhaps the best known articulation of this, in which writerly omission, done right, gives readers a 'feeling

---

72 Paul Zumthor, 'Brevity as Form', trans. Laurence Thiollier Moscato and William Nelles, *Narrative*, 24.1 (2016), 73–81 (pp. 75, 74).
73 Basseler, *An Organon of Life Knowledge*, p. 98.
74 Renate Brosch, 'English Summary of Short Story: Textsorte Und Leseerfahrung', *WVT Trier*, 2007, <http://www.wvttrier.de/top/summary%20(Short%20Story)%20_%20Brosch.pdf> (accessed 23 August 2022).

of those [omitted] things as strongly as though the writer had stated them'.⁷⁵ Writers often draw on this technique, and readers have come to expect it in their generic horizon of expectation when reading short stories. The short story's managed shortness means that there is often a lot of space for the reader to fill in, inviting them to draw both on their experience of the text and on their extra-textual knowledge to find ways of making sense. As Michael Chapman argues, the short story's 'brevity and elusiveness challenge[s] its audience to "complete" its suggestion and to seek coherence even when the experience, or the style, signals dislocation'.⁷⁶ The spaces, ellipses, ironies, and ambiguities that have come to characterise many short stories, however, put the reader in a difficult position, as filling in the gaps would be to move towards neutralising the short story's productive incompletion. This process will likely never exhaust the text, as there is no 'correct' solution. Rather, a short story, like Samuel Beckett's ideal artwork, is a 'a total object, complete with missing parts', and it is precisely its incompletion that makes it the kind of heuristic device it is.⁷⁷

While there is a temptation as a reader to think that the gaps have been 'filled in' and a solution found, it is more often in the process of discovering the insufficiency of our answers to the problem presented by the text that short stories do their most interesting work. In Paul March-Russel's words, '[r]eaders are increasingly made aware of the darkness that surrounds these narratives, a darkness to which they themselves are made responsible by the weight of interpretation being transferred from the author. In other words, an ethical imperative underlines these fictions.'⁷⁸ Where this becomes particularly interesting in a South African context is that the kind of self-projection onto the unknown that this imperative requires is so ethically and politically volatile in the country's history of political and aesthetic representation. This is one part of the short story's political purchase, as is forces readers to consider the ethics of this kind of projection, to try to reach beyond the known while recognising the fraught and partial nature of such attempts.

75 Ernest Hemingway, *Death in the Afternoon* (New York: Charles Scribner's Sons, 1932), p. 192.
76 Chapman, 'A Case of Story', p. 5.
77 Samuel Beckett, *Proust and Three Dialogues with Georges Duthuit* (London: Jonathan Calder, 1965), p. 101.
78 March-Russell, *The Short Story*, p. 21.

Shortness further calls out for particular modes of reading, or perhaps particular kinds of reader. The shorter the work, the more its details seem to spring out as significant, asking readers to notice detail in a way that differs from its usual function in longer texts. While longer texts are often replete with detail, using it to furnish the world of the text and so create its reality effect, detail in short texts often has the opposite effect. Rather than smoothing the edges of the fictional world, allowing greater immersion and a more ready acceptance of the text's premises, detail in short works often wrests us from the diachronic line of reading, slowing us down, and calling rather on synchronic patterns of meaning formed from accumulated details. In Suzanne Hunter Brown's words, 'brevity inclines readers to organize works as configurations rather than as successive structures'.[79] On the one hand, this requires short story readers to learn how to meet the genre's aesthetic demands, but it also perhaps helps develop sensitivity to detail and how seemingly disparate phenomena might relate to one another in the world outside the text.

How, then, might these various attributes bestowed by shortness – a tension between allegorisation and particularity; a foregrounding of implication; and an increased sensitivity to detail – allow us to think about the world outside the text? One useful way to begin thinking about this question is offered by Austin M. Wright in his essay 'Recalcitrance in the Short Story', in which he proposes that the experience readers have when reading short stories is, at least in part, a product of what he calls their 'formal recalcitrance', which occurs between 'the force of a shaping form and the resistance of the shaped materials'.[80] Wright is here arguing in quite strictly formal terms, as the effects of recalcitrance are thought to affect the relationship between writer, reader and story, with the reader's frustrated desire prompting further textual interrogation and exploration.

However, is it not the case that short stories might also generate a different kind of recalcitrance, a political recalcitrance, which could manifest in a sense of dissatisfaction that pushes the reader to 'recalculate and reconsider' the world in which the story is being read, as much as

---

79 Suzanne Hunter Brown, 'Discourse Analysis and the Short Story', in *Short Story Theory at a Crossroads*, ed. Susan Lohafer and Jo Ellyn Clarey (Baton Rouge: Louisiana State University Press, 1989), pp. 217–48 (p. 234).

80 Austin M. Wright, 'Recalcitrance in the Short Story', in *Short Story Theory at a Crossroads*, ed. Susan Lohafer and Jo Ellyn Clarey (Baton Rouge: Louisiana State University Press, 1989), pp. 115–29 (p. 115).

the world of the story?⁸¹ Following Wright, the formal disconsolation of these curtailed forms serves as an affective spur to further textual exploration, but this restless dissatisfaction orients readers to the world depicted in the text only. For *The Short Story after Apartheid*, this world is often asymptotic with South Africa, and so the recalcitrant operations of shortness might inform a reading of society in quite direct ways, namely to encourage dissatisfaction with the determinations of the present. However, even when the text's materials are not identifiably South African, the desire for *more* that shortness kindles can shape the reader's orientation to the world outside the text. Particularly because short stories often leave readers not knowing what it is that they don't know, the feeling of dissatisfaction becomes an affective free radical, liable to attach itself to whatever is at hand, and shaping our orientation towards it. However, as much as we might be tempted to solve the puzzle of the text (and so the political quandary it raises), to do so would be to attribute a political argument to texts that is disallowed by their formal intractability. In this regard, these stories' political recalcitrance is *to* politics, a refractory unwillingness to be held responsible to the expressly political obligations that have historically determined both the production and reception of South African literature. Shortness can then be seen as a means to make a particular kind of reader, one who is sensitive to both the aesthetic workings of curtailed forms and to how this can inform extra-textual understandings. Valerie Shaw's intriguing question, 'What can a short story do particularly well *because* it is short?', might then receive one answer that foregrounds how shortness is at once a means of orienting readers towards one text, a crash course in the mode of attention the genre requires, and a prompt to extra-aesthetic thought which never collapses literature into its social function.⁸²

The Short Story in South Africa: A Brief History

Before turning to the analyses that make up the chapters of *The Short Story after Apartheid*, it might be useful to outline a brief history of the short story in South Africa. More precisely, what I outline is the history of the anglophone short story. This caveat pinpoints one of

81 Ibid., p. 121.
82 Valerie Shaw, *The Short Story: A Critical Introduction* (Abingdon: Routledge, 2014), p. 21.

this book's most evident shortcomings in as linguistically diverse a context as South Africa. The short story has a rich history in South Africa's various languages – particularly in Afrikaans, to which I give some brief mention in footnotes below – and I wish this book could better testify to what Andries Walter Oliphant calls the 'multilingual fact' of South Africa.[83] I can only hope that my contribution will serve as an invitation to others better equipped to write on the short story's multilingual history. In the history I outline below, at least until the end of the apartheid period, writing by authors who were classified as white is discussed in separate paragraphs from that by authors otherwise classified, while drawing points of connection between them. This is to recognise the very different opportunities available to these groups, and to acknowledge the distinctiveness of these writing traditions while also troubling the idea that these bodies of writing developed independently. This decision brings with it compromises, particularly in emphasising distinction over imbrication and risking reinscribing racial categories, but my aim is to foreground the tension between mutual influence and state-sanctioned separate development that was imposed by apartheid's distortions. While offering a fully integrated history might avoid these problems, it would bring its own, in underplaying the dramatically different conditions under which these authors wrote, and the markedly uneven access to publication that they were afforded.

From the earliest oral narratives, through the beginnings of the written form in the mid-1800s, through its development in the *Drum* decade in the 1950s, and into the transformed political landscape of the post-apartheid period, the short story has played a crucial role in South African literature. One consequence of this longevity is a body of stories as various as it is substantial. It is not my aim to attempt a full survey of this corpus here, or to offer an overarching developmental narrative, but rather to give a sense of the generic backdrop against which the stories that I discuss in detail emerge. There is clearly a risk of presenting this process of historico-generic change as one of progress, turning texts into what David Attwell calls 'coloured pins on a battle map', each 'allegorized as representing particular phases or periods'.[84]

---

83 Andries Walter Oliphant, 'Nonidentity and Reciprocity in Conceptualising South African Literary Studies', *Journal of Literary Studies*, 19.3–4 (2003), 237–54 (p. 241).

84 David Attwell, *Rewriting Modernity: Studies in Black South African Literary History* (Pietermaritzburg: University of Kwa-Zulu Natal Press, 2005), p. 9.

However, as even the rather cursory overview I have space for here will show, while some very broad patterns might emerge, there is no unilinear development, and even within specific periods there is too much variety for any single text to become representative.

The entwined history of traditions in South Africa complicates even some of the earliest of the country's written stories. These are undatable oral narratives from San and Khoi languages, which were transcribed by civil servants and missionaries in the nineteenth century.[85] Of particular note is the Bleek and Lloyd Collection, a large ethnographic archive assembled between 1870 and 1884 which includes phonetically transcribed |Xam and !Kung folklore and stories, which were translated into English. This archive brings into sharp focus the unstable boundary between oral and written modes that informs much South African short fiction, and vividly depicts the multiple authorings that texts often go through before appearing in the form in which we can now access them. As Hedley Twidle observes, the Bleek and Lloyd texts are best considered not as giving direct access to a pre-modern oral culture, but rather as a 'language event of great complexity, difficulty, beauty, and unexpectedness'.[86] Short stories in the late nineteenth and early twentieth centuries tended to appear in newspapers and journals, and some of the earliest examples of short stories written by black authors include R.R.R. Dhlomo's contributions to the journal *Sjambok* from 1929 to 1931, and A.S. Vil-Nkomo's 'Mhlutshwa Comes to Johannesburg', published in *Bantu World* in 1933.[87]

Early individual stories by white writers began to appear in journals and periodicals from the late 1840s, with several collections appearing from the 1860s onwards. Volumes such as R. Hodges's *The Settler in South Africa and Other Tales* (1860) and A.W. Drayson's *Tales at the Outspan, or Adventures in the Wild Regions of Southern Africa* (1862) were followed by several collections by women, such as *Tales*

---

85 There is a much longer history to be told about the oral story in South Africa, some of which is covered in the opening section of Attwell and Attridge (eds), *The Cambridge History of South African Literature*.
86 Hedley Twidle, '|Xam Narratives of the Bleek and Lloyd Collection', in *The Cambridge History of South African Literature*, ed. David Attwell and Derek Attridge (Cambridge: Cambridge University Press, 2012), pp. 19–41 (p. 21).
87 I am indebted here to Rob Gaylard, 'R.R.R. Dhlomo and the Early Black South African Short Story in English', *Current Writing*, 17.1 (2005), 52–69; Gaylard, 'Writing Black'.

Written in Ladybrand (1885) by Marguerite de Fenton, Mary Anne Carey-Hobson's *South African Stories* (1886), and Olive Schreiner's *Dreams* (1891) and *Dream Life and Real Life* (1893). W.C. Scully's *Kafir Stories* came out in 1895, and many collections began to appear by authors such as Perceval Gibbon, Francis Carey Slater, Pauline Smith, Aegidius Jean Blignaut, and Herman Charles Bosman from the late 1800s up till the 1950s. This part of the history of the South African short story is covered admirably by MacKenzie, and many of the tropes that are established in these collections – race relations, the pull between rural and urban environments, the tension between the spectacular and the ordinary – continued, and indeed continue, to inform the writing of later decades.[88] One of the most striking features of many of these early stories is their use of a frame narrator, a formal device which suggests straightforward truth-telling while in fact offering authors rich possibilities for 'metafictional play [...] literary self-consciousness', and other forms of irony that are more readily – if mistakenly – associated with later writing.[89]

The 1950s saw a remarkable increase in short story writing by authors classified by the apartheid state as black and coloured. This change was driven by the founding of *Drum* magazine, which promoted short stories through its competitions and became a 'symbol of the new African who, in opposition to apartheid, asserted a city identity', as Bernth Lindfors writes.[90] *Drum* published early writing by Sophiatown Renaissance authors such as Bloke Modisane, Can Themba, Arthur Maimane, Casey Motsitsi, and, from the District Six School, Richard Rive, James Matthews, and Alex La Guma. Although the District Six writers were more overtly political, both camps were producing varieties of engaged writing, what Chinua Achebe memorably calls 'applied art'.[91] The city setting of these stories, Michael Chapman notes, is crucially important when considered as the assertion of an urban identity in the context of Hendrik Verwoerd's concurrent promotion of retribalisation through

---

88 MacKenzie, *The Oral-Style South African Short Story*.
89 Ibid., p. 5.
90 Bernth Lindfors, 'Post-War Literature in English by African Writers from South Africa: A Study of the Effects of Environment upon Literature', *Phylon*, 27 (1966), 50–62 (p. 52).
91 Chinua Achebe, 'The Novelist as Teacher', in *Morning Yet on Creation Day: Essays* (Garden City, NY: Anchor, 1975), p. 72.

the Department of Native Affairs.⁹² In a societal context of black citizens being institutionally depicted as inherently rural, the claim to a coherent black urban identity was particularly urgent. The short story in the 1950s offered black writers a way of affirming the modern subjectivity the government denied them, while providing a quickfire means of responding to their growing societal marginalisation. For many writers of the 1950s–1980s, fiction writing and journalism were pursued in parallel, with articles often appearing in the same magazines in which their stories were published. Anne McClintock describes the aesthetic of the *Drum* writers as being 'by all appearances the style of individual heroics', while Rob Nixon draws attention to their distinctive township idiom and strong American influence, which borrows both from the experimentalism of the Harlem Renaissance and the schlocky bravado of Hollywood gangster films.⁹³

While black short story writers in the 1950s were mainly published in South African magazines, as Walter Ehmeier notes, 'most of the major white writers' of the period – Nadine Gordimer, Dan Jacobson, and Jack Cope are three notable examples – 'turned to overseas journals to publish their work'.⁹⁴ This decision was, in part, financially motivated, as such journals offered much higher rates than those in South Africa, but it also signalled their aesthetic preferences, and perhaps a degree of cultural cringe. The *Drum* writers were in constant dialogue with a burgeoning black culture in America, including its imbrication with a multifaceted global modernism, and white writers were also strongly influenced by the Anglo-European literary tradition, which itself drew on African, American, and African-American aesthetics.⁹⁵ The politics

---

92 Michael Chapman (ed.), *The Drum Decade: Stories From the 1950s* (Pietermaritzburg: University of Natal Press, 2001), p. 187.

93 See McClintock, *Imperial Leather*, p. 335; Rob Nixon, *Homelands, Harlem, and Hollywood: South African Culture and the World Beyond* (New York: Routledge, 1994), particularly ch. 1, 'Harlem, Hollywood, and the Sophiatown Renaissance' (pp. 11–42).

94 Walter Ehmeir, 'Publishing South African Literature in English in the 1960s', *Research in African Literatures*, 26.1 (1995), 111–31 (p. 116).

95 There is a much longer story to be told about the pathways of influence between European modernism, the Harlem Renaissance, and black and white writers in South Africa, which sadly I do not have space to pursue here. Parts of this network are explored in Nixon, *Homelands, Harlem, and Hollywood*; Shane Graham, 'Cultural Exchange in a Black Atlantic Web: South African Literature, Langston Hughes, and Negritude', *Twentieth-Century Literature*,

of white writing in the 1950s were most visible, as Dorothy Driver argues, in an 'engagement with the social transformations wrought by apartheid and its social engineering, or by the related processes of urbanisation'.[96] Racism and its effects were central concerns, and their stories often feature an encounter between a white and a black character, as is the case in Gordimer's well-known early story 'Is There Nowhere Else We Can Meet?' (1952). The influence of the liberal tradition is strong in short stories by white authors in the 1950s, visible in what Stephen Watson calls their 'appeal to the moral consciences and emotions of [their] readers', their focusing of the action through the consciousness of an individual, and their tendency to sideline political analysis in favour of eliciting 'a purely emotional identification with the suffering hero'.[97] Some of these tropes reappear in various guises in the stories I analyse, particularly in the interracial encounters that structure stories by Gordimer, Wicomb, and Rose-Innes. The presence of such tropes – albeit in highly mediated and adapted forms – and the elision of explicit political positions in the stories I analyse make them in some ways the more immediate heir of their liberal 1950s antecedents than some of the politically strident stories in the decades that followed.

By the 1960s *Drum* had stopped publishing short stories. This loss was in some measure mitigated in the early 1960s by the magazine *Fighting Talk* until its demise in 1963, when the mantle was taken up by *The New African*, particularly from 1965 when Lewis Nkosi became literary editor. The aesthetic of these politically engaged stories was, in Elleke Boehmer's words, increasingly 'upfront, hard-hitting, [and] mimetic'.[98] Some black and coloured authors, such as Ezekiel (later Es'kia) Mphahlele and Richard Rive, published in international

60.4 (2014), 481–512; and Julius Bailey and Scott Rosenberg, 'Reading Twentieth Century Urban Black Cultural Movements through Popular Periodicals: A Case Study of the Harlem Renaissance and South Africa's Sophiatown', *Safundi*, 17.1 (2016), 63–86.

96 Dorothy Driver, 'The Fabulous Fifties: Short Fiction in English', in *The Cambridge History of South African Literature*, ed. David Attwell and Derek Attridge (Cambridge: Cambridge University Press, 2012), pp. 387–409 (p. 391).

97 Stephen Watson, '*Cry, the Beloved Country* and the Failure of Liberal Vision', *English in Africa*, 9 (1982), 29–44 (pp. 40, 33).

98 Elleke Boehmer, 'Endings and New Beginnings: South African Fiction in Transition', in *Altered State? Writing and South Africa*, ed. Elleke Boehmer, Laura Chrisman, and Kenneth Parker (Hebden Bridge: Dangaroo, 1994), pp. 43–56 (p. 46).

magazines, including those in other African countries, such as *Black Orpheus*, *Transition*, and *Présence Africaine*.[99] As a general tendency, however, the 1960s saw a decline in short fiction, with the tide of cultural expression for black authors largely turning from prose to poetry, aided in some measure post-1968, when 'a number of literary magazines (*Contrast*, *New Coin*, *Ophir*, *Bolt*, *Izwi*, the *Classic*) started to publish poems by black writers'.[100] As I return to at various points in this book, the dynamics of magazine publication remain important to the post-apartheid short story, not only in the variant versions of stories it often leads to, but also in that paratextual information comes to inform interpretation.

If the location of black literature in the 1950s was the city, in the 1960s it became the place of exile, as authors such as Nkosi, La Guma, and Bessie Head were forced from the country. The Suppression of Communism Amendment Act of 1965 prohibited the publication of writing by banned authors, affecting, among others, Modisane, Themba, Mphahlele, Nkosi, Todd Matshikiza, and Nat Nakasa, many of whom had made their name writing journalism and short stories in *Drum* in the 1950s. International publication became a necessity for black authors, and imports of their books had to evade the South African censors.[101] As Gordimer observes, '[t]hrough this kind of censorship, the lively and important group of black writers who burst into South African literature in the 1950s and early 1960s disappeared from it as if through a trap-door'.[102] Future generations of authors could no longer access the writings of those that had come before them, cutting a literary tradition off at the root.

In the late years of the 1950s and into the 1960s, white authors increasingly turned in one of two directions. Either they embarked on what Paul Rich calls 'a more sophisticated exploration of the moral choices available to individuals in a situation of evolving inter-racial relations', or they ventured into 'a more politicised realism which

---

99 Ehmeir, 'Publishing South African Literature', p. 116.
100 Gaylard, 'Writing Black', p. 220.
101 James Currey, 'Representing South Africa in the African Writers Series', *English in Africa*, 34.1 (2007), 5–20 (p. 8). See also Peter D. McDonald, *The Literature Police: Apartheid Censorship and Its Cultural Consequences* (Oxford: Oxford University Press, 2009).
102 Nadine Gordimer, 'English-Language Literature and Politics in South Africa', *Journal of Southern African Studies*, 2 (1976), 131–50 (p. 132).

emphasised the power not of individual manipulation but of collective resistance to white power'.[103] The early part of the decade was largely characterised by the former approach, although the repercussions of the 1960 Sharpeville Massacre and the realities of political repression, banning, and censorship soon prompted an interrogation of the ethics behind this choice. Cope, Gordimer, and Jacobson continued to dominate white short story publication in the 1960s, with Gordimer's stories gradually turning against the assumptions that underlay progressivist, liberal solutions, and the aesthetic of liberal realism that accompanied them.[104] As Rich continues, '[w]hile [liberal realism] emphasised the autonomy of competing and autonomous individuals, it ignored the essential loci of political power'.[105] Frustrated by this, by the time of an interview in 1974, Gordimer went so far as to say that '[l]iberal is a dirty word. Liberals are people who make promises they have no power to keep.'[106] Both literature and literary criticism were becoming increasingly disaffected with its philosophy, culminating in 1974 in the anti-liberal sentiment of the Cape Town 'Poetry '74' conference. At this event, Mike Kirkwood launched an attack on 'Butlerism', named for Guy Butler and characterised by its nostalgia towards the past and its faith in achieving racial harmony through individual action rather than structural change.[107] The terms of this debate are pertinent to the short story in particular, in that the form tends towards depicting isolated individual experience rather than large-scale group dynamics.

In the 1970s prose writing among black authors began to regain the ground it had lost to poetry in the 1960s, and after the 1976 Soweto

---

103 Paul Rich, 'Liberal Realism in South African Fiction, 1948–1966', *English in Africa*, 12 (1985), 47–81 (p. 70).

104 The boom in experimental Afrikaans short stories in the 1960s was notable. See Martin Trump, 'South African Short Fiction in English and Afrikaans Since 1948' (unpublished PhD thesis, School of Oriental and African Studies, University of London, 1985), pp. 209–86 <https://eprints.soas.ac.uk/28643/1/10672803.pdf> (accessed 17 May 2022).

105 Rich, 'Liberal Realism in South African Fiction'. p. 49.

106 Gordimer, cited in Tony Morphet, 'Stranger Fictions: Trajectories in the Liberal Novel', *World Literature Today*, 70.1 (1996), 53–58 (p. 54).

107 Dorothy Driver, 'Modern South African Literature in English: A Reader's Guide to Some Recent Critical and Bibliographic Resources', *World Literature Today*, 70.1 (1996), 99–106 (p. 99). For a reassessment of Butler's legacy, see Christopher Thurman, 'Beyond Butlerism: Revisiting Aspects of South African Literary History', *English Studies in Africa*, 51.1 (2008), 47–64.

uprising, 'prose fiction picked up again with a political vengeance'.[108] Writers such as Mtutuzeli Matshoba and Mothobi Mutloatse found a ready outlet for their short stories in *Staffrider* magazine. Founded in 1978, *Staffrider* in its early days featured a democratised editorial policy, in which submissions were by region or writers' collective rather than under the names of individual authors, a structural rejoinder to the individualist politics of liberalism. It featured writing that was often quite different from both the extroverted bravado of the *Drum* writers and from the history of the liberal tradition, in which, as Michael Vaughan describes, 'the category of "the individual" was central, and literary themes were mediated by a concern with sensitively *individualized* experiences and interactions'.[109] The dis-individuation and regional collectivism of *Staffrider* offered a pronounced sense of class consciousness and a rootedness in place that worked against the centrifugal exilic movement of the 1960s. Short stories in the early *Staffrider* were often generically unstable, hovering between fiction and reportage, and sharing the page with photography, poetry, journalism, and other forms. The stories often have an explicit political message, with many authors exploring ideas prominent in Black Consciousness, such as shared oppression, collective resistance, the question of violence, and the need for movements and organisations solely for black people. During this decade, Bessie Head's *The Collector of Treasures: And Other Botswana Village Tales* (1977), Ahmed Essop's *The Hajji and Other Stories* (1978), and Bal Ganesh's *Stories About My People* (1974) represented rarities in short story publication, which was dominated, at least in terms of collections, by male authors classified as black or white.

While the majority of short stories by white writers in the 1970s remained strongly marked by the dominant current of realism, more formally experimental modes were emerging, a feature that would grow in prominence from the 1980s and 1990s onwards. Sheila Roberts' collection *Outside Life's Feast*, which won the Olive Schreiner Prize in 1976 just one year before she left South Africa for the United States, was grittily realist, and informed by her understanding of the intersection

---

108 Mbulelo Mzamane, 'Introduction', in *Hungry Flames and Other Black South African Short Stories*, ed. Mbulelo Mzamane (London: Longman, 1986), pp. ix–xxvi (p. xxi).
109 Michael Vaughan, '*Staffrider* and Directions within Contemporary South African Literature', in *Literature and Society in South Africa*, ed. Landeg White and Tim Couzens (London: Longman, 1984), pp. 196–212 (p. 197).

between a stark poor white background and her commitment to feminism. In contrast to Roberts' hard-bitten realism, Peter Wilhelm's *LM and Other Stories* (1975) is notable for hallucinatory stories such as 'Lion' and 'Pyro Protram', which foreshadow elements of Vladislavić's writing in the 1980s. Gordimer's style became markedly more elliptic and experimental, a dimension of her artistic practice that would reach its apogee in the post-apartheid writing that I discuss in Chapter 1.

In 1965 Nkosi had damned the black writing of the 1950s, proclaiming that '[w]ith the best will in the world it is impossible to detect in the fiction of black South Africans any significant or complex talent which responds with both sufficient vigour of the imagination and sufficient technical resources, to the problems posed by conditions in South Africa'.[110] His opinions were little changed in his 1998 assessment of writing of the 1980s and early 1990s, when he described the 'colonial status of black writing in South Africa', referring to 'its formal insufficiencies, its disappointing breadline asceticism and prim disapproval of irony'.[111] This assessment is perhaps more interesting in terms of what it tells us about Nkosi's literary preferences rather than for the validity of its conclusions. Experimentalism of various kinds has been present in black South African writing from its inception, but even in the immediate context of Nksoi's comments, it hard to see how his position could account for the short stories in the 1980s of Joël Matlou, Bheki Maseko, Njabulo Ndebele, and Miriam Tlali.[112] Gaylard, citing Attwell, observes that Ndebele's and Wicomb's writing brought a higher degree of '"experimentalism" [...] into the tradition of the black South African short story, but an experimentalism that [wa]s "both socially connected

---

110 Lewis Nkosi, *Home and Exile, and Other Selections* (London: Longman, 1983 [1965]), p. 130.
111 Lewis Nkosi, 'Postmodernism and Black Writing in South Africa', in *Writing South Africa: Literature, Apartheid, and Democracy 1970–1995*, ed. Derek Attridge and Rosemary Jane Jolly (Cambridge: Cambridge University Press, 1998), pp. 75–90 (p. 77).
112 Although Matlou's collection, *Life at Home, and Other Stories* (Johannesburg: COSAW, 1991) came out in 1991, three of these stories were published in 1979, 1980, and 1987 in *Staffrider*. Several of Bheki Maseko's stories were also first published in the 1980s in *Staffrider*, *Ingolovane*, and *TriQuarterly*. Bheki Maseko, *Mamlambo and Other Stories* (Johannesburg: COSAW, 1991); Njabulo S. Ndebele, *Fools and Other Stories* (Johannesburg: Ravan, 1983); Zoë Wicomb, *You Can't Get Lost in Cape Town* (London: Virago, 1987).

and aesthetically reflexive'".[113] In terms of the direction the short story takes post-apartheid, it is interesting to note not only the increasing formal experimentalism during this period, but also that both Ndebele's *Fools* (1983) and Wicomb's *You Can't Get Lost in Cape Town* (1987) are short story cycles, a form that has become more common in post-apartheid writing.[114]

Greater experimentalism, combined with growing political commitment, also characterised the short stories of a number of white authors during the 1980s, with Gordimer's *Something Out There* (1984) and Vladislavić's *Missing Persons* (1989) in particular pushing towards new means of expression while sustaining a heightened political urgency. There was greater convergence during this period between the black and white short story traditions, as both sought out new forms that could maintain political purchase without sacrificing the 'vigour of the imagination' and technical capacity that Nkosi promoted.[115] From the early 1990s onwards there has been a visible move in the South African short story away from the explicitly political stories of earlier decades, which showed the brutalities committed by the government and its agents and the acts of rebellion they provoked, towards stories in which social issues are engaged in more oblique ways.[116]

While the short story was a favoured form for black authors during much of the apartheid period, the same cannot be said for the early part of the post-apartheid period. Margaret Lenta observed in 2011 that '[f]ew, if any black men have published collections of stories in the last decade'.[117] Although Lenta was correct that there were not

---

113 Gaylard, 'Writing Black', p. 318, citing Attwell, *Rewriting Modernity*, p. 179.
114 For more on cycles, see Susan Marais, '(Re-)Inventing Our Selves/Ourselves: Identity and Community in Contemporary South African Short Fiction Cycles' (PhD thesis, Rhodes University, 2014), <http://hdl.handle.net/10962/d1016357> (accessed 16 September 2022).
115 In Afrikaans short story writing in the 1980s, Taurus and other presses published work of a formal experimentalism to rival that of the Sestigers, and with greater political purchase. Some examples include Dan Roodt, Karin Konsentrasiekamp, John Miles, M.C. Botha, Lettie Viljoen, and Koos Prinsloo. See Ian Barnard, 'The "Tagtigers"? The (Un) Politics of Language in the "New" Afrikaans Fiction', *Research in African Literatures*, 23.4 (1992), 77–95.
116 As ever, there are exceptions, such as Alan Kolski Horwitz, *Meditations of a Non-White White* (Johannesburg: Dye Hard, 2012).
117 Margaret Lenta, 'Introduction', *Current Writing*, 17 (2005), i–iv (p. ii).

many collections by black authors in the 1990s and 2000s, there were some, and since her comments many more have been published. For example, Sindiwe Magona's *Living, Loving, and Lying Awake at Night* (1991) and *Push-push and Other Stories* (1996), and Mandla Langa's *The Naked Song and Other Stories* (1996) are notable in the earlier part of this period, and Zachariah Rapola's 2007 collection *Beginnings of a Dream* combines formal experimentation with techniques from orature in fascinating ways, and would reward a more substantial engagement than I have space for here. It is difficult to know with any certainty why interest in the short story waned somewhat in the period directly after apartheid. There are perhaps some material aspects to consider: improved access to education and a growing black middle class were probably contributing factors, as both a greater facility with English and financial stability would likely aid writing longer forms. As Wicomb notes, until at least the 1990s, 'material conditions contributed to the black preference for the short story', among which she identifies several possible contributing factors, such as English proficiency, '[l]ack of means, lack of privacy in overcrowded housing conditions, geographical instability', and funding available for 'low-cost pocket-size publications of collections and anthologies'.[118] As well as these factors, there is also the combination of a proportionally small number of black authors with publishing companies' general reluctance to publish short stories. Many publishers in South Africa will not accept short story collection submissions by first-time authors, with novels and non-fiction being the preferred forms, an issue I return to in the Conclusion.

Since around 2010 many more collections have appeared, which along with online initiatives such as *The Johannesburg Review of Books* and the LongStorySHORT, offer a picture of the short story regaining ground after a brief post-apartheid hiatus.[119] What is most exciting in this recent surge of short fiction is its sheer variety, with styles ranging from speculative fiction to oral storytelling, and sometimes blending English with Afrikaans, isiXhosa, Sesotho, and other languages. This

---

118 Zoë Wicomb, 'South African Short Fiction and Orality', in *Telling Stories: Postcolonial Short Fiction in English*, ed. Jacqueline Bardolph (Amsterdam: Rodopi, 2001), pp. 157–70 (p. 162).

119 See Kgauhelo Dube and others, 'LongStorySHORT: Decolonising the Reading Landscape – A Conversation with Kgauhelo Dube', in *The Short Story in South Africa: Contemporary Trends and Perspectives*, ed. Rebecca Fasselt and Corinne Sandwith (Abingdon: Routledge, 2022), pp. 226–41.

heterogeneity is present across the board in short story writing after apartheid.[120] In the collections I examine in detail in the following chapters, as well as in many others that I was not able to include, it is the sheer range of ambition and approach that is most immediately striking. Collections range geographically from South Africa to Europe and beyond, as is the case for Wicomb's *The One That Got Away* (2008), Vladislavić's *The Loss Library and Other Stories* (2011), or S.J. Naudé's *The Alphabet of Birds* (2015). There are stories that engage explicitly with the aftershocks of apartheid, those that do so implicitly, and those that focus elsewhere. There are formally experimental stories, genre stories, flash fiction, and everything in between. This welcome resurgence in the short story is, as I suggest in the Conclusion, perhaps a result of the expansion of MFA programmes in South African universities; many authors currently being published either studied creative writing or now teach in creative writing departments, where the short story is often used as a model for composition. Whatever the reason, it seems that the short story is currently thriving in South Africa, despite the caginess of some publishers.

One aspect of the short story not examined in detail in this book is the role of the anthology. All of the authors in this study have had their stories anthologised, and when a story is placed in such a volume, it enters into dialogue with those around it. It begins, in Michiel Heyns's formulation, 'confirming, contradicting, qualifying, relativising'.[121] Anthologies are fascinating documents, whether presented in national terms, such as Stephen Gray's *The Penguin Book of Contemporary South African Short Stories* (1993) or Michael Chapman's gargantuan *Omnibus of a Century of South African Short Stories* (2007), or according to some other logic of organisation. Andries Walter Oliphant's *At the Rendezvous of Victory* (1999) seeks to 'provide a perspective on narrative

---

120 Notable collections that I do not analyse in detail include Siphiwo Mahala's *African Delights* (2011) and *Red Apple Dreams and Other Stories* (2019), Dianne Awerbuck's *Cabin Fever and Other Stories* (2011), Reneilwe Malatji's *Love Interrupted* (2012), Makhosazana Xaba's *Running and Other Stories* (2013), Liesl Jobson's *Ride the Tortoise* (2013), Niq Mhlongo's *Affluenza* (2016), *Soweto, Under the Apricot Tree* (2018), and *For You, I'd Steal a Goat* (2022), Mohale Mashigo's *Intruders* (2018), Fred Khumalo's *Talk of the Town* (2019), and Terry-Ann Adams's *White Chalk* (2022).

121 Michiel Heyns, '"Separate Families, Separate Worlds, the Same Native Space": Aspects of the South African Short Story', *Current Writing*, 17.1 (2005), 167–84 (p. 168).

responses to recent changes in South Africa', while *Touch: Stories of Contact* (2010) clusters its texts around the multiple meanings of a single word.[122] As Elke D'hoker notes, '[f]ar more than a mere solution to the problem of publishing short fiction, the anthology is a literary form which plays a major part in the production, promotion, reception, evaluation and understanding of the short story'.[123] An analysis of the relations of 'power, ideology, institution, and manipulation' involved in the publication of South African anthologies surely demands further investigation, but this analysis must wait until a later date.[124]

Book Structure

Chapter 1 focuses on Nadine Gordimer, one of the most fêted figures in the South African short story, and one of the most important voices in the twentieth- and twenty-first-century short story more broadly. Across her career, but particularly from the 1990s onwards, her writing became more difficult to interpret and more self-reflexive. In her three post-apartheid collections, Gordimer uses non-linear plots to stage scenes of retrospection that are reflections on the country's past and on her own authorial legacy. Gordimer's formal experimentation in her post-apartheid work interrogates her prior strategies for political writing, showing the temporal contingency of engaged stylistics, and inviting others to think what modes of writing are fit to articulate the political present.

In Chapter 2, I analyse three of Ivan Vladislavić's stories from 1989 to 2019, showing how they offer new ways of conceiving the role that artworks play in the 'future of the past'. To do this, I track Vladislavić's changing depiction of monuments across his stories and

122 Stephen Gray (ed.), *The Penguin Book of Contemporary South African Short Stories* (Johannesburg: Penguin, 1993); Michael Chapman (ed.), *Omnibus of a Century of South African Short Stories* (Johannesburg and Cape Town: Ad Donker, 2007); Andries Walter Oliphant, *At the Rendezvous of Victory and Other Stories* (Cape Town: Kwela, 1999), p. 7; Karina Magdalena Szczurek (ed.), *Touch: Stories of Contact* (Cape Town: Struik, 2010).
123 Elke D'hoker, 'The Short Story Anthology', in *The Edinburgh Companion to the Short Story in English*, ed. Paul Delaney and Adrian Hunter (Edinburgh: Edinburgh University Press, 2019), pp. 108–24 (p. 117).
124 André Lefevere, *Translation, Rewriting, and the Manipulation of Literary Fame* (London: Routledge, 1992), p. 2.

how the relationship to the past implied by these totems of memory is informed by the experience of reading short fiction. As the Rhodes Must Fall movement has brought into sharp focus, monuments are charged symbols of how historical narratives are shaped by their public representation and are an important means through which the relationship between the individual and the state is mediated. The monuments Vladislavić describes are artworks of a special kind, that both encode and project particular understandings of history, statehood, and citizenship. The brevity of the reading experience of these stories, and the apophatic aesthetics they adopt, position the short story as a form of counter-monument to those of the national imaginary.

Chapter 3 argues that Zoë Wicomb makes use of the short story's elliptical tendency to mediate one of South Africa's most volatile political issues, namely, the 'problem of class'.[125] This 'problem' is in one sense societal – her stories in *The One That Got Away* (2008) depict how class intersects with race and other markers of identity to shape experience – but it is also literary, concerning how the elliptic, aporetic, and isolated short story articulates class experience, and what happens when these are arranged in a loosely linked cycle. By looking at class through dual sociological and aesthetic lenses, I draw attention to a crucial societal concern, while showing that the stylistic and formal tendencies of the modern short story both facilitate and impede engaged writing.

In Chapter 4, I examine how Phaswane Mpe's posthumously published short story collection *Brooding Clouds* (2008) offers experiences of form that allow a thinking through of the forms of violence, both structural and spectacular, that still disproportionally affect black South Africans. This violence appears in individual shocking acts – murders, suicides, and robberies – but is also a cumulative and crushing accretion of poverty, racism, curtailed education, stifled opportunity, disappointed hope, and the psychological harms that these factors cause. Mpe finds in the short story a form through which to express a political consciousness that comprehends singular acts of oppression as part of a distributed climate of disenfranchisement. Mpe's short fiction articulates this condition through what he calls 'brooding', a state which is sometimes a cast of mind, sometimes an orientation towards the world, sometimes a threatening or melancholy atmosphere in which life plays out. It is precisely the difficulty of disentangling the multiple

---

125 Zoë Wicomb, *The One That Got Away* (Cape Town: Umuzi, 2008), p. 126.

vectors of brooding that creates its formal effect, and this in turn constitutes the heuristic device that it offers: a model of complexity that shuns monocausal explanations.

Chapter 5 reads Henrietta Rose-Innes's short story collection *Homing* (2010), arguing that it sustains a productively unresolved tension between the aesthetic demands of the short story's spatial form and the spatially segregated post-apartheid nation. The chapter outlines why the land- and cityscape are crucial to understanding contemporary South Africa, and discusses how South African literature has responded to these spatial concerns. It then proposes an expanded concept of Joseph Frank's theory of spatial form, in which divergent understandings of literary space are put into dialogue, before looking in detail at how these factors play out in Rose-Innes's work. Analysing three stories from her collection *Homing*, I examine how these texts tack between the dehistoricising tendencies of spatial form and the historicised contexts in which the stories take place. These stories participate in a tradition in the South African short story in which setting becomes active in producing character and plot. The three spaces I look at – the mall, the luxury hotel, and the beach – all bring with them norms of behaviour as much as they serve as indices of inner states, and these resonate and clash with the stories' formal and symbolic logics.

The Conclusion thinks back over the previous five chapters, analysing how each author has worked with, developed, and altered the possibilities of the short story form in the years after apartheid. In their short stories, they have made substantial contributions to South African literature, and more broadly have contributed to the global development of the form. The Conclusion then returns to the possibilities that formal and generic analysis offers to postcolonial studies, to think synthetically about the intersections of the short story with these theoretical models in light of the authors discussed. It reflects on how strategies of engaged writing, the negotiation of the past, the imbrication of class and race, and the politics of place appear in short narratives, as they are imagined through the short story's preference for discontinuity, aporia, ellipsis, and spatial form. Further, it explores the expansion of creative writing programmes in South African universities, a development that has shaped and will surely continue to shape the generic contours of the short story in years to come.

At the time of writing, it is nearly thirty years since apartheid's end, and during this time the political terrain of the country's literature has changed. Many authors have staged what Shaun Irlam calls a 'modulated "retreat" from a strident political role of the writer'.[126] However, this does not mean that they no longer write politically. Rather, as post-apartheid societal concerns have become increasingly complex in their aetiology, authors have adopted new formal and stylistic means of responding to them. By attending to questions of form, genre, and style, we gain a clearer picture of how these texts gain their political purchase in ways that are particular to literature, and also why these stories exceed any solely political interpretation. These stories are not symptoms of a prior social form, static carriers of information, or allegories of the social, but rather offer a means of co-creating knowledge. The authors I examine have decisively shaped the short story in South Africa and offer some of the most compelling examples of how the form might contribute to addressing the ethical and political challenges posed by life after apartheid.

---

126 Shaun Irlam, 'Unravelling the Rainbow: The Remission of Nation in Post-Apartheid Literature', *South Atlantic Quarterly*, 103.4 (2004), 695–718 (p. 714).

CHAPTER ONE

Nadine Gordimer
Past, Present, and Future

Nadine Gordimer opens her 1968 essay on the short story, 'The Flash of Fireflies', by pondering the short story's longevity. 'Why is it', she asks, 'that while the death of the novel is good for post-mortem at least once a year, the short story lives on unmolested?'[1] If the novel is suffocated by an excess of critical attention, the short story, 'like a child suffering from healthy neglect [...] survives'.[2] She answers by noting that the short story has always been 'more flexible and open to experiment than the novel'.[3] To her mind, the novel requires a 'prolonged coherence of tone' that would be intolerable if it was too experimental, the sustained note of coherence transforming into an irritating 'high pitched ringing in the reader's ears'.[4] Short-story writers, for their part, offer 'flashes of fearful insight alternating with near-hypnotic states of indifference', they 'see by the light of the flash; theirs is the art of the only thing one can be sure of – the present moment'.[5] Gordimer's comments suggest an essential difference between the novel and the short story, and one that would be difficult to sustain in light of the novel's wild experiments from its earliest examples. However, her claim does offer some insight into how she thinks of her short story writing. 'Writers of short stories', she says, having invested less time than novelists in writing, have 'more

---

1 Nadine Gordimer, 'The Flash of Fireflies', in *The New Short Story Theories*, ed. Charles E. May (Athens, OH: Ohio University Press, 1994), pp. 263–67 (p. 263).
2 Ibid., p. 263.
3 Ibid., p. 264.
4 Ibid., pp. 264, 265.
5 Ibid., p. 265.

chance of working without compromise'.[6] This suggests that Gordimer saw her short fiction as the domain in which she could pursue her experimentation to its furthest reaches.

In her last three collections, *Jump* (1991), *Loot* (2003), and *Beethoven Was One-Sixteenth Black* (2007), Gordimer's experimentation extends the formal exploration of her previous work. These fragmentary, gestural texts offer readers stripped-back, meta-textual experiences through which to conceive of a present moment – the firefly's flash – that is occupied by the past. The short story's accommodation of temporal compression and dilation plays an important role in how she does this. Both thematically and formally, her stories become increasingly preoccupied with the passage of time, and specifically the past's immediacy to the present in post-apartheid South Africa. This has been a common concern of post-apartheid literature, but Gordimer's case presents a particularly interesting example. Not only do her transition and post-apartheid stories appear in the wake of apartheid's end, and so constitute a formal response to its lingering presence, they also allow her to reflect on the aesthetic strategies of her own writing, and so offer a challenge to engaged writing after apartheid. In these stories we see not only the formal engagement of the social world or an individual consciousness, but also a working through of the affordances that different modes of writing might offer to a project of political writing in a dramatically changed political landscape.[7]

Gordimer's career spanned the apartheid era and beyond, and included some fifteen novels and over two dozen collections of stories published across a lifetime of artistic and political commitment. To Gordimer's mind, commitment was not only a matter of politics, it was also a question of finding a 'thread of order and logic in the disorder, and the incredible waste and marvellous profligate character of life'.[8] In transforming the excess of experience into pattern or design, Gordimer foregrounds both the workings of form and the demands of social reality.

---

6 Ibid., p. 266.

7 I elsewhere explore Gordimer's late-career experimentation as a navigation of 'late style'. Graham K. Riach, 'The Late Nadine Gordimer', *Journal of Southern African Studies*, 42.6 (2016), 1077–94.

8 Nadine Gordimer and Jannika Hurwitt, 'Nadine Gordimer, The Art of Fiction No. 77', *Paris Review*, summer 1983, <https://www.theparisreview.org/interviews/3060/the-art-of-fiction-no-77-nadine-gordimer> (accessed 12 January 2021).

For Gordimer, there was no easy compromise to be made between the two, and each of her works reads as a site of struggle, filtered through a vivid writerly imagination. In one of her most famous essays, she describes the writer's 'essential gesture', namely the 'transformation of experience' that comes about from 'the lifting out of a limited category something that reveals its full meaning and significance only when the writer's imagination has expanded it'.[9] From the 1970s onwards, this imaginative transformation took an ever-more experimental direction in novels such as *The Conservationist* (1974), *Burger's Daughter* (1979), and *July's People* (1981), right through to *No Time Like the Present* (2012), which would be her last.

While her novels are perhaps her best-known works, throughout her career Gordimer found in the short story a highly flexible and adaptable form. *Face to Face* (1949) and *Beethoven Was One-Sixteenth Black* (2007) bookend a remarkable career as a short story writer, an aspect of Gordimer's oeuvre that is often overlooked. Gordimer held the form in high esteem, yet Rob Nixon observes that her stories are 'critically remaindered as if they were five-finger exercises', a judgement justified in that several major studies, such as those by Stephen Clingman and Judie Newman, either underplay the importance of her stories or omit them altogether.[10] However, while this may have been true at the time Nixon wrote, there has been more interest in her short stories since, although still less than in her novels. Dominic Head's *Nadine Gordimer*, in a chapter on Gordimer's short fiction, makes a convincing case for the increasing 'sophistication' of her later stories, pointing to their 'increasingly destabilised narrative texture' and productively fragmentary form.[11] A 2016 part special issue of the *Journal of Southern African Studies* and a 2019 special issue of *Commonwealth Essays and*

---

9 Nadine Gordimer, 'The Essential Gesture', in *Telling Times: Writing and Living, 1950–2008* (London: Bloomsbury, 2010), pp. 409–23 (p. 422).

10 Rob Nixon, 'Nadine Gordimer', in *British Writers, Supplement II*, ed. George Stade (New York: Scribner, 1992), pp. 1–28 (p. 9); Stephen Clingman, *The Novels of Nadine Gordimer: History from the Inside*, 2nd edn (Amherst: University of Massachusetts Press, 1992); Judie Newman, *Nadine Gordimer* (London: Routledge, 1988).

11 Dominic Head, *Nadine Gordimer* (Cambridge: Cambridge University Press, 1994), p. 181. Robert F. Haugh's *Nadine Gordimer* also argues for Gordimer's abilities as a short story writer, but his study is marred by its failure to acknowledge her changing concerns from the 1960s onwards. Robert F. Haugh, *Nadine Gordimer* (New York: Twayne, 1974).

Studies were devoted to Gordimer, with several articles on her short fiction. Ileana Dimitriu has published perceptive pieces on Gordimer's post-apartheid short fiction, in which she 'challenge[s] interpretations of Gordimer's short-story writing as ideologically less significant and/or artistically less accomplished than her novels'.[12] Rita Barnard brilliantly explores the relationship between realism and modernism in her short stories, and Graham Huggan focuses insightfully on the political traction of Gordimer's short fiction, judging in the last instance that the 'concentrated form of the short story' makes the 'enormity of [societal] discrepancy' felt more keenly, and so provides Gordimer with a form that 'may well cut deeper than the ostensibly political novel into the fabric of society'.[13] While it is perhaps unnecessary to pit the two forms against one another in terms of their political efficacy, it is true that Gordimer's short stories are characterised by an intensity of focus and a compression of form that is less pronounced in her novels. Both her short stories and her novels share common interests and techniques, but the short story's shortness and density create a sense of simultaneity between past, present, and future that well suits the odd temporality of the post-apartheid period, and that is perhaps less present in her post-apartheid novels.

As Dorothy Driver observes in her introduction to *Nadine Gordimer: A Bibliography of Primary and Secondary Sources*, 'recent developments in the South African political situation' mean that it is now time to 'read the relations between art and politics in Gordimer's writing not simply at the level of content but also at the level of form'.[14] Postcolonial criticism, and criticism of Gordimer in particular, has at times foregrounded analysis of content and historical situatedness over that of poetics.[15] So, as Anne Collett writes, it is now time to pay greater

12 Ileana Dimitriu, 'Shifts in Gordimer's Recent Short Fiction: Story-telling after Apartheid', *Current Writing: Text and Reception in Southern Africa*, 17.1 (2005), 90–107 (p. 90).
13 Rita Barnard, 'Nadine Gordimer's Transitions: Modernism, Realism, Rupture', *Cycnos*, 34.3 (2018), 19–33; Graham Huggan, 'Echoes from Elsewhere: Gordimer's Short Fiction as Social Critique', *Research in African Literatures*, 25.1 (1994), 61–73 (p. 71).
14 Dorothy Driver and others (eds), *Nadine Gordimer: A Bibliography of Primary and Secondary Sources, 1937–1992* (London: Hans Zell, 1994), p. 5.
15 For more on this tendency of postcolonial criticism, see Jane Hiddleston, 'Introduction', in *Postcolonial Poetics: Genre and Form*, ed. Patrick Crowley and Jane Hiddleston (Liverpool: Liverpool University Press, 2011), pp. 1–12;

attention to the 'aesthetics' of Gordimer's fiction, the 'construction of writing at the most fundamental level of word order and word choice, sentence structure, and rhythm'.[16] It is not entirely true that criticism of Gordimer has so resolutely avoided the formal and stylistic dimensions of her writing. To take two influential examples, Clingman's field-defining work on Gordimer may emphasise her writing's historical dimension, but it is deeply concerned with how formal features, down to the stylistic level of the sentence in some cases, can open out onto social and historical thought.[17] Likewise, Barnard's equally influential work has always been alert to the formal characteristics of Gordimer's writing.[18] Nevertheless, it remains the case that Driver's and Collet's call for aesthetic attention to Gordimer is far from being answered in full, and particularly in relation to her short fiction. Before discussing this further, however, it may prove useful to outline some elements of Gordimer's short story practice, and the political coordinates of her writing.

Gordimer's career began in earnest in 1949 with her first published book, a collection of short stories titled *Face to Face*.[19] It appeared less than a year after the National Party came to power in June 1948. This temporal coincidence between authorial and political circumstance draws attention to a central concern of Gordimer's writing, namely, the relationship between writing and politics. Her books became increasingly responsive to the historical conditions in which she found herself, yet she maintains that it was not political involvement or 'the "problems" of [her] country' that 'set [her] writing'.[20] Rather, it was through a delicate literary excavation of the society around her that she

---

Dominique Combe, 'Preface', in *Postcolonial Poetics: Genre and Form*, ed. Patrick Crowley and Jane Hiddleston (Liverpool: Liverpool University Press, 2011), pp. vii–xii.

16 Anne Collett, 'Writing Freedom: Nadine Gordimer and *The New Yorker*', in *Experiences of Freedom in Postcolonial Literatures and Cultures*, ed. Annalisa Oboe and Shaul Bassi (Abingdon: Routledge, 2011), pp. 341–52 (p. 350).

17 Clingman, *The Novels of Nadine Gordimer*; Stephen Clingman, 'Surviving Murder: Oscillation and Triangulation in Nadine Gordimer's *The House Gun*', *MFS: Modern Fiction Studies*, 46.1 (2000), 139–58.

18 See, for example, chapters 2 and 3 of Rita Barnard, *Apartheid and Beyond: South African Writers and the Politics of Place* (Oxford: Oxford University Press, 2007).

19 Nadine Gordimer, *Face to Face: Short Stories* (Johannesburg: Silver Leaf, 1949).

20 Nadine Gordimer, 'A Bolter and the Invincible Summer', in *Telling Times:*

first came to political consciousness. She began to write by means of an 'apparently esoteric speleology of doubt, led by Kafka rather than Marx', a process that 'sent [her] falling, falling through the surface of "the South African way of life"'.[21] She remained adamant that she was 'not by nature a political creature', as she told the *Paris Review* in 1983, and yet her fiction and critical essays read like seismographs of societal change in the country she refused to leave, despite repeated government censorship and harassment.[22] The metaphor of a seismograph perhaps underplays, however, the extent to which Gordimer's writing is a conscious remodelling of language in a historically particular set of social and political conditions. The style of her writing from the 1970s onwards changed quite drastically from her earlier stories, which were influenced by the short stories of Anton Chekhov, Guy de Maupassant, and Ernest Hemingway as well as by the more local current of liberal realism, with its focus on the individual's interior life, commitment to addressing social problems through individual choice, and its attempt to invoke the reader's sympathetic engagement.[23] As a general tendency, from the 1960s and 1970s, accompanying her public disavowal of liberalism, her writing pursued a more experimental direction with increasingly fragmentary forms, and from the 1980s into the 1990s and beyond there was an intensification of meta-textual and postmodern aspects. However, while this trajectory holds in general terms, it might be more accurate to say that strands of liberal realism, modernism, and postmodernism (among others) coexist in her later works, and many of the short stories from her last three collections make the tension between these dimensions of her writerly practice an important feature of their operation.

In *Jump*, *Loot*, and *Beethoven*, Gordimer's stories not only return to scenes of retrospection on the apartheid past and the repercussions it has on the present, but they do so in prose increasingly marked by a self-reflexivity about her own writerly practice. In an interview,

Writing and Living, 1950–2008 (London: Bloomsbury, 2010), pp. 112–21 (p. 119).
21 Ibid., p. 119.
22 Gordimer and Hurwitt, 'Nadine Gordimer'.
23 See Peter Blair, 'The Liberal Tradition in Fiction', in *The Cambridge History of South African Literature*, ed. David Attwell and Derek Attridge (Cambridge: Cambridge University Press, 2012), pp. 474–99; Morphet, 'Stranger Fictions'; Rich, 'Liberal Realism'.

Gordimer commented on her erratic use of tenses, saying that she favoured 'chopping and changing from the present to the past because that's how we think. Do we ever live really in the present? I don't think so, not entirely, do you?'[24] This heightened sensitivity to the past's immediacy to the present is visible both thematically and at the level of form, where it is filtered through the short story's feeling of 'all-at-onceness'.[25] Gordimer's stories from this period formally negotiate the past's continuation in the present through their chaotic, yet paradoxically static depiction of time, but more than this, they call into question the aesthetic parameters of her own fictional project. While in *Jump*, the consequences of Gordimer's experimentation are largely to be deduced from her writing's formal characteristics, in *Loot* and *Beethoven* her authorial interventions become ever more explicit, offering a running commentary on stories as she tells them. This is fascinating both for what it can tell us about Gordimer's practice as a writer, but also in terms of how she hoped her fictions might be received and the work to which she thought they might be put by readers and writers.

'Jump': The Leap to Nowhere

Jump appeared in 1991, in the middle of what Gordimer, citing Gustave Flaubert, called 'the most difficult and least glamorous of all tasks: transition'.[26] It might have been expected that her first collection since the transfer of power began in 1990 would constitute a point of departure, a jump to a new mode of life as apartheid drew to a close. Instead, she opens the collection with a story first published in *Harper's* in 1989 that is marked by a temporal shuttling between past and present that leads to a sense of interminable stasis.[27] The opening stories of collections set the

---

24 Nadine Gordimer and Henk Rossouw, 'An Interview with Nadine Gordimer', *VQR: A National Journal of Literature & Discussion*, 2007 <http://www.vqronline.org/web-exclusive/interview-nadine-gordimer> (accessed 7 October 2022).

25 John Gerlach, 'Narrative, Lyric and Plot in Chris Offutt's *Out of the Woods*', in *The Art of Brevity: Excursions in Short Fiction Theory and Analysis*, ed. Per Winther, Jakob Lothe, and Hans Hanssen Skei (Columbia: University of South Carolina Press, 2004), pp. 44–56 (p. 44).

26 Nadine Gordimer, *Writing and Being* (Cambridge, MA: Harvard University Press, 1995), p. 134.

27 Nadine Gordimer, 'Jump', *Harper's Magazine*, October 1989, pp. 55–61.

tone for what follows, and with this choice Gordimer shows a suspicion of narratives of progress. In the context of Gordimer's oeuvre, the collection's title brings with it the existential resonances of a Kierkegaardian leap of faith, what Rita Barnard describes as an 'affiliation with the not-yet-become'.[28] This gesture of commitment to an as yet uncertain future appears in various guises throughout Gordimer's works. It is present in the ambiguous ending of 'No Place Like' in *Livingstone's Companions*, in which a woman in transit in an airport chooses not to board her connecting flight, and again in the apocalyptic ending of *July's People*, in which Maureen Smales runs towards an unmarked helicopter, unaware 'whether it holds saviours or murderers; and – even if she were to have identified the markings – for whom'.[29]

These earlier texts are essentially turned towards the future, and the collection's title suggests that it will share this orientation. However, *Jump* is Janus-faced, as concerned with the past as with what is to come. Many of the stories are set in the late 1980s and early 1990s, a historical juncture between an authoritarian past and an uncertain future when, although much of the institutional architecture of apartheid was being dismantled, the end was not yet in sight. The collection responds to the state of transition through a thematic and stylistic processing of the past's immanence to the present, leading to a state of suspension that persists until the collection's last words: 'Waiting. I'm waiting to come back home.'[30] The mode of this suspension hovers between the latent energy of future possibility and the stagnant morass of present difficulty, a suitably indeterminate state for what Johan U. Jacobs calls a 'post-apartheid but pre-democratic South Africa'.[31]

'Jump' describes the experience of a counter-revolutionary in an unnamed southern African country who has recently switched sides

28 Rita Barnard, 'Locating Gordimer: Modernism, Postcolonialism, Realism', in *Modernism, Postcolonialism, and Globalism: Anglophone Literature, 1950 to the Present*, ed. Richard Begam and Michael Valdez Moses (Oxford: Oxford University Press, 2018), p. 104.
29 Nadine Gordimer, *Livingstone's Companions* (London: Jonathan Cape, 1971); Nadine Gordimer, *July's People* (New York: Penguin, 1981), p. 158.
30 Nadine Gordimer, *Jump and Other Stories* (London: Bloomsbury, 1991), p. 257. All further references to this work are given parenthetically in the text until the end of this section.
31 Johan U. Jacobs, 'Finding a Safe House of Fiction in Nadine Gordimer's *Jump and Other Stories*', in *Telling Stories: Postcolonial Short Fiction in English*, ed. Jacqueline Bardolph (Amsterdam: Rodopi, 2001), pp. 197–204 (p. 199).

to join the national armed forces. The man sits in a room in 'what was once the hotel' (3), where he lives on room service deliveries while awaiting the outcome of the 'deal' (5), in which he is to be given a house and money to live on. Since changing sides, he has given press conferences to the international media, describing his childhood in the country, his imprisonment by the post-independence government due to having inadvertently photographed a politically sensitive building, and his actions to destabilise the country after his release. In a series of flashbacks to the conferences, he recounts his long-distance and ostensibly unwitting actions that contributed to a number of atrocities: 'cut[ting] off the ears of villagers [...] rap[ing] children and forc[ing] women at gunpoint to kill their husbands and eat their flesh' (13), in a process of 'destabilization' (14) conceived to bring down the revolutionary government. On one occasion he visited a training camp in the country, where he was faced with the repercussions of his actions. This included being offered one of the 'girls of twelve or thirteen' who had been brought in to 'satisfy' (16) the new recruits. The experience horrified him, leading to his defection.

The authorities have now used the protagonist's story, and seem to have lost interest in him – '[o]nce he's told everything [...] what use is he to them?' (18) – and the 'deal', with its attendant possibilities for moving on, shows little sign of being honoured. Towards the end of the story, a 'girl' (18) of undisclosed age with whom he is sexually involved appears from the adjoining bedroom. The sexual in Gordimer is always, in Bruce King's words, 'a microcosm for or related the political', and their relationship is at least in part determined by his access to power, and foreign currency.[32] He is taciturn and treats her callously, although it is left open whether it is the memory of the girls at the training camp that impedes his coming close to her. The girl invites the man to the beach, but he remains silent until she leaves. The man contemplates either committing suicide by throwing himself from the balcony or finally leaving his hotel room.

There is significant overlap between the story and real-world events. In a chapter by Gordimer in the BBC book *Frontiers*, there is evidence that the protagonist is based on Paulo Oliveira, a defector from Renamo

---

32 Bruce King, 'Introduction: A Changing Face', in *The Later Fiction of Nadine Gordimer*, ed. Bruce King (Basingstoke: Palgrave Macmillan, 1993), pp. 1–17 (p. 4).

in late 1980s Mozambique who Gordimer once interviewed.[33] Renamo was formed in 1976 by white Rhodesians seeking to quash Mozambique's efforts to support an attempt to overthrow the Rhodesian government, and was sponsored from the 1980s onwards by the South African Defence Force. The protagonist of 'Jump' bears an uncanny similarity to Oliveira, Renamo's sometime Head of Information in Europe. In 1988 Oliveira publicly defected from his Renamo post in Lisbon, and put himself at the disposal of the Mozambican authorities, including giving a press conference in Maputo on 23 March 1988, and several 'follow-up personal interviews'.[34] Gordimer's character, for his part, was formerly in a 'European city' (10), where he occupied a room with 'communications installations' (13) and received 'intelligence by fax and satellite' (17). He now wonders if he could find a position in 'information, public relations (with his international experience)' (5) and has given a TV conference and a series of interviews. Furthermore, both Oliveira and the story's central figure were once recreational parachutists.[35] In one sense, the close correlation between the two is of little importance to reading the story. Gordimer's protagonist is, at the most fundamental level, not Oliveira. At the same time, however, to ignore the similarities would be to miss the refracted image of the world that Gordimer offers. Although the protagonist is not Oliveira, he is some embodiment of what Gordimer felt someone *like* Oliveira represented, though 'more intense, compounded, and condensed in essence of personality than could exist materially'.[36]

The overlap between Oliveira and Gordimer's fictional protagonist does, however, raise an important issue about the operation of time in Gordimer's work, and it is one on which the story reflects. In essence, Oliveira and his fictional counterpart are both specialists in information, while Gordimer deals in stories, a distinction Walter

---

33 Judie Newman first spots this similarity in 'Jump Starts: Nadine Gordimer After Apartheid', in *Apartheid Narratives*, ed. Nahem Yousaf (Amsterdam: Rodopi, 2001), pp. 101–14 (p. 110); see Ronald Eyre and others, *Frontiers* (London: BBC Books, 1990).

34 Hans Abrahamsson and Anders Nilsson, *Mozambique, the Troubled Transition: From Socialist Construction to Free Market Capitalism* (London: Zed Books, 1995), p. 246, n. 96.

35 William Finnegan, *A Complicated War: The Harrowing of Mozambique* (Oakland: University of California Press, 1993), p. 190.

36 Nadine Gordimer, 'Adam's Rib: Fictions and Realities', in *Writing and Being* (Cambridge, MA: Harvard University Press, 1995), pp. 1–19 (p. 6).

Benjamin makes between time-specific 'information' and atemporal 'story'.[37] In Benjamin's figuration, the sudden increase in the dissemination of information has caused the decline of the oral storyteller, but it is only storytelling that can grant wisdom, with information being suitable only for the gratification of immediate needs. The protagonist's coming to self-knowledge through the incessant repetition of his story, given as oral testimony, then becomes a counter to the damage caused by his former role in information. As Gordimer puts it in 'Jump': 'Can't be explained how someone begins really to know. Instead of having intelligence by fax and satellite' (17). The contrast between story and information takes on a meta-textual resonance when we consider that Gordimer's story sits in relation to history as the protagonist's story does to the information in which he formerly dealt. Both story and information are true, albeit in somewhat different senses, yet for Benjamin it is story, through its greater psychological purchase, which achieves 'an amplitude that information lacks'.[38] It is as if the tension Gordimer felt between a responsibility to document immediate political reality and the desire to create timeless story was here transformed into the very substance of the story, a level of meta-textuality that came increasingly to the fore in her post-apartheid writing.

Arrested time permeates the story: the protagonist is shown with his back turned to 'the day pressing to enter' (3) through the curtains; a 'cold fried egg waits on a plate'; a 'jug of hot water has grown tepid'; and he sits 'telling, telling – telling over to himself' (14) his story up to the moment of narration. The story's narrative development is like that of a Möbius strip, in which forward progress is at once a return to the point of origin. This state of suspension is amplified through the story's recurring imagery of reflection and replaying. The man sits and stares at the 'dim, ballooned vision of a face, pale and full' reflected in the 'silvery convex of the TV screen' (4), with the hotel an 'echo chamber' (3). As he ruminates over the telling and retelling of his story, he plays, rewinds, and plays again a cassette of 'the music track from a film about an American soldier who becomes brutalized by the atrocities he is forced to commit in Vietnam' (4). As the story progresses, it becomes increasingly unclear whether the tape holds 'the

---

37 Walter Benjamin, 'The Storyteller: Reflections on the Works of Nikolai Leskov', in *Illuminations: Essays and Reflections*, ed. Hannah Arendt, trans. Harry Zohn (New York: Schocken Books, 2007), pp. 83–109.
38 Ibid., p. 89.

accompaniment the performance [of his story to the media] never had' (6), or the actual story itself: 'A crescendo comes in great waves from the speaker provided with the tape player: to win the war, stabilize by destabilization, set up a regime of peace and justice!' (15). He no longer has to listen, as now the 'tympani of conflict, the brass of glory [...] the maudlin strings of regret, the pauses of disgust – they come from inside him' (4). The musical development, from conflict and glory to regret and disgust, tracks his developing doubts about his past actions, with the endlessly replayed tape a figure for the protagonist's inability to escape his own conscience. Like the movement of the tape, the story's narrative shuttles between different times, and despite the lack of action in the present, a metonymic trajectory is established through the juxtaposition of what Jeanne Colleran calls '[p]ublic, social realities' with 'private, psychic obsessions'.[39] There is an implicit dynamic established between the protagonist's immobility and the political situation in which he finds himself, the emotional map of the one stretching to cover the coordinates of the other, and *vice versa*.

The curious temporality of written narrative, in which the future is already spatially *there* in the form of as yet unread pages in a book, is self-reflexively explored in 'Jump' through the metaphor of the tape, which plays as the protagonist recounts his life story. The tape player, as well as constituting the physical embodiment of a trapped consciousness, further serves as a figure of the temporality that is inherent to fiction, and which takes on a particular intensity in the short story. While readers of any narrative have the impression of time moving forwards, in point of fact everything that is yet to come is already accessible, separated spatially rather than temporally by the pages between the point of reading and the end. In Mark Currie's words, 'the future lies there to the right, awaiting its actualisation by the reading'.[40] The sense of temporal disjunction and the imminence of the end this provokes is intensified in the short story, in that its brevity forces a greater awareness of how little time remains.

After a description of the protagonist's colonial childhood, there comes

---

39 Jeanne Colleran, 'Archive of Apartheid: Nadine Gordimer's Short Fiction at the End of the Interregnum', in *The Later Fiction of Nadine Gordimer*, ed. Bruce King (Basingstoke: Palgrave Macmillan, 1993), pp. 237–45 (p. 238).

40 Mark Currie, *About Time: Narrative, Fiction and the Philosophy of Time* (Edinburgh: Edinburgh University Press, 2007), p. 18.

the event that – all at once, reeled up as the tape is filling its left cylinder on rewind – the experience that explained everything he had ever done since, everything that he was to confess to, everything he was to inculpate himself for [...] and to himself, in fiery dimness behind the curtains' embers, facing the fish-eye of the TV screen, surrounded by the music, alone.

Both the protagonist's story and the end of 'Jump' are fixed in the written text, with the last page the textual equivalent of the spool's end. Gordimer's story, like that of her protagonist, can never proceed beyond what has already been written, already been said. However, there is an implicit contrast established between the predetermined future in a text, and the as yet undetermined future that extends beyond the story's end for the reader. As Currie puts it, 'the already-there-ness of the future on the reel of a film, and by extension with the already-there-ness of the future in writing' sits in contradiction with '[t]he unreality of the future [in the world], its openness'.[41] Gordimer's story both acknowledges and disturbs this inevitable constraint of written narrative. On the one hand, her protagonist's life, like the tape on the spool, is doomed to play out in the same manner in perpetuity. He is arrested in a perpetual present in which the 'fiery dimness' outside is shunned for the *mise-en-abîme* 'fish-eye of the TV screen'. On the other, the story's final words, '[n]ot now; not yet' (20), point towards a future beyond the story in which change may come about. The political impetus of the story lies in the contrast between the end-stopped temporality of written narrative and its implied reader's capacity to live on once it has finished. This is, in effect, the main political affordance this story offers us: a formal experience that frames the contrast between the time-locked lives of her characters and the unfolding lives of the readers who engage them, a life in which choice can still be made.

It seems unlikely that the protagonist's future will fulfil the utopian possibility offered by the girl, standing in the threshold space of the doorway, inviting him to 'have a swim [...] eat some prawns' (19). He gives no answer, a 'wordlessness' that Colleran identifies as 'the only response possible to the devastating sense that life has outstripped any ability to account for it'.[42] Gordimer's silent characters, Colleran notes, are most often whites 'caught at the end of the Interregnum without an

[41] Ibid., p. 19.
[42] Colleran, 'Archive of Apartheid', p. 242.

expressible sense of future or commitment'.[43] Although the protagonist of 'Jump' is no longer obliged to stay in his room – '[o]f course, he can go out. Go where he likes, it was only for the first six months that he was restricted' (18) – he cannot leave because outside are those he left orphaned, mutilated, and 'beggared' (20). The past hangs heavy around his neck, and all he can imagine for the future as he looks from his balcony is the 'stunning blow of the earth as it came up to flexed knees, the parachute sinking silken' (20), either a suicidal jump or an abortive leap to faith, '[n]ot now; not yet' (20). The text ends with the protagonist in this suspended state, in which the future is tangible yet tantalisingly out of reach. While in Gordimer's earlier work such endings emphasised the radical openness of the future, in 'Jump' the balance falls more strongly on how the past can bar the future closed. This ending, a form of failed epiphany, is pervaded by a sense of opportunity missed, of an inability to turn fully towards the future. The protagonist has taken a first leap into the unknown by defecting, but finds himself not freed from the past, but rather unable to move on, caught in the grey ethics of the interregnum.

'Loot', 'Karma', and the Rebirth of the Author

Some twelve years passed between *Jump* and Gordimer's next collection, *Loot*, which came out in 2003. In the intervening years, several important societal changes had occurred. In 1999 Thabo Mbeki took up the country's presidency, the Truth and Reconciliation Commission produced its final report, and, as can be garnered from *Loot*'s fascination with malpractice, widespread corruption pushed the government to launch its National Anti-Corruption Programme and Public Service Anti-Corruption Strategy. If *Jump*, ironically, was often about standing still, then the temporal gap between it and *Loot* had led to stagnation, corruption, and decay. While *Jump* showed inaction in action, *Loot* is concerned with exposing the resulting rot. This appears in various forms, from the corruption of ideals in the first section of 'Karma', in which a former anti-apartheid activist is caught up in a bribery scandal, to the pungent decay of a recently buried corpse in 'L,U,C,I,E'. The collection is made up of texts as various in their styles as in their lengths. Some stories read as realist while others are jaggedly experimental, some

---

43 Ibid., p. 243.

span but a few pages while others approach novella length, but as Claire Messud notes, its 'cohesion lies in its engagement with death'.[44] *Loot* is dedicated to Reinhold Cassirer, Gordimer's husband who died in 2001, and the collection is heavy with loss and the awareness of finitude. As King observes to be true of Gordimer's later works more generally, *Loot* is troubled by the 'passing of youth, and failures to seize the day and make use of time'.[45] When a BBC World Service programme – bluntly titled 'Gordimer Looks Towards End' – asked her about the collection's preoccupation with death, she replied baldly: 'It's because I'm getting so old.'[46] It seems that important aspects of Gordimer's short story writing as she aged were the freedom the form granted her to experiment and the forum it provided for self-scrutiny.

Gordimer's texts from at least the 1960s onwards are stylistically challenging, shunning standard punctuation and dispensing with clear distinctions between interior monologue, narratorial voice, and direct speech: 'I simply cannot stand he-said/she-said anymore', as she put it in 1983.[47] However, while critics had once remarked on the 'lapidary' quality of her prose style, by the time *The House Gun* appeared in 1998, this style was rather characterised by its 'jagged abruptness'.[48] The stories in *Loot* are formally unruly, they change tone suddenly, while compiling discarded fragments of styles and registers to give a clinical, staccato, effect. This prompted an anonymous reviewer at *Publishers Weekly* to declare the stories 'tentative, as though they were straight out of Gordimer's sketchbook, and needed a layer of finish'.[49] Her stories in this collection are only occasionally driven by traditional linear plot, with most favouring symbolic, compact, demanding forms that reflect on their own representational practices.

44 Claire Messud, 'Lost Things Revealed', *The New York Times*, 4 May 2003, <http://www.nytimes.com/2003/05/04/books/lost-things-revealed.html> (accessed 16 January 2020).
45 King, 'Introduction: A Changing Face', p. 13.
46 'Gordimer Looks Towards End', *BBC*, 6 June 2003, <http://news.bbc.co.uk/1/hi/entertainment/arts/2966732.stm> (accessed 20 January 2015).
47 Gordimer and Hurwitt, 'Nadine Gordimer, The Art of Fiction No. 77'.
48 John Barkham, 'Nadine Gordimer', *Saturday Review*, 12 January 1963, 63; Jack Miles, 'A Crime of Passion: Review of *The House Gun*', *New York Times*, 1 February 1998, <http://www.nytimes.com/books/98/02/01/reviews/980201.01milest.html> (accessed 10 October 2022).
49 'Book Review: *Loot* by Nadine Gordimer', *PublishersWeekly.Com*, <https://www.publishersweekly.com/978-0-374-19090-3> (accessed 10 October 2022).

The collection's opening story, 'Loot', first appeared in *The New Yorker* in March 1999, just three months before Mbeki took over the country's presidency. The story turns out to be an allegory of greed and, fittingly for its moment of publication, one of regime change. However, its use of allegory is complex, referring at once to plural contexts of allegorisation, spanning from South Africa to South America. When asked to choose between calling it a 'moral fable' or a 'political allegory', Gordimer replied: 'I suppose it's a little bit of each. Maybe it's more of a political fable.'[50] There are a number of such allegorical or fable-like stories from *Jump* onwards: 'Once Upon a Time' and 'Teraloyna' in *Jump*, and 'Loot' and 'Look-alikes' in *Loot*. *Beethoven* offers 'Tape Measure', a tale told from the perspective of a recently evacuated tapeworm. The prevalence of allegory in Gordimer's later short stories should not come as a great surprise, as her fiction has explored allegorisation since at least *The Conservationist* (1974). As Rita Barnard argues, Gordimer's use of allegory is most interesting when it jumps between the allegorical and other modes and when its allegorical work goes beyond the national framework envisaged by Fredric Jameson in his much-discussed essay that I invoked in this book's Introduction.[51] This is certainly the case, as allegory in its most sophisticated form is not like a peach with a single kernel of meaning, but more like an onion, made up only of its multiple layers and the relations between them, and with its susceptibility to reinterpretation one of its most important features. 'Loot', in which Gordimer juxtaposes fictional modes, stages allegory's multiple hermeneutic affordances, and then juxtaposes allegory's mode of creating sense against that of realist description. Gordimer effectively tells the same story twice, once from a generalised allegorical perspective, and again drawing on particularised, historically specific information, although the two are intermingled to some extent throughout. What emerges is an allegorisation that is as much tied to historical circumstance as it is to the process of writing.

'Loot' is a variation on what Barnard calls Gordimer's 'blueprint stor[ies]', stories so 'stripped and resonant that [...] they are] in fact metafictional'.[52] Barnard is here discussing 'No Place Like', a story first

---

50 Nadine Gordimer and Hermione Lee, 'Nadine Gordimer with Hermione Lee', in *Writing Across Worlds: Contemporary Writers Talk*, ed. Susheila Nasta (London: Routledge, 2004), pp. 315–26 (p. 316).
51 Barnard, 'Nadine Gordimer's Transitions', p. 23.
52 Rita Barnard, 'Relocating Gordimer: Modernism, Postcolonialism, Realism'

published in 1971, so metafictional aspects are not unique to Gordimer's post-apartheid writing. It is not that Gordimer's writing post-1990 marks a clean break from what came before, but rather that certain characteristics are more emphasised than in her previous writing, and the degree of self-referentiality differs. While earlier works such as *July's People* and *Burger's Daughter* are, to some extent, metafictional in drawing attention to the artwork as an artefact, these novels are for the most part less concerned with the kind of self-reflexivity about writing that is visible in her later stories. 'Loot', for example, uses its very form to offer a textual performance of a tension that striates Gordimer's aesthetics: the need to articulate the particular while striving towards that which exceeds it.

Gordimer calls 'Loot' 'one of the very few stories of about two hundred or more I have written that was set off by a particular site and a particular occasion'.[53] She describes this event in some detail:

> I was in Chile a couple of years ago and went to the area where an earthquake took place. It was the biggest earthquake ever measured on the Richter scale and it had the extraordinary effect of changing the landscape forever [...] When people told me that there was this extraordinary event, that the sea drew back, and there was all this stuff there, I was absolutely fascinated.[54]

'Loot' similarly features an earthquake so powerful that it causes the ocean to draw back, 'as a vast breath taken'.[55] The treasures that this suck back reveals on the seabed prompt a voracious period of looting, as 'men, women and their children [...] heave out of the slime and sand what they did not know they wanted' (4). Engrossed in their gleaning, they do not hear 'a distant approach of sound rising as a great wind does' (4), as the sea returns to 'engulf them to add to its treasury' (4). The story is then retold from an individual's perspective, a collector who, rather than joining in the indiscriminate looting, is hunting for something

---

(talk given at Queen Mary University of London, 2014); Barnard, *Apartheid and Beyond*, p. 54.

53 Gordimer and Lee, 'Nadine Gordimer with Hermione Lee', p. 316.
54 Ibid., p. 316.
55 Nadine Gordimer, 'Loot', in *Loot and Other Stories* (London: Penguin, 2004), pp. 1–6 (p. 3). All further references to this work are given parenthetically in the text until the end of this section.

specific, though he does not yet know what it is. At last, 'stuck fast with nacreous shells and crenellations of red coral, is *the* object. (A mirror?)' (5). It transpires that the man is no everyman ('that bore', as Gordimer once called him), but is rather someone with a name 'well-known in the former regime circles' (6).[56] This does not spare him from the wave's all-engulfing rush. Immediately striking here is the tension established between the parable-like aspect of the text and its seeming specificity: the story opens 'once upon our time' (3), a turn of phrase that suggests the fairy-tale opening 'once upon a time' but also points to the historical time of Gordimer's writing.

Halfway through the story, the narrative mode partially switches from allegory to something much closer to realist description. This shifting between the universal and the particular and the narrative looping back to the beginning of the story that has just been told are disconcerting, as if the hermeneutic rug has been pulled out from beneath the reader's feet. A short account is given of the television, radio, and newspaper coverage that the event receives, of the 'bodies [...] the sea rejected, washed up down the coast somewhere' (4). The story then opens into an uneasy space in which references to real-world objects and events vie with their symbolic counterparts. A print of Hokusai's *The Great Wave* that hangs above the collector's bed, 'out of sight behind his head' (5), is doubled by its symbolic *doppelgänger*, the 'great wave' of change that sweeps the collector away. While the first half of the story presents the action at a distance from any individual character – there are just 'people [...] men, women, and their children' (3–4) – the second half focuses on one character who is, in a limited way, developed. The reader is plunged into the minutiae of his bedroom furnishings, and details of his home and relationships. This pits the allegorical perspective detailed in the first half of the story against a realism that seeks truth through the particular experienced over time. Gordimer strives to 'trace the trails made by ordinary lives' and so reveal the 'arcane pattern of abstract forces of which [those lives] are the fingerpainting'.[57] The theoretical pull in Gordimer's work, between commitment to material detail and the will to abstract from that material, is here made the substance and form of the story.

In 'Jump', this hermeneutic loop is embodied in the figure of the cassette tape, but in 'Loot' it is crystallised in the figure of the mirror,

---

56 Gordimer, 'The Idea of Gardening', p. 4.
57 Gordimer, 'The Essential Gesture', p. 412.

an object that becomes overdetermined by the symbolic resonances it is made to take on. The object of the collector's desire is at once an actual mirror, a figure for fiction's anamorphic reflection of reality, and, like Jacques Lacan's *objet petit a*, a figure for desire itself.⁵⁸ The bipartite structure of 'Loot' can be understood as a single image, with its perspective reversed across a central axis of allegorical and realist meaning. The presentation of each of these two modes as the reflection *of* the other, and so somehow inherent *in* the other, puts pressure on the tenability of an aesthetic divide that has animated Gordimer's writing life. This level of self-reflexivity and postmodernist *mise en abîme* shows an intensification of the aesthetics of her writing during apartheid. Further, it shows Gordimer establishing a critical perspective on her own literary output, while navigating the evolving politics of post-apartheid authorship, in which engagement has taken new, often more tangential forms.

When the wave arrives to wash the man away, it comes from 'behind his bed-head' (6), seemingly transforming the story into a dreamscape. However, Gordimer refuses to leave the story there, instead describing the seabed strewn with skeletons of the 'latest victims [...] dropped from planes during the dictatorship' (6), swaying the story again towards the historically particular. In fact, in an interview with Hermione Lee, Gordimer sharpens her historical focus further, describing this sentence as a 'reference to [...] that part of the world, especially Argentina, where political opponents were thrown into the sea'.⁵⁹ Gordimer's use of allegory allows her to speak to multiple contexts. On one level, the story is a national allegory of regime change and corruption in South Africa. But to reduce the story to meaning this alone would be to miss the sophistication of its working. The story also serves as a more generalised allegory of regime change and corruption, a realist description of the horrors in Argentina and a natural disaster in Chile, but also an allegory for the very workings of allegory, split between a timeless world of myth and fable and the outer realities to which it points. As Gordimer argues in her essay 'Adam's Rib', fiction is connected with real life, but is not a one-to-one relationship, with the author 'looting the character of living personages' to create stories.⁶⁰ As is so often the case for

---

58 Jacques Lacan, *Livre V: Les Formations de l'inconscient, 1957–1958*, ed. Jacques-Alain Miller (Paris: Seuil, 1998), p. 253.
59 Gordimer and Lee, 'Nadine Gordimer with Hermione Lee', p. 317.
60 Gordimer, *Writing and Being*, p. 18.

Gordimer, to write is not only to explore how the legacy of apartheid continues to shape the post-apartheid nation, but also to reflect on how a post-apartheid aesthetics might move beyond the determinations of previous decades.

This self-examination, combined with a growing preoccupation around how to end and how to begin, is foregrounded in *Loot*'s last cluster of stories, titled 'Karma'. It is difficult to know what to call this text, whether a short story, a sequence, or a novella. It is made up of six short texts, bound together by a narratorial consciousness, a transhistorical karmic entity that is reincarnated into different lives. In the first story, although at this stage the reader is not aware of the sequence's conceit, the narratorial entity manifests in the person of Arthur, husband of an ex-political activist Norma. The two now live in a Cape Dutch gabled house, and she becomes one of 'the comrades [...] now in Government and parastatal organisations' (160), before moving into the building sector and becoming embroiled in a corruption scandal. Arthur dies, and the second half of the story begins when the entity has been reborn into the person of a young black boy whose family buy the gabled house. The boy falls when riding his bicycle and dies under the wheels of a truck, only for the narrating conscience to be again reborn in the following stories.

Central to 'Karma' is the question of narratorial voice. There is a plenitude of speaking positions across the sequence: a relatively flat, unobtrusive, third-person narrator; a breathless, naïve, first-person narration by the young boy; a coloured woman who during apartheid finds an abandoned white child; a still-born twin; a lesbian considering becoming a mother; a young Russian boy killed in a concentration camp; and a Russian hotel maid. Strange resonances are set up between the stories, as Gordimer dons and sloughs these personalities, displaying an authorial virtuosity that draws attention to its own performativity. Mediating between them is the karmic entity, a gnomic meta-narrator and sometime authorial substitute. In the third story, an extended narration in the voice of the karmic entity becomes blurred with that of Gordimer. Echoing Gordimer's metaphor of the short story as the flash of fireflies, this narrator says: 'I flit about, I experience snatches of corporeal life of any and all of you, as I please' (194). Later, the identification between the entity and the author becomes more explicit, when it 'imagine[s] a corporeal life for [it]self', thinking 'maybe I would have been a writer; fiction, of course, because that's the closest a corporeal being can get to my knack of living other lives; multiple existences that are not the poor little opportunities of a single existence' (200). This trans-textual narratorial voice not only allows Gordimer to 'flit' between subject positions, it also disrupts the temporal inevitability of the short story, in which the ending weighs heavily on the story from its start. The karmic consciousness offers a literary device that attempts to defy the short story form by allowing individual stories to bleed into one another. The use of a frame narrator has a lineage in the South African short story, such as in Herman Charles Bosman's Oom Schalk Lourens, but Gordimer's figure differs in that as well as passing ironic comment on the lives in the stories, it actually lives those lives itself.[61]

In both 'Loot' and 'Karma', Gordimer uses the short story's horizon of generic expectation and its formal affordances to offer readers a way to conceive of the aesthetic challenges her writing seeks to address. In 'Loot', it is the short story's proximity to parable and allegory that is exploited to wrongfoot readers looking for a master-key of meaning with which to unlock her fictions. She does this by juxtaposing while interleaving allegorical and realist modes in a single story that is fashioned around a central axis. In 'Karma', she explores the possibilities for rebirth offered by apartheid's end, and does so through a reflection on the author's own capacity for perpetual rebirth in writing. As Gordimer works through the aesthetic affordances of her own short fiction, she uses the very dilemmas that inhered in her earlier work as both the form and substance of her post-apartheid works.

Beginnings and Endings: 'Beethoven Was One-Sixteenth Black' and 'Alternative Endings'

Even in comparison with *Jump* and *Loot*, many of *Beethoven Was One-Sixteenth Black*'s stories are texturally ravaged, more resistant to understanding, and the collection as a whole feels disjointed and fragmented. What coherence there is comes from a pervasive reckoning with the dynamics of loss. Characters go hunting through family archives, read over old letters, and decide which books to revisit before time runs out. The narrator of one story warns that '[c]aches of old papers are graves, you shouldn't open them', but the urge to dig in the

---

[61] For more on frame narration in South African short fiction, see MacKenzie, *The Oral-Style South African Short Story*.

past, even at the risk of unearthing grisly remains, is one that Gordimer seemingly cannot resist.[62]

In this collection, Gordimer's long-term commitment to formal and stylistic experimentation is at its most intense, a feature that draws into focus the temporal contingency of forms of activism. It is this very concern that animates the volume's opening story, 'Beethoven Was One-Sixteenth Black'.[63] It describes, in fragmentary and disjointed form, an event in the life of Frederick Morris, a white 'academic who teaches biology and was an activist back in the apartheid time' (3–4). The story is elliptic, the plot sparse, and the narrative shuttles back and forth between present and past, often in the space of a single paragraph. The text is littered with intrusive asides – 'a non-racial institution with a black majority (politically-correct-speak)' (4) – stylistic tics, and a gestural style that foregrounds the process of textual creation as central to the text. Alison Cohn thinks that the story offers 'a plot so sparse and a narrative voice so fractured as to seem like a burlesque of the psychological depth that has characterised her writing'.[64] In a story that questions whether forms of activism that once held currency still do – '[a]ren't there other tactics now? [...] all they can think of is use what we had' (10) – Gordimer's near parody of her previous writing puts the spotlight on the political efficacy or otherwise of her own aesthetic forms.

The pared-back plot concerns Morris's attempt to seek out black ancestors, a process initiated when he hears a radio presenter pronounce that 'Beethoven was one-sixteenth black' (3). This sets him on the genealogical track of possible black relatives, traces in the past that might serve his reinvention in the present: '[t]he standard of privilege', he knows, 'changes with each regime' (15). Questioning the motives behind his own search, Morris asks: 'Isn't it a try at privilege. Yes?

---

62 Nadine Gordimer, 'A Beneficiary', in *Beethoven Was One-Sixteenth Black and Other Stories* (London: Bloomsbury, 2007), pp. 115–35 (p. 115).

63 Nadine Gordimer, 'Beethoven Was One-Sixteenth Black', in *Beethoven Was One-Sixteenth Black and Other Stories* (London: Bloomsbury, 2007), pp. 1–16. All further references to this work are given parenthetically in the text until the end of this section.

64 Alison S. Cohn, 'Nobel Winner's "Beethoven" an Uneven Performance', *The Crimson*, 2007, <http://www.thecrimson.com/article/2007/12/14/nobel-winners-beethoven-an-uneven-performance/> (accessed 20 February 2020).

One up towards the ruling class whatever it may happen to be?' (15). In particular, Morris is looking for descendants of his great-grandfather, the remarkably named 'Walter Benjamin Morris' (5), a diamond prospector in Kimberley who may or may not have had sexual relations with his black washerwomen. Morris is fascinated by the 'immovabl[e] confiden[ce] [...] [o]f virility' (6) that he sees in his great-grandfather's face, framed in an 'oval frame under convex glass' (9). Morris uses his Easter break to drive to Kimberley, 'to see the Big Hole' (11) he tells his colleagues, but really intent on using a phonebook to search for the elusive missing Morrises. In Kimberley, he meets a group of men in a township bar, and although he finds some camaraderie with them, he has little luck finding any leads. Morris abruptly returns to the university, where he shares a joke with his colleagues about his trip as the 'protests against academe as the old white male crowd' (4) continue.

In Gordimer's story, post-apartheid whiteness, although clearly still a marker of privilege, lacks the cachet that black relatives would bring. As Gordimer states in an interview, '[i]t's almost become fashionable among [...] whites who were part of the freedom struggle to say "My great, great grandmother was Xhosa, or Zulu"'.[65] The seemingly altered societal valence of race is introduced on the first page, in sketch-like prose and a scraggy *mise en page*:

> Beethoven was one-sixteenth black
>   the presenter of a classical music programme on the radio announces along with the names of musicians who will be heard playing the String Quartets no. 13, op. 130, and no. 16, op. 135.
>   Does the presenter make the claim as restitution for Beethoven? Presenter's voice and cadence give him away as irremediably white. Is one-sixteenth an unspoken wish for himself.
>   Once there were blacks wanting to be white.
>   Now there are whites wanting to be black.
>   It's the same secret.

The startling first line sits at the top of the page, unpunctuated and floating. As in 'Jump' and 'Loot', there is a sense of unsettled, non-linear temporality. This is emphasised as the passage continues, switching to

---

[65] Nadine Gordimer and Ángel Gurría-Quintana, 'Taking Tea with Nadine Gordimer', *Prospect*, 21 July 2014, <http://www.prospectmagazine.co.uk/world/taking-tea-with-nadine-gordimer> (accessed 6 September 2022).

the present tense and then the future passive 'will be heard'. All new paragraphs in the story are indented, but the text after the first line is set even further in, creating uncertainty over the relationship between the opening words and their continuation. The effect is primarily one of eccentric timing, as if an extra beat had been inserted into a musical bar to catch the unwary listener off guard.

Equally unexpected is the question of Beethoven's 'restitution', although the passage suggests why this might be required. The presenter is 'irremediably white', implying a societal context in which binaries of racial value have been reversed. The lack of a question mark after '[i]s one-sixteenth an unspoken wish for himself' shows the words to be half a question, half a statement of fact. While '[t]o be white in apartheid days', as a character in *Loot* puts it 'was to be – everything',[66] after they ended, not only can a 'shades-of-black' become 'a big businessman' (12), but blackness becomes a marker of 'privilege', an indicator of 'the ruling class' (15). However, it is important not to miss the extent of Gordimer's irony here. It is outrageous to suggest that the inclusion of a small black minority into the sphere of economic privilege constitutes a reversal of racial prejudice, and raises the question of who, at this point, speaks. The opinions seem closest to those of a white academic at a university with ongoing 'protests against academe as the old white male crowd' (4), as he faces his increasing marginalisation.

Such attempts to reshape the past in the service of the present take on additional meaning when the implications of Morris's great-grandfather's name – Walter Benjamin Morris – are taken into account. Morris observes that '[t]he past is only valid in relation to whether the present recognises it' (7), a conception of history taken from Benjamin, who contends that 'every image of the past that is not recognised by the present as one of its own concerns threatens to disappear irretrievably'.[67] By naming Morris's great-grandfather in this way, Gordimer draws attention to how those in the present make use of the past, whether to acquire black ancestors or to assure an authorial pedigree. Benjamin's 'angel of history' has his back turned to the future, his wings battered by the storm of progress. Morris's trip to Kimberley to find Walter Benjamin Morris is a means of facing up to the past, but the 'Big Hole'

---

66 Nadine Gordimer, *Loot and Other Stories* (London: Penguin, 2004), p. 176.
67 Walter Benjamin, 'Theses on the Philosophy of History', in *Illuminations: Essays and Reflections*, ed. Hannah Arendt, trans. Harry Zohn (New York: Schocken Books, 2007), pp. 253–64 (p. 255).

takes on the character of the chaotic past itself, a synchronous mess rather than teleological progression. The Big Hole at Kimberley is, in one sense, a literal opening onto the past, its story of exploitation only one of many in the country's history of disparity. However, the 'great gouged-out mouth of the diamond pipe formation' (11) is equally a figure of the past's voracious, de-differentiating maw.

Returning to the university staffroom, Morris talks with his colleagues:

—Oh and how was the Big Hole?—
—Deep.—
Everyone laughs at witty deadpan brevity. (16)

His response is at once amusing and horrifying. The Big Hole of the past is deep indeed, and the idea of reckoning with such depths triggers something akin to the historical sublime, before which we can only stand in recognition of our own incapacity and incomprehension. Morris's response is, on the one hand, flippant, making light of the past's failure to render the present intelligible. On the other, he is deadly serious, an ambivalence created by the dashes, which mark unstable silences. These dashes indicate comic timing, but equally betray reticence about reckoning with bigger questions than he or his colleagues are prepared to countenance. Everyone laughs at 'witty deadpan brevity', the pun on 'deadpan' recalling both Walter Benjamin Morris's panning for diamonds and Frederick Morris's panning in the past for black relatives. However, the impossibility of finding sense in the past when seen from the present is an occasion for both wonder and horror. Morris looks to the past as a way of finding himself in a changed present, but can only stare into the depths.

Like *Loot*, *Beethoven Was One-Sixteenth Black* ends with a grouped cluster of stories, this time titled 'Alternative Endings'. The three stories that make it up are all told in a largely realist mode, each describing a couple in which one partner betrays the other. What makes the stories unusual is the narratorial framing that precedes them, in which Gordimer seems almost to speak in her own voice, or at least the voice of her non-fictional essays. In it, she describes the process by which a writer decides what to transpose from reality into fiction, where to start and where to end a story, and how to portray the experiences they describe. She observes the arbitrariness of the writer's method, who 'picks up an imagined life at some stage in the human cycle and leaves it at another.

Not even a story from birth to death is decisive' (139). The task of the writer is to give shape to the mess of life, as 'the continuity of existence has to be selectively interrupted by the sense of form which is art' (139). In other words, by giving form to a morass of experience, the writer does not simply present that experience, but creates the conditions under which experience comes to be understood as experience. Likewise, the sense of form comes about through its coincidence with that experience. In Robert Kaufman's words, 'material [...] gets to count as material in the first place by virtue of its relationship to an act – provisional though it may be – of framing, an act of form. By the same token, the formal gets to be formal only by its momentary, experimental coincidence with the material.'[68] In framing these otherwise realist stories with a reflection on the relationship between content and form, Gordimer draws attention to the artifice of realist writing, as if to warn readers that its workings are every bit as complex as those of the collection's more overtly experimental texts. As Barnard, drawing on Jameson, notes, realism might itself be thought of as the 'name for any narrative organized around the very interrogation of realism and the realistic itself', and Gordimer here uses an authorial prologue to make this aesthetic point an explicit feature of the story's formal architecture.[69]

In repeating what is effectively the same story told with different details, Gordimer works against realism's commitment to particularity, making the stories feel more like those that Vladimir Propp uses to delineate the structural functions of folk tales.[70] But instead of dragons and knights, Gordimer offers us a typology of bourgeois life: the unfaithful husband, the successful woman whose husband is left behind, the charismatic man who strays from home only to return. What draws the typological nature of these characters into view is both the meta-textual preface and the repetition of a similar story three times in quick succession. Such repetition, Maurice Shadbolt notes in a vivid metaphor, turns short stories into 'performing seals, doing the same tricks over and over', something that is 'more evident in the short story than in any other form of literature'.[71] What is important here is that the

---

68 Kaufman, 'Everybody Hates Kant', p. 135; cited in Marjorie Levinson, 'What is New Formalism?', *PMLA*, 122.2 (2007), 558–69 (p. 561).
69 Barnard, 'Nadine Gordimer's Transitions', p. 23.
70 Vladimir Yakovlevich Propp, *Morphology of the Folktale*, trans. Laurence Scott, 2nd edn (Austin: University of Texas Press, 1968).
71 Maurice Shadbolt, 'The Hallucinatory Point', in *The New Short Story Theories*,

typological nature of these characters, emphasised by their recurrence in quick succession, suggests the eventual substitutability of the individual actors in the structure. And yet this structuralist perspective is counterbalanced by the accumulation of realist detail in the stories, and the reader's implied sympathetic response to the stories presented. We are encouraged to feel with the wife who discovers her musician husband's infidelity as she hears his cello 'saying something passionately angry in its deepest bass' (166). If Gordimer once participated in a mode of liberal realism that insisted on particularised circumstances and what Richard Peck calls the 'appeal to the lump in the throat', here we find not exactly a rejection of that mode, but rather a staged interrogation of its premises that allows for both its deployment and ironisation.[72]

As Gordimer reached the end of her writing career, she thought back over the modes of writing with which she had strived to fulfil the 'necessary gesture' of national testimony and the 'essential gesture' of transforming experience into art.[73] These twinned gestures once operated implicitly in her works, but in the post-apartheid short stories I analyse above they increasingly become the subject of the story, and are expressed through their form. From *Jump*, through *Loot*, to *Beethoven Was One-Sixteenth Black*, Gordimer strives to find a style fit to articulate the past's strange hold on the present in transition-era and post-apartheid South Africa, dissecting both the body politic and her own body of work. Given Gordimer's reputation as an engaged writer, and her centrality to the South African short story, her meta-analysis of her own aesthetic practice in her last collections might be understood as her challenge to engaged authors in the post-apartheid nation. If the necessary gesture was once to a national framework, it expands in these stories to encompass a more global frame, and her essential gesture transforms from a first-order instantiation of her aesthetic practice to a second-order reflection on it. Much like Morris, the ex-activist white academic protagonist of 'Beethoven Was One-Sixteenth Black', she seems to ask: 'Aren't there other tactics now?' (10). There are the existing methods – those that Gordimer created, used, and sometimes discarded – each of which offered writers and readers a set of resources to draw on

---

ed. Charles E. May (Athens, OH: Ohio University Press, 1994), pp. 268–72 (p. 270).

72 Richard Peck, *A Morbid Fascination: White Prose and Politics in Apartheid South Africa* (Westport, CT: Praeger, 1997), p. 95.

73 Gordimer, 'The Essential Gesture'.

for societally oriented thought. But what path will be followed by those that write after her?

The following chapter explores one possible answer to this question. Ivan Vladislavić shares Gordimer's concern for the continuing presence of the past in the post-apartheid nation, and for the dynamic between realism, allegory, and experimentalism. He also, in his most recent work, shares Gordimer's interest in reflecting on his own artistic practice. Vladislavić's approach differs, however, in that he uses the short story's aporetic aesthetics and relation to other art forms – monuments, illustrations, collages, photographs, and pieces of performance art – to explore the dynamics of societal memory.

CHAPTER TWO

A Moment's Monument
Counter-Monuments in Ivan Vladislavić

In March 2015 a statue of Cecil Rhodes that occupied a prominent position on the campus of the University of Cape Town became the subject of a series of protests. The protestors wanted the statue removed, considering it an oppressive symbol of imperialism and racist white supremacism; the statue's defenders wanted it to remain, their reasons ranging from accusations of revisionism or censorship to wholehearted support of Rhodes's legacy.[1] These events marked the beginning of the Rhodes Must Fall movement, which evolved to encompass calls for the removal of statues worldwide, efforts to address institutional racism, and demands to increase access to education. Even before Rhodes Must Fall, iconography of Rhodes had become a lightning rod for social protest: in May 2014 an image of 'The Man in the Green Blanket' had been stencilled on the statue along with the text 'Remember Marikana', in reference to Mgcineni Noki, the miner and strike leader who was killed during the 2012 Marikana massacre. Hedley Twidle recounts how the bust of Rhodes had been variously 'wrapped in black trash bags and swaddled in green fabric' and 'repeatedly daubed, spattered, and even necklaced', while the statue itself was 'pelted with shit'.[2] The statue was eventually

---

1 Interestingly, the statue has been a focal point of protest since at least the 1950s, when Afrikaner students called for its removal over Rhodes's derogatory comments about and attitudes towards Afrikaners.
2 Hedley Twidle, 'To Spite His Face: What Happened to Cecil Rhodes's Nose?', *Harper's Magazine*, 11 November 2021, <https://harpers.org/archive/2021/12/to-spite-his-face-what-happened-to-cecil-rhodes-statue-nose/> (accessed 21 September 2022). . Necklacing is a means of unofficial execution in which a petrol-doused tyre is placed round a victim's neck and set alight.

removed from the campus in April of the same year, a moment vividly described by Twidle: 'He was unbolted from the platform and hoisted up with a crane, not so much falling as ascending or levitating. It was an uncanny thing to see: something that had been so still, such a fixture for so long, suddenly beginning to move, wobbling in the harness of a crane.'[3]

These events brought the question of what to do with South Africa's statues firmly into the centre of public consciousness, but Ivan Vladislavić's interest in these displays of public memory goes back much further. From his earliest collection, *Missing Persons* (1989), right through to 'Save the Pedestals' (2019), he has explored how monuments become charged symbols of historical narratives that are shaped and reshaped over time, and constitute an important dimension of how the relationship between the individual, memory, and the state is mediated. Interviewed some months after the Rhodes statue had been removed, Vladislavić noted that the increased attention had 'the potential [...] to make people think hard about how the society represents itself, what the power is of representing certain ideas in the form of a statue or a monument', noting that '[i]f we are going to represent anything in our public spaces [...] the least one would hope for is that we construct something complex and something that asks questions rather than delivers answers, delivers final position on things'.[4] His interest in monuments has attracted quite some critical attention, but surprisingly little has been made of the short story form in which he often writes about them. And yet the formal characteristics of his stories frame the monuments he describes in interesting ways, offering aesthetic experiences that run counter to those of the monuments that his stories describe.

Vladislavić is often portrayed as a central figure in post-apartheid literature, yet when asked what he thought of this, he questioned whether the distinction between the 'new' and the 'old' South Africa could ever be quite so neat:

> I might be [a post-apartheid writer] in the sense that I write after apartheid, or the beginnings of the end of it, but I'm not a

---

3 Ibid.
4 Ivan Vladislavić and Corina van der Spoel, 'Ivan Vladislavić Believes Society's Monuments Should be Complex, with a Sense of Irony', *Penguin SA @ Sunday Times Books LIVE*, <http://penguin.bookslive.co.za/blog/2015/12/01/ivan-vladislavic-believes-societys-monuments-should-be-complex-with-a-sense-of-irony-podcast/> (accessed 21 September 2022).

post-apartheid person − not in terms of my history [...] history doesn't work like that; no matter how spectacular the transitions and changes are, it doesn't fall into neat compartments and chapters. And certainly, in one's lived experience, it's a much greyer, more muddled process.[5]

Born in 1957, Vladislavić spent most of his early life under apartheid rule, so his wry observation that he is 'not a post-apartheid person' is, in a sense, true. However, it may well be exactly his experience of both apartheid and its aftermath that gives him purchase on the paradoxical temporality of the post-apartheid era. Vladislavić's post-apartheid short stories stand out for their formal innovations, which offer structures for thinking through the complications and contradictions of post-apartheid life. His writing has always had an orthogonal quality: in the 1980s, with a State of Emergency in place and violent government repression reaching new lows, the dominant literary mode in English-language writing was a serious and hard-hitting form of realism. With hindsight, those years can appear as the climactic death rattle of a regime in crisis, but Vladislavić, reflecting on the period, observes that '[f]or people living through the mid-1980s in SA, it didn't look like apartheid was going to end − the feeling was of something interminable'.[6] Vladislavić's response was *Missing Persons*, an intense, fretful short story cycle that responds to the societal turbulence of the 1980s in wildly imaginative literary forms.[7] His mode of experimentalism may in part be influenced by his knowledge of Afrikaans literature, among other things. He recognises a certain affinity with 'the Afrikaans writers of the seventies' − writers such as Etienne Leroux, Breyten Breytenbach, and John Miles − as well as with 'Don Barthelme, John Barth, Richard Brautigan, and Kurt Vonnegut'.[8] He elsewhere mentions that by 1984 he had 'discovered the light political touch of writers like [Zbigniew] Herbert, [Milan]

---

5 Thurman, 'Places Elsewhere', p. 91.
6 Christopher Thurman, '"I Take up My Spade and I Dig": Verwoerd, Tsafendas and the Position of the Writer', in *Marginal Spaces: Reading Ivan Vladislavić*, ed. Gerald Gaylard (Johannesburg: Wits University Press, 2011), pp. 46–69 (p. 56).
7 Some individual stories had previously appeared in *Sesame*, *TriQuarterly*, *Stet*, *Staffrider*, and the *English Academy Review*.
8 Vladislavić and Warnes, 'Interview with Ivan Vladislavić', p. 276.

Kundera and [Danilo] Kiš'.[9] His influences are then resolutely both local and global, as much in dialogue with innovative Afrikaans writing as with the möbial fictions of American mid-century postmodernists or the oblique political satires of their Eastern European contemporaries.

In this chapter, I track two interrelated movements in Vladislavić's short fiction. The first concerns the monuments his stories describe, and how Vladislavić uses them as a foil to think through questions of memory from the dying days of apartheid in the late 1980s through to the late 2010s. Monuments are artworks of a special kind that often deflect responses attuned to their aesthetic properties in favour of their presentation of history, even though their formal features are central to how their historical narratives are constructed. In the monuments Vladislavić describes, there is a movement from more traditional examples – large imposing statues and so on – to what James E. Young has termed 'counter-monuments', creative interventions that are 'ethically certain of their duty to remember, but aesthetically sceptical of the assumptions underpinning traditional memorial forms'.[10] In 'We Came to the Monument', the geometric severity of the monument, modelled on the Voortrekker Monument outside Pretoria, portrays a rigid relationship between citizens and the panoptical and paranoid apartheid state. I read this story within the embattled siege mentality of the 1980s and in relation to the current of allegorical futurity that flows through 1980s South African fiction. 'Cold Storage', meanwhile, contains a range of monuments, each less substantial than the last, a dematerialisation that is engaged through an increasingly flindered text. I pay particular attention to the presentation of Micha Ullman's public sculpture *Bibliothek*, arguing that its aesthetic of absence can be helpfully understood in relation to the short story's use of implication. In 'Save the Pedestals', an unoccupied pedestal offers a site of troubled nostalgic reflection and an opportunity to consider the lure of acceding to power. The story's style blends the stylistic virtuosity of Vladislavić's early writing with the leaner prose of his later work, turning it into a consideration of his own past as a writer as much as an engagement with the changed dynamics of monumentalisation in the wake of the Rhodes Must Fall movement. As the political antagonist of South African

---

9 Ivan Vladislavić, 'Staffrider', *The Chimurenga Chronic*, <https://chimurengachronic.co.za/staffrider/> (accessed 12 October 2022).

10 James E. Young, 'The Counter-Monument: Memory against Itself in Germany Today', *Critical Inquiry*, 18.2 (1992), 267–96 (p. 271).

writing becomes less distinct, the monuments Vladislavić describes, and the forms in which he describes them, have increasingly offered an alternative canon of monumentalisation, a counter-narrative to the temporality of both state-sanctioned monuments and the 'counter-monuments' his stories describe.

The second movement, which is an extension of the first, examines the developed intermedial aspect of Vladislavić's short stories. This appears both in the stories' extended ekphrastic descriptions of monuments and in their appearance alongside visual media. In the first story I discuss, 'We Came to the Monument', Vladislavić describes a marble frieze through a textual ekphrasis that sits in a complicated relationship to the object it describes. Vladislavić uses the short story's capacity for lyrical intensity to create what Dante Gabriel Rossetti, on the sonnet, calls a 'moment's monument' that runs counter to the temporal perpetuity that the gargantuan building described in the story projects.[11] In 'Cold Storage' from *The Loss Library*, the lyricism of Vladislavić's earlier writing has cooled into a flatter, less affectively charged style. This pared-back, minimal mode perhaps suggests a more restricted purview for art's potential to alter the world, but in so doing it also draws on the short story's capacity for implication to engage the apophatic monuments it describes. The story not only describes an array of counter-monuments, but has also been published in multiple editions, appearing unillustrated, accompanied by collages by Sunandini Banerjee, and beside haunting photographs by Abrie Fourie.[12] These different editions allow an exploration of how absence in different forms can be both generative of meaning and risk collapse into meaninglessness.

The neatness of this trajectory – from lyrical density to sparsity – is tempting as a model for Vladislavić's own development as a writer, from an early dense and hallucinatory style towards a leaner, more cool-headed style later in his career. While there is some truth in this, I suggest that a more accurate picture would include currents of hot lyric density and cool realist minimalism flowing together from his earliest

---

11 Dante Gabriel Rossetti, *Ballads and Sonnets* (London: Ellis and White, 1881), p. 161.
12 As I discuss elsewhere, 'Propaganda by Monuments' appeared in *Staffrider* magazine in 1992 alongside illustrations by Andrew Lord. See Graham K. Riach, 'Sticking Together: Ivan Vladislavić's Collage Practice', *Safundi*, 16.1 (2015), 78–95.

works.¹³ 'Save the Pedestals' (2019) begins with only an empty pedestal and no monument at all. It evinces a fascinating synthesis of these two sides of Vladislavić's writing practice, offering a mode that combines the documentary and the speculative. In this way, Vladislavić's stories not only show properties of these monuments that were already there, but also allow for what Curt Cloninger calls 'apparatal entanglements', processes through which readers and artworks co-create meaning. This holds true equally for the monuments in the stories as for the stories themselves.¹⁴ The story was published in the *Yale Review*, appearing beside different artworks in the online and print versions. These intermedial engagements foreground the importance of contexts of publication to how short stories might be received, and crucially they thicken and complicate how the stories negotiate questions of memorialisation.

The Lyrical Gesture of 'We Came to the Monument'

One story from *Missing Persons*, 'We Came to the Monument', offers both a way to think through the seemingly unassailable determinations of the 1980s, and an invitation to think beyond them.¹⁵ The story describes a war-torn landscape through which a group is making its way back to their deserted home city. On their way they set up camp next to a large hilltop monument, and eventually move inside it. The story is told by two alternating narrators, distinguished on the page typographically, with the first narrator italicised, the second in a regular font. It becomes clear that the first narrator is a sentient statue that, faced with the threat of being toppled during the revolutionary war which precedes the story,

13 *101 Detectives* presents an interesting case, as while the collection was published in 2015, the stories that appear in it were written, or at least begun, from the early 1990s to the date of publication. This could well explain the very different styles between different stories.
14 Curt Cloninger, *Some Ways of Making Nothing: Apophatic Apparatuses in Contemporary Art* (Santa Barbara, CA: Punctum Books, 2021), p. 18.
15 It is difficult to say exactly when 'We Came' was written, but when another story from *Missing Persons*, 'The Prime Minister is Dead', was printed in *Tri Quarterly* in 1987, it describes Vladislavić as having 'just finished a collection of short stories', suggesting that 'We Came' was written at some point before then. Ivan Vladislavić, 'The Prime Minister is Dead', *Tri Quarterly*, 69 (1987), 447–53.

sprang to life, and made his way from the city to become part of the monument. Before leaving the city, the statue had fallen in love with a girl, and is delighted to find she is part of the group that arrives many years later and sets up camp outside. This girl, the second narrator, is the daughter of the group's leader, Steenkamp, whose name means 'Stone Camp' in Afrikaans. The group ethos is stiflingly conservative, and in protest against its reverence for the past the daughter breaks into the museum under the monument to put its artefacts to use in the present. However, her act of rebellion has little effect, and the group decides to move from the area outside the monument to inside the structure. Unwittingly, she sets her bed up under her stony admirer, who by now has left his post as a sentinel on the outside of the monument to take a place, back turned, *'among the vanquished'* on the marble frieze inside.[16] Although she is unaware of the statue's feelings towards her, she is intrigued by the figure, and thinks of it as her friend. The group members abandon their plan to return to the city, and 'never go farther than the monument' (71). The story ends with the two narrators imagining apocalyptic scenes of 'storms and floods', and 'lightning striking upwards' (80).

This gargantuan monument, an unforgiving 'black block on the broken hills' (71), is an outward projection of everything that is wrong with the group's suffocating dynamic. The colossal structure memorialises a violent conquest carried out by the group's ancestors, and this behaviour is normalised, even celebrated, through its triumphal and panoptical hilltop location. By coming to the monument, the group symbolically adopts the principles for which it stands. Steenkamp's daughter at first defines herself only through a group identity, 'we', that is understood through its relation to the monument, and by extension to her father: '[o]ur leader's name was Steenkamp; I am his only daughter' (69). Her self-assimilation into patriarchal power, a patriarch whose name associates him with the immobility of the monument, reveals something of the suffocating effect of the group's conservative dynamic. The stone of the monument is 'not a passive element. It sucked them in, it cunningly enslaved them, while allowing them the illusion of liberty' (71). Steenkamp's daughter confesses that as a child, faced with the monument's cathedral atmosphere, and its marble frieze depicting a

16 Ivan Vladislavić, 'We Came to the Monument', in *Missing Persons* (Cape Town: David Philip, 1989), pp. 69–81 (p. 80). All further references to this work are given parenthetically in the text until the end of this section.

broad historical sweep 'of origins, of pioneers, of battles and massacres', she was filled with 'a small, private horror' (71). If, as Henri Lefebvre claims, monuments provide 'a collective mirror more faithful than any personal one', this monument provides a reflection of a group identity that, in its individual instantiations, is calcified, stifling, and overbearing.[17]

The story's characters are purposely undeveloped, which, coupled with the story's lack of historical and geographic specificity, invites an allegorical interpretation in which the group's return to the monument is a formal figuring of the perpetuation of hegemonic societal forms. The ancestors depicted in the frieze are 'frozen, half in and half out the stone' (74), a calcification of the body into the monument that is a continuing threat: the female narrator has to crack herself loose after sitting for too long against the structure. Although on this occasion the girl manages to resist the fixity of the monument, she only narrowly escapes incorporation into its narrative of war and conquest, of 'hooves trampling the bodies of [...] fallen enemies' (71), and the subjugation of a kneeling people. While this broadly allegorical reading is certainly one way of understanding the story, as with Gordimer's 'Loot', when the story's place and time of publication is borne in mind, a more complicated picture emerges, somewhere between allegory and a description of the concrete phenomenal world.

It is clear from the monument's hilltop location, cavernous spaces, and marble friezes that this 'tomb with a view' is not just an allegorical abstraction, but is also a description of the Voortrekker Monument that overlooks Pretoria.[18] The structure was inaugurated in December 1949, just one year after D.F. Malan's National Party was voted into power, and was conceived, in Alta Steenkamp's words, 'to represent the cultural and bodily struggle for territory of a select group of white inhabitants of South Africa, namely the Afrikaner'.[19] The Voortrekker Monument's symmetrical form, constructed almost solely by white labour in a

17 Henri Lefebvre, *The Production of Space* (Oxford: Blackwell, 1991), p. 220.
18 Barbara Kirschenblatt-Gimblett, 'Objects of Ethnography', in *Exhibiting Culture: The Poetics and Politics of Museum Display*, ed. Steven D. Lavine and Ivan Karp (Washington, DC: Smithsonian Institution, 1991), pp. 386–433 (p. 416).
19 Alta Steenkamp, 'Apartheid to Democracy: Representation and Politics in the Voortrekker Monument and Red Location Museum', *Arq: Architectural Research Quarterly*, 10.3–4 (2006), 249–54 (p. 250).

farcical attempt to preserve its racial purity, attempts to depict architecturally the triumph of Western civilisation.[20] Its straight lines and geometric shapes were intended to represent the rational architectural antithesis of the traditional African round hut or *rondavel*.[21] There was a belief that the formal properties of the monument could embody an entire mode of thought.

The similarities between the monument in Pretoria and the monument in the story are striking. The Voortrekker Monument is '[a] great grey colossus [that] can be seen from all directions as you approach Pretoria';[22] Vladislavić's monument, for its part, '[e]ven when the sky faded to grey', persists as a 'black block on the broken hills' (71). The Voortrekker Monument vaunts its 'unique marble Frieze [that] is an intrinsic part of the design', while Vladislavić describes 'walls inside [...] lined with marble friezes' (70).[23] The architects of the Voortrekker Monument clearly understood the semiotics of form, but they could not have anticipated Vladislavić's contribution to South African fiction lying in his ability to, in Ken Barris' words, 'imagine the country through its existing symbols, while subverting them to his own ends'.[24] Vladislavić here takes the monumental symbol of mythologised Afrikaner nationalism and transforms it into a prison of the movement's own making.

By introducing this real-world structure into what reads as an allegorical framework, 'We Came to the Monument' not only draws attention to the story's form – as Vladislavić observes in a later text, 'it is almost impossible to describe literary structures without resorting to

---

20 The only exceptions to the white labour rule came when black labourers were brought in for 'subsidiary tasks such as mixing concrete and cleaning the site' after building costs spiralled. Elizabeth Rankin and Rolf Michael Schneider, *From Memory to Marble: The Historical Frieze of the Voortrekker Monument. Part I: The Frieze* (Berlin: De Gruyter, 2019), p. 69.
21 Steenkamp, 'Apartheid to Democracy', pp. 250–51; Vicki Leibowitz, 'Making Memory Space: Recollection and Reconciliation in Post Apartheid South African Architecture' (unpublished master's thesis, RMIT University, 2008), <https://researchrepository.rmit.edu.au/esploro/outputs/9921861490601341> (accessed 10 August 2022).
22 'The Voortrekker Monument', *VTM* <https://vtm.org.za/en/the-voortrekker-monument/> (accessed 8 October 2022).
23 Ibid.
24 Ken Barris, 'Fiction of Ideas', *Southern African Review of Books*, 3.6 (1990), 6–7 (p. 6).

architectural metaphor'[25] – but also creates a temporal strangeness in allegory's workings. As I discussed in Chapter 1, Gordimer is concerned with allegory's relationship to realism, and Vladislavić here attempts to maintain allegory's timeless quality without sacrificing the historical particularity of work that more obviously describes the world in which it was produced. The layering of two kinds of temporal reference is particularly visible in a passage that performs an ekphrasis of one panel from the monument's frieze:

> [o]ne of our early leaders sits on the left. Behind him stand our people, his people. Some of them hold rifles; all of them wear hats. Our leader looks at the man opposite him, but he appears not to see him. He looks through him to the distant mountains […] To [a woman's] left, a priest. He holds a Bible. He looks at the man with determined tenderness.
>
> The enemy […] He looks like a man who has never sat on a chair before […] He is about to make a cross on the document which our leader pushes towards him […] He looks at the end of the quill. Behind him, his people kneel. (78–79)

The scene on the frieze can be understood on the one hand as a generic metaphor for the violence of colonialism, the rifles and the Bible representing physical force and religious ideology as instruments of conquest. On the other, this is also a description of Piet Retief's 1838 meeting with Dingane to sign a land treaty, as depicted on the twelfth panel of the frieze of the Voortrekker Monument.[26] While the veracity of the treaty, which granted the Voortrekkers a large area of land, is highly dubious, in Elizabeth Rankin and Rolf Michael Schneider's words, 'the frieze reflects none of these uncertainties. Even more convincingly than

---

25 Ivan Vladislavić, 'Frieze', in *The Loss Library and Other Unfinished Stories* (Calcutta: Seagull, 2012), pp. 47–54 (p. 49).

26 For comparison, this is part of a description of the frieze panel: 'In the centre […] two quite different men sit facing each other: the Zulu king Dingane in full regalia, and across the table the Voortrekker governor Piet Retief in trekker clothing […] Behind Dingane, his advisors and confidants kneel or crouch, and next to Retief stands a group of trekkers […] A little apart, marking the liminal zone between Zulu and trekkers, stands the English missionary, the Rev. Francis Owen, identified by his clerical collar and Bible.' Rankin and Schneider, *From Memory to Marble*, pp. 260, 209.

any certified copy of the treaty, the marble representation confirms its existence.'[27] Making use of classical marble, the monument suggests a stony permanence that fixes a historical narrative in place.

By offering a vivid representation of a real-world object, this passage operates in different terms to those of simple allegory. Rather than an extended metaphor that points to a meaning lying outside the confines of the narrative, 'We Came to the Monument' folds the ekphrastic description of a real-world artwork into a broadly allegorical framework. By blurring the edges of allegory in this way, Vladislavić maintains a degree of materiality sufficient to allow engagement with the world outside the text, while avoiding the future obsolescence of so-called protest literature. In so doing, he treads a very fine line. The ekphrasis of this panel provides a literary mediation of an already aesthetically mediated historical event, and in so doing draws attention to the formal workings of different art forms. However, this is perhaps at risk of enacting what Clive Barnett calls a 'politically duplicitous escape from historical reality'.[28] Vladislavić's adoption of this complex strategy is at once a product of, and an attempt to go beyond, what Neil Lazarus calls the 'ever more restricted terrain to which, by virtue of its situation, [white South African writing in the 1980s] [was] condemned'.[29] Vladislavić uses the formal properties of the Voortrekker Monument and its marble frieze as figurations of the social forms he experiences, and in so doing raises the question of what modes of thought his own literary forms make possible. An air of stagnation hangs over the story, and as the group comes to settle inside the monument, it gives a sense of formal hermeticism to the story, what Fredric Jameson calls the 'windless closure of the formalisms'.[30]

However, the following passage concludes the female narrator's account:

> It seems to me sometimes as if the earth stopped dead on its axis then, like a globe blocked by a child's hand, and slowly began to

---

27 Ibid., p. 264.
28 Cited in Andrew van der Vlies, *South African Textual Cultures: White, Black, Read All Over* (Manchester: Manchester University Press, 2011), p. 146.
29 Neil Lazarus, 'Modernism and Modernity: T. W. Adorno and Contemporary White South African Literature', *Cultural Critique*, 5 (1986), 131–55 (p. 131).
30 Fredric Jameson, *The Political Unconscious: Narrative as a Socially Symbolic Act* (Ithaca, NY: Cornell University Press, 1981), p. 27.

revolve in the opposite direction. It gathers up the long thread of history, so carelessly unwound into space. A wind is blowing in the hourglass, and it lofts the grains of sand into the night. When the people are asleep the sand settles in the blood, the streets. I try to resist, by dreaming up storms and floods.[31]

Faced with stasis at best, or worse, regression, the sole response the narrator can muster is to 'try to resist' with a biblical dream of storms and floods, implying the narrator's unwitting reaffirmation of her group's values, even as she would seek to oppose them. The circular aspect of the narrative, combined with the arresting of the group's movement at the monument, suggest the formal manifestation of a societal impasse. Elleke Boehmer, discussing late apartheid fiction, notices a trend in literature from the 1980s to conclude with a sense of 'a suspension of vision, a hemming in as opposed to a convinced and convincing opening up or testing of options'.[32] The imagery of arrested movement, rewinding, and the settling sands of time certainly give a sense of entropy or futility. As in Gordimer's 'Jump', the past weighs heavily on the present, impeding forward movement. And yet the prose at this point shifts in register, a lyrical intensification that points the reader towards a symbolic register of interpretation, not showing new events but rather investing existing ones with greater significance. In this moment of lyrical pause, there is an affective intensification for the reader, and a glimpse of an alternative temporality to that of the monument's stultifying logics.

And so, formally at least, the story ends on a tentative note of hope, suggesting something of what Nick Visser sees in some 1980s fiction: the possibility of projecting a vision of the future, or at least of 'positioning readers in a certain way in relation to [the future]'.[33] Steenkamp's daughter and the statue may be visited by oneiric visions of 'storms and floods', and 'lightning striking upwards' (80), but these catastrophes are tempered by the statue's unnamed hope, which 'digs its claws into the earth, and howls her name' (81). The statue's *'hopes and hungers as improbable as birds take flight against a steep grey sky and disappear'*,

---

31 Vladislavić, 'We Came to the Monument', p. 80.
32 Boehmer, 'Endings and New Beginnings', p. 44.
33 Nicholas Visser, 'The Politics of Future Projection in South African Fiction', in *Black/White Writing: Essays on South African Literature*, ed. Pauline Fletcher (Cranbury, NJ: Associated University Presses, 1993), pp. 62–82 (p. 63).

but one hope remains, which '*digs its claws into the earth, and howls her name. It turns on me its ancient face of joy and grief. It will not let me go*' (81). Howling and the digging in of claws, if nothing else, are at least acts of antagonistic struggle, what Walter Benjamin describes as an 'attempt [...] to wrest tradition away from a conformism that is about to overpower it'.[34] The conformism he rails against is the kind of conservatism represented by the hilltop monument, a reified form of tradition, defined and transmitted by those in power.

In contrast, Vladislavić's story shows how literary form offers a structure through which political thought might move. His turn to a lyrical register in the story's final lines turns our attention to the lyric's fundamental subject: time. In stilling the narrative progress of the story, this lyrical intensification offers a temporal alternative to the world it describes. If the monument offers an experience of time that reifies historical narratives, and subjects those who interact with the structure to its calcifying logics, then the story here offers a temporal experience that reaches beyond such logics, suggesting that an imaginative alternative might be within reach.

This line of thought implies a powerful argument for art's agency in the world, a model in which art *matters*. This lyrical cry to the transcendent power of love, poetry, hope, and imagination over the determination of societal structure is perhaps naïve, but rather than dismiss it, we might rather consider how this lyrical protest might have registered when the story was published. As Barris observes in an early review of the story, '[t]he political statement of the story is subtle, quite sublimated within its poetry', and in this regard it offers an aesthetic rejoinder to a more utilitarian model of art's political efficacy that marked much writing and critical debate in the 1980s.[35] The lyrical turn at the story's end provokes a feeling of frustration for readers seeking a more explicit project of political action, but in so doing it asks us to participate in imagining a world beyond the determinations of such models of efficacy, while ironising the hopelessness of its own gesture. However, underlying this is the paradox Sharon Cameron identifies in the lyric: 'If there is a victory in the form of the lyric – the stunning articulation of the isolated moment – despair underlies it. It is despair of the possibility of complete stories, stories whose conclusions are

---

34 Benjamin, 'Theses on the Philosophy of History', p. 255.
35 Barris, 'Fiction of Ideas', p. 6.

known, and consequently it is despair of complete knowledge.'[36] By refusing both the efficacy of political writing and the transcendence of the unbridled imagination, this story leaves both characters and readers on the brink of an as yet unrealised moment of resolution. This fiction of disconsolation insists, although guardedly, on a life after apartheid.

'Cold Storage' and Monumental Apophasis

By 2011, when Vladislavić published *The Loss Library and Other Unfinished Stories*, he was well established as one of South Africa's major writers of short fiction, but also of novels, creative non-fiction, essays, and other forms. In the intervening years he had published one other collection of stories, *Propaganda by Monuments*, and several other texts. The word 'stories' in *The Loss Library*'s title is somewhat misleading: these texts are generic oddities, hovering somewhere between elliptic short stories and exploratory essays. David Winters describes how the collection 'doesn't read like something straightforwardly "written". Instead, it is brought into being by the tension between being written and unwritten, where neither ever overwhelms the other.'[37] *The Loss Library*, described by S.J. Naudé as 'clear-eyed lament[s] for failed, lost or unwritten stories', appeared in a South Africa that had for seventeen years been working through the complications of democracy, while coping with apartheid's legacy of inequity.[38] Perhaps appropriately for thinking through apartheid's unfinished business, *The Loss Library*'s stated mandate is to 'deal with unsettled accounts', by telling the stories of stories that remain incomplete.[39] The texts in the volume 'concern stories [Vladislavić] imagined but could not write, or started to write but could not finish' (1). They come close to what Janette Turner

---

36 Sharon Cameron, *Lyric Time: Dickinson and the Limits of Genre* (Baltimore, MD: Johns Hopkins University Press, 1981), p. 71.
37 David Winters, 'Literature is What We Are Lost In', *3:AM Magazine*, 18 March 2012, <http://www.3ammagazine.com/3am/literature-is-what-we-are-lost-in/> (accessed 25 March 2021).
38 S.J. Naudé and Ivan Vladislavić, 'In Conversation: S.J. Naudé and Ivan Vladislavić', *Granta*, 12 December 2014, <https://granta.com/in-conversation-s-j-naude-and-ivan-vladislavic/> (accessed 29 July 2021).
39 Vladislavić, *The Loss Library*, p. 1. All further references to this work are given parenthetically in the text until the end of this section.

Hospital wished for in a review of Alice Walker: 'a different literary form, a new kind of polemic [...] perhaps something akin to Pascal's *Pensées*, an episodic collage of documentary fact, scholarly opinion and lyrical monologue'.⁴⁰ If the allegorical stagnation of 'We Came to the Monument' inspires a lyrical means of thinking through the harm inflicted by calcified societal insularity, the loose essayistic form of 'The Cold Storage Club' suggests a mediated response to what Andrew van der Vlies calls the 'disappointments, temporal and affective' of the post-apartheid period.⁴¹

In such an end-weighted form as the short story, the inability to finish might be thought fatal, but Vladislavić makes a virtue of this shortcoming. Edgar Allan Poe once pondered 'how interesting a magazine paper might be written by any author who would – that is to say, who could – detail, step by step, the processes by which any one of his compositions attained its ultimate point of completion', and Vladislavić here takes him almost at his word.⁴² Vladislavić's approach, however, differs, in that his text's ultimate goal is not completion as such, but a kind of completion-in-incompletion. Rather than showing a gradual progression towards a finished object, it is the very means of writing, the 'wheels and pinions', which become the story's end.⁴³ In each section, he gives a synopsis of an idea for a story from his notebook, and then explains why that story was never written. Some of them never really got off the ground, some were incorporated into larger works; one was even 'drafted and then lost, and [his] attempt to reconstruct it failed' (1). Vladislavić approaches these unfinished texts tangentially, explaining their interrupted genesis through suggestive digressions and meanders.

The book's combination of tipped-in collages, italicised passages from notebooks and dated diaristic entries creates a scrapbook quality wholly appropriate for describing these works-no-longer-in-progress. Each 'case study' (1) plunges the reader straight into a new time, place,

---

40 Janette Turner-Hospital, 'What They Did to Tashi', *New York Times Book Review*, 28 June 1992, p. 12.
41 Andrew van der Vlies, *Present Imperfect: Contemporary South African Writing* (Oxford: Oxford University Press, 2017), p. 23.
42 Edgar Allan Poe, 'The Philosophy of Composition', in *The New Short Story Theories*, ed. Charles E. May (Athens, OH: Ohio University Press, 1994), pp. 67–69 (p. 68).
43 Ibid., p. 68.

and set of concerns, and within the texts the topic often jumps suddenly from one paragraph to the next. The short texts are also stuffed with things – photographs, sculptures, hats, birds, and of course books – that are described but never shown, a spectral plenitude of absent objects. The objects described and the physical support the book provides vie for the reader's attention, and yet the texts in this collection feel less disjointed than those in *Missing Persons* or *Propaganda by Monuments*. Despite the abrupt changes of topic, the textural and stylistic movements are for the most part more gradual, the tone is cooler, more distanced and wry, and the reading experience feels calmer. *The Loss Library*'s more distanced tone frames the playoff between presence and absence, giving a form built around a ghostly scaffolding. In returning to the 'failed' (1) stories of his past, Vladislavić evokes some of the challenges facing authors almost twenty years into the post-apartheid period, and reassesses the optimism of the years directly after liberation. These texts constitute admissions of missed opportunities, but are equally acts of recuperation, attempts to see how one might build anew on the political and aesthetic ruins of the past. The unfinished stories he describes are but a few from 'hundreds' (3) that were never written, and he finds in them the materials with which to try again, by exploring how the unrealised futures that the past holds might be put to use in the present.

'Cold Storage' begins with an italicised, dated paragraph, describing an unwritten story (101). This present marker of an absence hovers at the top of the page like words on a gravestone, marking the entrance into the text as a moment of both loss and memory. In Maurice Blanchot's words, in which he considers how language both uses and instigates absence, 'when we speak, we are leaning on a tomb'.[44]

> *Only amateurs collect books in order to read them. The professionals wrap their investments in archival plastic and put them away in the safe. Idea: a syndicate of pros, old friends and rivals, buy a defunct meat-processing plant and use its refrigeration rooms to store their books. Reconstruct the minutes of the Cold Storage Club.*
>
> *(2005)*

---

44 Maurice Blanchot, *The Gaze of Orpheus*, ed. P. Adams Sitney, trans. Lydia Davis (Barrytown, NY: Station Hill, 1981), p. 55.

Vladislavić's 'account' of this unrealised story takes the form of a series of meditations on a range of topics suggestively related to it. These include the 1933 Opernplatz Nazi book-burning and Micha Ullman's public sculptures, including *Bibliothek* (1995), in memory of the burnings; *Aberntstern* (1996), a diminutive memorial to Claus von Stauffenberg, who failed in an attempt to assassinate Adolf Hitler; and *Löffel* (1997), a spoon set in a paving stone. Also discussed are a grandiose Nazi memorial and the acts of civic defiance it provoked; Bruno Wank's *Argumente* (1995), a sculptural tribute to those acts of resistance; and Goran Tomasević's 1999 photograph of a NATO-bombed convoy of Albanian refugees. As this dense description suggests, there is a lot packed into a text that barely spans 11 pages. The account jumps paratactically, and the text integrates journal entries and snatches of overheard conversations. A text that describes monuments and photographs, forms haunted by absence, and that adopts an aesthetic strategy that plays on the dynamic between being written and unwritten offers a formal structure through which a new politics of memory can be articulated, while offering an artistic response to the unfulfilled promises of liberation.

The monuments in 'Cold Storage' are, for the most part, quite different from those in Vladislavić's earlier works. The earlier monuments – the giant geometric building in 'We Came to the Monument' and an enormous stone head of Lenin in the case of 'Propaganda by Monuments' – were built on an imposing scale. The Nazi memorial Vladislavić describes in Munich, an 'altar-like memorial tablet, surmounted by a swastika and eagle, rows of flags and wreaths, and a huge torch' (110), might be thought of the same species, in that it uses massive presence to impose a societal narrative and suggest its permanence. Ullman's works, on the contrary, are 'small, unobtrusive things, sometimes underfoot, sometimes overlookable' (105). *Bibliothek* is an underground room lined with empty bookshelves, visible through a small glass panel on the ground. The von Stauffenberg memorial is 'a hollow the size of a cup that sometimes fills with water' (105). The absences they memorialise, of books, of people, become a constitutive feature of their design. Rather than filling that absence with presence, these monuments leave physical and conceptual space, and the viewer is challenged to respond to it. James E. Young calls such works 'counter-monuments', creative interventions that are 'ethically certain of their duty to remember, but aesthetically sceptical of the assumptions underpinning traditional memorial forms'.⁴⁵ This scepticism often appears formally through, in Quentin Stevens, Karen A. Franck, and Ruth Fazakerley's words, 'the inversion of traditional monumental forms' by foregrounding:

> voids instead of solids, absence instead of presence [...] dark rather than light tones, and an emphasis on the horizontal rather than the vertical. Forms may be sunken rather than elevated [...] shifted off-axis, or dispersed or fragmented rather than unified in a single, orderly composition at a single location.⁴⁶

If this description is fit for the monuments his stories describe, it might also be used for the short story forms that Vladislavić develops in this collection, which increasingly draw on oblique, fragmentary, and apophatic means of addressing the 'duty to remember', or perhaps better for these stories, an instinct, urge, or desire to do so. While in 'We Came to the Monument' monumental grandeur is set against the short story's diminutive frame and lyrical temporality, in 'Cold Storage', the aesthetic mode of the stories is closer to that of the monuments it describes, using withdrawal, implication, and suggestion, and leaving even greater interpretational freedom to the reader.

The changing nature of the monuments is accompanied by a different relationship between text and visual media, a feature that first became apparent in the 2012 edition of *The Loss Library* in which 'Cold Storage' is preceded by a tipped-in collage by the volume's illustrator Sunandini Banerjee.⁴⁷ While the frieze in 'We Came to the Monument' maintains a dense stony presence, even in a story that features mobile statues, this collage overlays images and pieces of text of varying

---

45 Young, 'The Counter-Monument', p. 271.
46 Quentin Stevens, Karen A. Franck, and Ruth Fazakerley, 'Counter-Monuments: The Anti-Monumental and the Dialogic', *The Journal of Architecture*, 17.6 (2012), 951–72 (p. 956).
47 Unlike the relationship between text and image in *TJ & Double Negative*, in which Vladislavić wrote a text that was published alongside pre-existing photographs by David Goldblatt (although Vladislavić says he did not look back at the photographs when writing the book), these collages were added 'after the fact' of writing. See Ivan Vladislavić and Jan Steyn, 'Interview with Ivan Vladislavić', *The White Review*, 2012, <http://www.thewhitereview.org/interviews/interview-with-ivan-vladislavic/> (accessed 10 June 2019); Ivan Vladislavić and David Goldblatt, *TJ & Double Negative* (Cape Town: Umuzi, 2010).

degrees of transparency and ephemerality. With some decryption, most of the images become identifiable after reading the story. There is a signpost from Berlin, a blurred image of *Schalechet* (*Fallen Leaves*), one of Ullman's sculptures, and some half-erased text superimposed with the words 'RAY BRADBURY' and 'FARENHEIT 451' in a larger font, taken from the cover of the first edition of Ray Bradbury's novel, running perpendicular to it.[48] In the centre is a seated, puckish George Groszian cartoon figure. There is little planar space here, but the palimpsestic overlaying of times and places creates, paradoxically, a feeling of depth and diachrony, but also of that depth's being flattened, and so temporal extension's collapse into synchrony. The overlaying of text and images from different times creates a collage that feels as temporal as it is spatial. The resulting pull between surface and depth, chronology and achronology, primes the reader for the text to follow. These collages were present only in the 2012 Seagull Books hardback edition, published for the international market and distributed by the University of Chicago Press, the book having previously been published without them as an Umuzi paperback in South Africa in 2011. While the collages were added as a supplement after the book had been written, it is still difficult not to feel that international readers were being offered the complete package. As well as its publication in *The Loss Library*, 'Cold Storage' was also published beside a series of photographs in *Oblique*, an artist's book by South African artist Abrie Fourie, published two years after a 2009 solo exhibition of the same name. These editions make different 'claims on our attention', in George Bornstein's words, as literary work 'might be said to exist not in any one version, but in all the versions put together'.[49] There is then a strong case to be made for reading these versions alongside one another.[50]

---

48 Ray Bradbury, *Farenheit 451* (New York: Ballantine, 1953). Aptly for a story about book burning, Bradbury's novel is named after what he thought to be the auto-ignition point of paper. See Robin Anne Reid, *Ray Bradbury: A Critical Companion* (Westport, CT: Greenwood, 2000), p. 53.
49 George Bornstein, *Material Modernism: The Politics of the Page* (Cambridge: Cambridge University Press, 2001), p. 6.
50 This is further complicated when online editions are taken into account. I first came across Fourie's accompanying photographs on his website. See Abrie Fourie, 'Oblique', *Abriefourie.Com*, <http://www.abriefourie.com/oblique_01.html> (accessed 10 April 2021).

Vladislavić's writing can be read in light of these multiple versions by using the text and photographs in Fourie's book as starting points for reading 'Cold Storage' in *The Loss Library*. Fourie observes that '[a] print, for all its materiality, stands in the place of and points to something that is absent. I hint at that silent tension between absence and presence, those oblique and surprise perspectives that highlight the play between abstract and real forms.'[51] The aesthetic affinity that this project has with Vladislavić's work in *The Loss Library* is evident. Vladislavić states in an interview that because he gives 'detailed descriptions of images' in *The Loss Library*, to include those images 'would have defeated the object'.[52] Yet when described in such detail, these images still seem to hover about the text. Although the 'real forms' of the images he describes are not there, there is nevertheless a 'silent tension' established between the text and the missing images.

The photographs that accompany 'Cold Storage' in *Oblique* further enrich the possibilities for interpreting the text, although they offer little by way of explanation. As Vladislavić observes of W.G. Sebald's use of photographs, the images that sit beside 'Cold Storage' are also 'always less than or more than illustrative', and '[t]heir purpose is less to define than to disrupt, to create ripples and falls in the beguiling flow of prose. They are pebbles and weirs.'[53] One such photograph in *Oblique* is titled 'Rykestraße, Berlin, Germany, 2008', and shows what appears to be a rusting shutter door, bearing an abstract shape that is spectrally incomplete, as if a previously existing image had been rubbed out. Like Ullman's works on paper, which Vladislavić also describes, this image is 'barely there on the surface [...] as if someone had carried the solid objects from a room that had not been dusted for years'.[54] The rust and faded shape evoke feelings of nostalgia and transience, inspiring a yearning for the missing object's restoration, along with an awareness that this thing of beauty could only have come about through a process of disappearance and decay. When the works of Fourie and Vladislavić are juxtaposed, they both complement and complicate one another. Fourie's photograph has come about through the imperfection caused by entropy; Vladislavić's story is premised on the latency of unfinishedness. The aesthetic pull between presence and absence that

---

51 Ibid.
52 Vladislavić and Steyn, 'Interview with Ivan Vladislavić'.
53 Vladislavić, *The Loss Library*, p. 54.
54 Ibid., p. 107.

this collaborative project creates leads to a contradictory mixture of hope and lost hope, possibility and disappointment.

In the case of the 'We Came to the Monument', the ekphrasis of a monument's frieze and the short story's accommodation of the lyrical offer alternative temporal experiences from both the stifling temporality of rigid monumentalism and the political urgency of some 1980s writing. *The Loss Library*'s 'Cold Storage', for its part, puts the short story in dialogue with apophatic monuments and photographs, using these absences as a formal invitation for readers think to through the impasses and frustrations of the time after apartheid, and to try to find meaning in what remains.

Heavyweight History in 'Save the Pedestals'

In 'Save the Pedestals' (2019), Vladislavić revisits and develops many of the concerns and aesthetic strategies from across his previous writing. The story was written after the Rhodes Must Fall movement, which brought the politics of monumentalisation into the centre of South African public discourse. The story features two ageing 'veterans', Comrade A and Ma Z, who meet once a month to collect their pensions and go for something to eat.[55] One week before the meeting recounted in the story, a statue of the country's former president, the Old Man, had been removed, leaving only the pedestal in its place. The removal was 'very civilised' (169), despite 'all the fighting that went before' (169). Unlike some other statues with which it is compared in the story, such as Saddam Hussein's, the Old Man's statue was not toppled, but rather, much like the Rhodes statue at UCT, gently lifted off by crane. The only part of the statue that remains, except for the pedestal, are the guards carved around the base, 'men with beards', 'four sentries draped with bandoliers' (169). Above them is a 'man-shaped hole in the air whose headspace was troubled by the quick grey smudges of pigeons, claws outstretched, reaching for the vanished perch of a hat brim' (170). Ma Z observes that '[o]nce you've pulled something off a pedestal it must be very tempting to jump up there yourself' (169), but they resist that temptation, rather imagining what might replace

---

55 Ivan Vladislavić, 'Save the Pedestals', in *The Yale Review* (Hoboken, NJ: Wiley Blackwell, 2019), pp. 165–86 (p. 167). All further references to this work are given parenthetically in the text until the end of this section.

the statue. Perhaps a 'hero of the struggle', a 'professional man ... [i]n a three-piece suit', a 'VIP', or more abstractly 'Just an idea. Let's say: enterprise' (170). The suggestions keep coming fast, 'one of our mining magnates [...] our billionaire philanthropists' (170), a worker in overalls, 'on all fours with his head hanging down between his shoulders' (171). The characters think back to their earlier lives: Ma Z visiting Sofia, Comrade A working in a factory and growing up in the same neighbourhood as the Old Man, and a memory they share, seemingly of a romantic relationship that is rekindled at the story's close. The pair later find a shape covered in tarpaulin on the pedestal and, having failed to see much underneath it, they decide to go to the unveiling, but then mix up the dates and miss it. The story ends with the two holding hands and looking up at the new statue that stands in place of the Old Man.

In 'Save the Pedestals', the location retains a somewhat otherworldly or indistinct character, but several cues suggest Pretoria's Church Square.[56] The 'Palace of Justice, Old Parliament, the General Post Office, the Opera House' (171) can mostly still be found on Church Square, save the Opera House, which is no longer there. The statue that has been removed bears some resemblance to that of Paul Kruger, a *voortrekker*, President of the South African Republic from 1883 to 1900, and controversial figurehead of the Boer cause during the Second Anglo-Boer War. Much like the real statue, the statue in 'Save the Pedestals' was previously located at the railway station before being moved to the large square; both have a distinctive hat; and both are framed by statues of citizen militias with bandoliers. However, the shrouded figure of the new statue, 'three times bigger' (180) than the old one, hints at the giant Nelson Mandela statue that replaced that of J.M.B. Herzog outside the parliamentary Union Buildings, and the description that the Old Man had 'stirred crowds to insurrection against their Imperial masters' (180) ambiguously refers to both Kruger and Mandela. Clearly, in a story that considers the ephemerality of seemingly immovable structures – the

---

56 Vladislavić, best known as a documenter and chronicler of Johannesburg, also often includes Pretoria in his writing: the monument in 'We Came to the Monument' alludes to the giant monument outside the city; 'Propaganda by Monuments' features Boniface Khumalo sitting on what was then Strijdom Square. His most substantial Pretoria work is *The Distance* (2019), which is entirely set there.

title of the story refers to Stanisław J. Lec's aphorism 'When smashing monuments, save the pedestals – they always come in handy'[57] – this ambiguity is wholly intentional.[58]

The story has appeared next to two different images, each of which guide the reader's perception of it. In the online version, there is a detail from *Three Pedestals with Draperies* by lithographer and painter Léon Laroche (c. 1885–95). The full painting, held at the Rijksmuseum, shows three pedestals with greyed-out figures on top. The image is seemingly designed to demonstrate how to drape fabric around a pedestal – the pedestals are in colour and are sharply defined, in contrast to the gestural outline of the statues above them. In the detail from the image that illustrates 'Save the Pedestals', the image has been cropped and converted to black and white, showing one of the shadowy, semi-opaque greyscale busts on top of a clearly defined plinth. The bust seems almost to dissolve into the grain of the empty space behind it, but is still visible. There is clearly an aesthetic overlap here with Fourie's work, as presence and absence are held in tension.

The print version of the story in the *Yale Review*, however, shows quite a different image: a full-colour photograph of René Magritte's *The Future of Statues* (1937). The original work was made from a commercial plaster copy of Napoleon Bonaparte's death mask, which Magritte painted with a vivid blue sky on which shining white clouds float. This suggests Napoleon's vison, perhaps his lofty arrogance, but the object is also a *memento mori*, a material reminder of the emperor's finitude in contrast with his usual overbearing monumentalisation. The clouds that pass across his face both suggest the transience of his earthly glory and portray him as something like a blank space onto which other narratives might be projected. The concerns this artwork raises, of earthly embodiment against a monumental will to the eternal, and of how monuments become screens onto which societal dynamics are projected, are both integral to 'Save the Pedestals', in which ageing revolutionaries see the transformation of a public imaginary.

---

57 Stanisław Lec, *Unkempt Thoughts*, trans. Jacek Gałązka (London: Minerva, 1962), p. 50.

58 Vladislavić came across this aphorism when I sent it to him in an email some years before the story's publication, hence why the story is dedicated to me. I mention this not only because I am grateful for the dedication, but also to illustrate the fruitful cross-pollination between Vladislavić's writing and the theoretical apparatus of academia.

'Save the Pedestals' goes even further than Vladislavić's previous writing in exploring the work of time and memory as they operate in monuments, artworks, and the experience of the short story. In 'We Came to the Monument', the compression of the short story, its mobilisation of lyrical suspension, and its parable-like quality offer an alternative temporal account to that of the monument it describes. 'Cold Storage' adopts a retrospective temporal structure that tries to put past failure to use in the present, using the apophatic aspect of counter-monuments, the short story, and photographs to draw the reader into a process of thought. 'Save the Pedestals', for its part, overlays the willed eternal temporality of overbearing monuments, the fluxional or perspectival temporality of how these monuments come to be reinterpreted, the lived temporality of the span of a life, the recurring temporality of an author's revisited oeuvre, and the temporal experience of reading the story. This story not only deals with the kinds of temporal work performed by monuments, it also shows Comrade A and Ma Z as involved in their own struggles with time. This story presents a struggle with memory, forgetting, and the march of history, but also with biological time, a current that runs with but is existentially decoupled from that of history taken in its long span. It is precisely through the juxtaposition of these modalities of time that this story offers readers a formal means through which to conceive of their temporal situatedness.

The story reveals a further dimension of Vladislavić's thinking about the politics of monuments, but also turns his investigation into memory more fully on himself and on the reader of his fictions. As I argued was the case for Gordimer in Chapter 1, Vladislavić here revisits the aesthetic strategies and thematic concerns of his earlier work. But he is also concerned in this story with the process of ageing, and what place memory and nostalgia have in the context of an individual life and how it intersects with a national imaginary. Andrew van der Vlies, in his consideration of Vladislavić's writing, reads it through Svetlana Boym's theory of 'restorative' and 'reflective' nostalgia, with the first an almost pathological attempt to hold on to the past, and the second, in which Vladislavić's work is thought to participate, a more critical position that allows the feeling of longing while foregrounding its risks.[59] This is certainly a productive framework for thinking about Vladislavić's fictions, and particularly up to *Double Negative*, the most recent novel that was available when van der Vlies's study was published in 2017.

59 Van der Vlies, *Present Imperfect*, p. 100.

Since then, Vladislavić has taken a somewhat more sceptical position on nostalgia in any form. In an interview with the *Johannesburg Review of Books* in 2019, he observes that 'I was once interested in the notion of a "critical nostalgia", but I'm no longer sure what that means. I hear Zoë Wicomb's sceptical commentary on how easily nostalgia fades into "plain old fond remembrance".'[60] In 'Save the Pedestals', forms of public memory are doubled by nostalgic and even sentimental acts of personal and private memory, both at the level of character and in a writerly revisioning of how such concerns have been treated in previous works.

The overlap between these different kinds of memory come into view at one moment when the two protagonists are discussing the fate of Soviet-era statues in contemporary Russia.[61] Ma Z says, 'people are fond of them. There's Old Vladdie, they'll say, as if he were a great-uncle they used to visit in the school holidays' (177). Vladdie here is, of course, Vladimir Lenin, but is perhaps equally Vladislavić looking back on the pasts of his written self. This story offers a sampler of the tonal palette from his previous writing: sometimes it is lyrical, elsewhere ironically distant, sometimes guardedly nostalgic, elsewhere wackily postmodern. The story maintains something of the intensity of *Missing Persons*, and particularly 'We Came to the Monument', as both feature lyrical italicised passages and reflections on the contrast between the rigidity of monuments and the softness of human bodies. There is equally something of the wonky, zany comedy of *Propaganda by Monuments* – for example, the image of Saddam Hussein's toppled statue rebounding 'like one of those donkeys with elastic bands for joints' (169) – and a return to the listing that was everywhere in his earlier works.[62] And yet

---

60 Ivan Vladislavić and Jennifer Malec, '"The Fallible Memory is Surely at the Heart of Writing Fiction"—Jennifer Malec Interviews Ivan Vladislavić about His Latest Novel, *The Distance*', *The Johannesburg Review of Books*, 2019, <https://johannesburgreviewofbooks.com/2019/05/06/the-fallible-memory-is-surely-at-the-heart-of-writing-fiction-jennifer-malec-interviews-ivan-vladislavic-about-his-latest-novel-the-distance/> (accessed 20 September 2022). The citation is from Zoë Wicomb, '"Good Reliable Fictions": Nostalgia, Narration, and the Literary Narrative', in *Race, Nation, Translation: South African Essays, 1990–2013*, ed. Andrew van der Vlies (New Haven, CT: Yale University Press, 2018), pp. 203–16 (p. 203).

61 This is, of course, the question that animates his well-known story 'Propaganda by Monuments'.

62 He notes in a 2012 interview that 'The lists and deconstructive exercises in some of my stories may have become too much for sensitive readers, myself

the prose elsewhere has a more stripped back and tannic quality, more in the mode of his later writing. In fact, all of these aspects have been present in Vladislavić's writing from his earliest works, something he touches on in an interview, in which he notes that his writing has always contained 'a range of voices or registers, with relationships between them that I can diagrammatize', elaborating that '[t]here are half a dozen voices I can identify in my first story collection, *Missing Persons*, and I can take one of them and trace it through the later work. It gets picked up in this story, and then in that novel, and then in this new piece I'm working on.'[63] What is perhaps unique about 'Save the Pedestals' is that these different registers are co-present in such a compressed way. This leads to the text performing its own formal and stylistic memory work in revisiting aspects of Vladislavić's previous writerly practice. The pedestal, then, performs a double metaphoric function as both the location of successive regimes' will to power and the short story's capacity as a vehicle for different styles of an author's aesthetic development.

Asked about his work with other artists, Vladislavić notes that working in this way forces him to navigate the 'magnetic field of another imagination and meet with or assert a productive resistance'.[64] While in this interview he is discussing the process of writing, this might be extended to think about what happens when readers experience the stories as well. 'Save the Pedestals' is filled with references to other artworks: the statue on the pedestal, poems by Mafika Gwala, Lionel Abrahams, Zbigniew Herbert, Miroslav Holub, and Pablo Neruda, and a work by conceptual artist Christian Jankowski.[65] The artwork described at the end of the story, Jankowski's *Heavy Weight History* (2013), involved the artist photographing and filming eleven top Polish weightlifters as they attempted to lift up monuments in Warsaw while sports commentator Michał Olszański provided unscripted

---

    included, but I've moved on in that respect too.' Vladislavić and Steyn, 'Interview with Ivan Vladislavić'.

63 Ivan Vladislavić, Peter Beilharz, and Sian Supski, 'Ivan Vladislavić – A Tale in Two Cities', *Thesis Eleven*, 136.1 (2016), 20–30 (p. 28).

64 Naudé and Vladislavić, 'In Conversation'.

65 In fact, the Lionel Abrahams poem that is alluded to is 'Place (A party of white Johannesburgers reads Zbigniew Herbert, Holub and other poets at the foot of a mine dump, Summer 1969)', which itself alludes to Herbert and Holub among others, and which is about the failures of memory. Further, this poem is also alluded to in *Portrait with Keys*, p.134.

commentary. Some of the monuments come loose from their bases and seem to hover before being set down again; others refuse to move at all. Jankowski's website describes the work as follows: 'In a city like Warsaw, which was almost completely destroyed during World War II, memorials function as signs of identities old and new [...] Jankowski decided to rupture that historical narrative, to introduce lightness to a subject with such gravity.'[66] Olszański's commentary provides moments of unexpected insight, such as when the weightlifters fail because they are 'overwhelmed by history', or when their successes are celebrated: 'In this way, before our eyes, new history is created!' The statue of Ronald Reagan outside the US Embassy is one they could not lift. One interviewed weightlifter explains that 'It's a symbol, as you said, we owe him our freedom [...] We feel somehow ... greatly honoured.' Olszański replies, 'So, in the end it's good that Ronald Reagan stays firm [...] [O]ur sportsmen had to leave this monument with the feeling of failure, but it's not really a failure.'

The relationship between weightlifter and monument offers a useful way of thinking about the short story's role in relation to the weight of history, as embodied in monuments of this kind. While it is very rare that a work could overcome this weight, it allows a momentary glimpse of what it might look like if it could, and so invites readers to take on their own projects of conceptual refiguration. In this context, art's failure to enact change might look, if not like a success, then at least like an invitation to think through the nature of that failure and how this very process might constitute one of its social affordances. 'Save the Pedestals', like *Heavy Weight History*, implicates the reader in the politics of memory, not as a distanced observer but rather as an immediate participant, bearing the weight of history on their own shoulders, and left to consider how they think back on the 'bad old days' (178).

The struggle of the weightlifters to move the monuments, which results more often in failure than in euphoric success, offers a useful foil for thinking through art's role in political thought. Even a failure to succeed, by posing the question of what success would have looked like, allows a more reflective engagement with the terms of the world we occupy. The short story, marginal and insubstantial, does not aspire to replace the larger narratives it engages, but in creating a

---

66 'Heavy Weight History', *Christian Jankowski*, 2017, <https://christian-jankowski.com/works/2013-2/heavy-weight-history/> (accessed 1 October 2022).

moment's monument it might open a space in which they could be better understood. Frank O'Connor characterises the short story as a 'struggle with [...] the novelist's Time [...] an attempt to reach some point of vantage from which past and future are equally visible'.[67] Short stories, then, in formally evincing the tension between narrative time and a point outside it, offer readers a conceptual apparatus with which to think through the fact of our time-bound lives and our attempts to make sense of this state. Moreover, short stories, and particularly the short stories by Vladislavić that I have analysed here, offer a further heuristic device, one that affords thought on the pull between worldly events and art's attempts to help us make sense of them.

---

[67] Frank O'Connor, *The Lonely Voice: A Study of the Short Story* (Cleveland, OH: World Publishing, 1963), p. 105.

CHAPTER THREE

Zoë Wicomb and the 'Problem of Class'

Zoë Wicomb's short stories have a 'problem of class'.[1] The turn of phrase is Wicomb's own, taken from her 2008 collection, *The One That Got Away*, and in what follows, I suggest that class analysis has been largely absent from criticism of Wicomb's work, despite its importance in her writing. This requires framing her oeuvre in the context of the apartheid government's creation of a class hierarchy through the racially determined distribution of public services. In light of this, I analyse two of Wicomb's short stories – 'In the Botanic Gardens' and 'There's the Bird that Never Flew' – arguing that reading for class in these stories is complicated by her formally and stylistically experimental prose and the generic tendencies of the short story. In 'In the Botanic Gardens', Wicomb makes particular use of ellipsis, allowing her to pose political and ethical questions through what is unsaid. However, while ellipsis allows for a suggestive opening of political possibilities, it also precludes commitment to an identifiable political position. Wicomb is clearly aware of this paradox and foregrounds its contradictions in her work, allowing for a reading that puts pressure on modes of criticism that exaggerate the political affordances of gaps and absences and that determine the value of artworks by the frankness of their political commitments. 'There's the Bird that Never Flew' foregrounds other dimensions of class, namely the role that cultural capital plays in class identity and the overdetermined classification of artworks. Many of Wicomb's stories, as is the case for the stories by Ivan Vladislavić I analysed in the previous chapter, are concerned with intermedial questions about the nature of art, and about how artworks might be analysed: Wicomb's short stories, like the artworks that appear in them, are at once bearers of political content, commodities, a means of expressing class identity through a

---

1 Wicomb, *The One That Got Away*, p. 126.

performance of taste, and, crucially, sites of aesthetic experience that allow a thinking through of these concerns.

The analysis of social class has been less common in post-apartheid literary criticism than it was during apartheid. Critics have paid close attention to race, gender, and sexuality in Wicomb's writing, but class has been largely neglected, even though it permeates her oeuvre.[2] There are a few passing references: Dorothy Driver observes that '[t]he subordinations endemic to the discourses of race, class and gender insistently interrelate in Wicomb's critical thinking'; Andrew van der Vlies warns against an easy cosmopolitanism that is 'blind to race, gender, sexuality, and material need'; and Pamela Sculley sees 'analytic gaps' around 'class, social justice, and gender' when discussing cosmopolitanism in Wicomb's writing.[3] Although all recognise that class is at issue in her work, none takes this observation any further, even though they rightly note, as Wicomb does herself, 'the "bound-upness" of race with other modalities. For instance, with the exploitation of gender, and with economics.'[4] The lack of critical discussion of class in her work is perhaps partly rooted in how her texts deflect analysis in these terms. In the short stories I discuss below, Wicomb's aporetic prose uses ellipses, ambiguities, and partial gestures that are far from the more explicitly engaged tenor of some South African writing from the 1970s and 1980s. By preferring ambiguity to certainty, by gesturing towards class while never making it explicit, the style of these short stories is bound up with its political affordances. As I discuss below, art's role in the construction and performance of class identity is one of Wicomb's enduring preoccupations, and this can be understood on a number of levels. On the one hand, characters' engagements with artworks are often described in

---

2 See, for example, Andrew van der Vlies, 'Zoë Wicomb's Queer Cosmopolitanisms', *Safundi*, 12.3–4 (2011), 425–44; Hugh William Macmillan and Lucy Valerie Graham, 'The "Great Coloured Question" and the Cosmopolitan: Fiction, History and Politics in David's Story', *Safundi*, 12.3–4 (2011), 331–47.

3 Dorothy Driver, 'The Struggle Over the Sign: Writing and History in Zoë Wicomb's Art', *Journal of Southern African Studies*, 36.3 (2010), 523–42 (p. 526); van der Vlies, 'Zoë Wicomb's Queer Cosmopolitanisms', p. 442; Pamela Scully, 'Zoë Wicomb, Cosmopolitanism, and the Making and Unmaking of History', *Safundi*, 12.3–4 (2011), 299–311 (p. 302).

4 Aretha Phiri and Zoë Wicomb, 'Black, White and Everything In-between: Unravelling the Times with Zoë Wicomb', *English in Africa*, 45.2 (2018), 117–28 (p. 118).

terms of a pull between untethered aesthetic appreciation, the cultural capital attached to their appreciation, and the ways art can frame our understanding of the social. On the other, these same questions are a component of the reading experience. Wicomb's stories can then be thought of as in part a self-directed meditation on the class of thing they are: untethered acts of the imagination, a means of projecting class identity, or, in Albie Sachs's words 'a weapon of struggle'.[5]

The fracture between art's autonomy from the world and its inescapable embeddedness in it are not only critical concepts through which to read Wicomb's work, they are integral to her writing. Driver pinpoints a key aspect of Wicomb's work in describing its 'double aesthetic and political direction'.[6] In Driver's estimation, while Wicomb's fiction 'yearns for a writing released from "history" and "meaning"', it remains committed to 'truth-telling about varieties of subordination', a bifurcated movement she memorably calls the 'struggle over the sign'.[7] In this struggle, there is 'on one hand [...] a desire either to stand outside history or to inhabit a different history [...] and on the other hand, the recognition of the inevitable and ongoing interconnections of self and text with history'.[8] There is a conflict between the autonomous artwork, often tending towards undecidability and uniterability while arguably sacrificing societal purchase, and the committed artwork, with a more confident claim to worldly agency, but risking, in Lewis Nkosi's words, 'disappointing breadline asceticism and prim disapproval of irony'.[9] In Wicomb's own words, we must acknowledge 'the bivalency of art, by which it is at the same time transparent and opaque, and inhabits the realm of ambiguity, of the equivocal, resists a literal or utilitarian translation into public good'.[10] An analysis of Wicomb's fiction must be supple enough to show how the material effects of class and the way they are depicted interact, so that neither an analysis of social class nor the particularity of the literary effects used to describe its operations occlude each other. For Driver, '[Wicomb's]

---

5 Albie Sachs, 'Preparing Ourselves for Freedom', in *Spring Is Rebellious: Arguments about Cultural Freedom*, ed. Ingrid de Kok and Karen Press (Cape Town: Buchu, 1990), p. 19.
6 Driver, 'The Struggle Over the Sign', p. 523.
7 Ibid., p. 523.
8 Ibid., p. 523.
9 Nkosi, 'Postmodernism and Black Writing in South Africa', p. 77.
10 Phiri and Wicomb, 'Black, White and Everything In-between', p. 125.

ends are political, they are also aesthetic; in her art – at its best – there is no difference', and in what follows I explore how these twin desiderata interface and interfere with one another in her short fiction.[11]

Wicomb, like Nadine Gordimer and Ivan Vladislavić, is known for both her short fiction and her novels, as well as for her insightful literary criticism.[12] In an interview with Devi Sankaree Govender, Wicomb speaks about why she began her writing career with the short story, and the reasons she gives are at once aesthetic and pragmatic: '[w]riting short stories', she says, 'seemed less ambitious [...] I was still a mother and had a full-time job and somehow I loved the economy of the short story.'[13] Wicomb's association of the short story's 'economy' with the burden of domestic labour is echoed by fellow short story writer Alice Munro, for whom writing short stories was 'simply a matter of expediency. I had small children, I didn't have any help [...] So I wrote in bits and pieces with a limited time expectation. Perhaps I got used to thinking of my material in terms of things that worked that way.'[14] The short story has often been seen to be responsive to depicting the kind of societal disenfranchisement that women – and, for that matter, other marginalised groups – often face. Frank O'Connor argues that the short story is the form in which 'submerged population groups' can be made visible, and the form has been, for Clare Hanson, 'a vehicle for [...] knowledge which may be in some way at odds with the "story" of dominant culture'.[15]

Wicomb's and Munro's comments are particularly interesting in the immediate link they make between domestic labour and literary form, with writing practices and aesthetics directly emerging from the compressions of time such work requires. Wicomb observes, discussing

---

11 Driver, 'The Struggle Over the Sign', p. 538.
12 Her fictional works include *You Can't Get Lost in Cape Town* (1987), *David's Story* (2000), *Playing in the Light* (2006), *The One That Got Away* (2008), *October* (2014), and *Still Life* (2020). Her critical essays were brought together in Zoë Wicomb, *Race, Nation, Translation: South African Essays, 1990–2013*, ed. Andrew van der Vlies (New Haven, CT: Yale University Press, 2018).
13 Zoë Wicomb and Devi Sankaree Govender, 'A Girl in Short', *Sunday Times*, 8 April 2001, p. 12.
14 Alice Munro and Cara Feinberg, 'Bringing Life to Life', *The Atlantic*, December 2001, <http://www.theatlantic.com/magazine/archive/2001/12/bringing-life-to-life/303056/> (accessed 3 December 2015).
15 Clare Hanson, 'Introduction', in *Re-Reading the Short Story*, ed. by Clare Hanson (London: Macmillan, 1989), pp. 1–9 (p. 6).

You Can't Get Lost in Cape Town, her first published work, that 'material conditions dictated the form for me: with a small child and no room of my own (let alone the so many guineas per year) the short story was the obvious choice', but elaborates that she then 'grew interested in the gaps between the stories, the negative semantic space that is my protagonist's life'.[16] My aim in pointing this out is, on the one hand, to show the hard realities in which such brilliant work was produced, but equally to argue that the short story's elliptical unfinishedness can be a positive quality in articulating certain kinds of experience. Adrian Hunter, borrowing from Gilles Deleuze and Félix Guattari, thinks of the short story as a form of 'minor literature', that is, a literature that 'self-consciously maintains its ec-centric, "minority" position' in relation to the norms of a dominant culture.[17] Wicomb has twice described herself as a 'minor writer' – once in 2002 when asked about her place in a South African canon, and once on winning the Windham-Campbell Prize for Fiction in 2013[18] – and Hunter's model offers a useful perspective on how this comment might be understood. This is not minority as lack, but is rather a position that, like the elliptical short story, is consciously disaligned from majority discourses and so sustains a productive distance from them.

This 'ec-centric', perhaps better 'ex-centric', position would not appear obvious from Wicomb's reception, particularly in recent years. Unusually for a contemporary South African author, she has had three academic conferences devoted solely to her, with journal special issues and a collected edition based on them. Her collected essays were published by Yale University Press in 2018, edited by Andrew van der Vlies, and as I mentioned above she was awarded the 2013 Windham-Campbell Prize. The only contemporary South African author to receive more attention is perhaps J.M. Coetzee, one of the three, along with Nadine Gordimer and André Brink, who Wicomb described in 2002 as the 'major writers' who 'whether they like it or not, constitute

---

16 Stephan Meyer and Thomas Olver, 'Zoë Wicomb Interviewed on Writing and Nation', *Journal of Literary Studies*, 18.1–2 (2002), 182–98 (p. 185). *You Can't Get Lost in Cape Town* is sometimes read as a novel, but is now more often seen as a short story cycle.
17 Hunter, *Cambridge Introduction to the Short Story*, p. 140.
18 See Aaron Bartels-Swindells, 'The Metapragmatics of the "Minor Writer": Zoë Wicomb, Literary Value, and the Windham-Campbell Prize Festival', *Representations*, 137 (2017), 88–111.

the new antiapartheid canon'.[19] Wicomb observes that her work will likely be received doubly, once, 'in accordance with apartheid', in a lineage of coloured writers – Peter Abrahams, Alex La Guma, Richard Rive, and Bessie Head – and again as part of post-apartheid literature, and in both cases she says she will be received as 'a minor writer'.[20] I am not suggesting that Wicomb desires obscurity or that she considers her work as somehow inferior to that of these authors. On the contrary, when *Guardian* critic John Dugdale commented that the Windham-Campbell prize-winners were 'ethnic, sexual, political, and aesthetic outsiders', Wicomb found his comments 'humiliating'.[21] However, a strategic form of minority allows a certain leverage while pointing out the insufficiency of structures that accord value to certain authors.

Although one must be wary of reading Wicomb's slippery fictions as crudely autobiographical, there do seem to be elements of her experience that are negotiated in her work. In an interview with Eva Hunter in 1990, Wicomb describes how her own experience informed her first book, *You Can't Get Lost in Cape Town*:

> Yes, in a sense I have travelled great distances economically and psychologically and I feel extraordinarily comfortable with that. I don't feel that I should be groping around for working-class roots because I feel perfectly happy with my roots, and with the people I come from [...] In a sense I wanted to write about the kind of alienation that comes through education.[22]

It is rare to hear Wicomb describe herself as feeling 'extraordinarily comfortable', a turn of phrase that, *pace* Wicomb, perhaps belies a certain unease. Further, the 'kind of alienation' that education brings is, of course, tightly bound up with class mobility. Wicomb attended

---

19 Meyer and Olver, 'Zoë Wicomb Interviewed on Writing and Nation', p. 188.
20 Ibid., pp. 187–88.
21 Zoë Wicomb and Derek Attridge, 'Zoë Wicomb in Conversation with Derek Attridge', in *Zoë Wicomb & the Translocal: Writing Scotland & South Africa*, ed. Kai Easton and Derek Attridge (Abingdon: Routledge, 2017), pp. 209–19 (p. 215). I have been unable to locate the original article by Dugdale to which Wicomb refers in this interview.
22 Eva Hunter and Craig MacKenzie (eds), *Between the Lines II: Interviews with Nadine Gordimer, Menán Du Plessis, Zoë Wicomb, Lauretta Ngcobo* (Grahamstown: National English Literary Museum, 1993), p. 91.

secondary school in Cape Town, and 'after completing an Arts degree at the University College for Cape Coloureds, Western Cape', in 1970 she 'came to England [...] and studied English Literature at Reading University'.[23] Wicomb may have travelled 'great distances economically and psychologically' from her South African birthplace, but the host culture still remains at a remove: 'In some ways', she says, 'I have acculturated in Britain – I'm middle class, educated and in a sense grew up there – but in another sense I will always be an outsider.'[24]

Wicomb has spent most of her adult life in Scotland, a country that has long-standing historical links with South Africa, but where she has never felt as though she wholly belongs: in Scotland, she says, 'I feel like I am in a glass bowl.'[25] The ties between the two countries shape *The One That Got Away*, appearing in characters who travel between them, and in the strange echoes of South Africa in the buildings, place names, and monuments that bespeak Scotland's troubled imperial history. There is a sense in Wicomb's work of characters caught between conflicting identities, of feeling out of place both at home and abroad, and this arises from a knot of complications formed from class, race, and other factors. Some possible reasons for these complications, and the anxieties they cause, can be found in how class operates in tandem with race in South Africa, and how the coloured community was manoeuvred into a liminal position during the last two decades of apartheid.[26]

23 Wicomb, *You Can't Get Lost in Cape Town*, back cover.
24 Hunter and MacKenzie (eds), *Between the Lines II*, p. 87.
25 Zoë Wicomb and Hein Willemse, 'Zoe Wicomb in Conversation with Hein Willemse', *Research in African Literatures*, 33.1 (2002), 144–52 (p. 149).
26 The term 'coloured' in South Africa has a complicated history. Often glossed as 'mixed-race', the term is better understood as referring to a group, many of whom were classified as Coloured (capitalised to distinguish this category from contemporary usage) by the apartheid state, made up of, in Andrew van der Vlies's words, people of 'mixed-race and autochthonous ancestry'. Andrew van der Vlies, 'Zoë Wicomb's South African Essays: Intertextual Ethics, Translative Possibilities, and the Claims of Discursive Variety', in *Race, Nation, Translation: South African Essays, 1990–2013*, ed. Andrew van der Vlies (New Haven, CT: Yale University Press, 2018), pp. 3–33 (p. 13). For more, see Mohamed Adhikari, *Not White Enough, Not Black Enough: Racial Identity in the South African Coloured Community* (Cape Town: Double Storey, 2005); Mohamed Adhikari, *Burdened by Race: Coloured Identities in Southern Africa* (Cape Town: Double Storey, 2009).

A Class Apart

The analysis of class in South Africa has become less prominent in South African studies since apartheid's end – Jeremy Seekings and Nicoli Nattrass warn that 'class appears to be in danger of falling off the map of South African studies'[27] – but when it does appear it is most usefully analysed in its articulation with race. Seekings and Nattrass stress that class and race are intricately bound up in South Africa, a conclusion supported by Murray Leibbrandt et al., at least in strictly economic terms, in a working paper published in 2010: 'The poverty rankings by race are completely robust. At any poverty line, Africans are very much poorer than Coloureds, who are very much poorer than Indians/Asians, who are poorer than whites.'[28] This should be of particular concern, as despite the ANC's 'clear public commitment to, and [...] political interest in mitigating inequality [...] income inequality in South Africa [...] may in fact have worsened since the end of apartheid'.[29] This concern has been particularly pressing in the years since 1994, during which, despite a transition from a white government to a largely black one, a failure to address deep systemic inequalities has perpetuated class divisions that closely adhere to the racial demarcations of previous decades.[30] In 2015, for example, 47% of households headed by black Africans were living below the poverty line, falling to 23% for coloured households, just over 1% for Indian households and less than 1% for white households.[31]

---

27 Jeremy Seekings and Nicoli Nattrass, *Class, Race, and Inequality in South Africa* (New Haven, CT: Yale University Press, 2006), pp. 28–29.

28 Murray Leibbrandt and others, *Trends in South African Income Distribution and Poverty since the Fall of Apartheid* (Paris: Organisation for Economic Co-operation and Development, 28 May 2010), p. 15, <http://www.oecd-ilibrary.org/content/workingpaper/5kmmsot7p1ms-en> (accessed 13 May 2013).

29 Seekings and Nattrass, *Class, Race, and Inequality*, pp. 28–29, 3–4; Andries Bezuidenhout, Christine Bischoff, and Ntsehiseng Nthejane, 'Is Cosatu Still a Working-Class Movement?', in *Labour Beyond Cosatu*, ed. Andries Bezuidenhout and Malehoko Tshoaedi (Johannesburg: Wits University Press, 2017), pp. 48–61.

30 See Boike Rehbein, 'Social Classes, Habitus and Sociocultures in South Africa', *Transience*, 9.1 (2018), 19

31 Yul Derek Davids and others, 'Race and Class Perceptions of Poverty in South Africa', in *Paradise Lost: Race and Racism in Post-Apartheid South Africa*, ed. Gregory Houston, Modimowabarwa Kanyane, and Yul Derek Davids (Leiden: Brill, 2022), pp. 200–29 (p. 203).

The class make-up of post-apartheid South Africa was formed in important ways by government policies during the last decades of apartheid. By the mid-1970s it had become clear to reformist leaders in the National Party that the support of coloured and Indian South Africans was 'crucial to any successful counterrevolutionary project'.[32] This realisation led them to implement a policy of 'embourgeoisement' of the coloured population, which Ian Goldin breaks down into investment in 'housing, infrastructural development, health facilities, and schooling, as well as promising a degree of inclusion within the framework of representative democracy'.[33] Education was perhaps the most important of these, as '[u]pward occupational mobility among coloured and Indian people was based on improved public education'; Seekings and Nattrass cite the impressive statistic that '[t]he number of coloured and Indian students at residential universities rose from fewer than 2,000 in 1960 to more than 14,000 in 1983'.[34] The class hierarchy these policies created both fragmented interracial alliances and led to infra-racial fissures. Social mobility within the coloured population became more common, a phenomenon that exacerbated the social one-upmanship Richard Rive had earlier seen in 'upper class Coloureds with electric stoves, refrigerators and Venetian blinds on their windows'.[35] By providing different population groups with differing access to public services, the government promoted a politics of divide and rule, and so established the foundation of post-apartheid class divisions.

In considering the relationship between race and class, Seekings and Nattrass analyse the role of public policy, the 'distributional regime', and particularly the role of education.[36] They cite structural continuities between the apartheid and post-apartheid periods as generative of recurring patterns of societal inequality, which allowed some sections of the population to acquire the 'advantages of class that allowed them to sustain privilege in the market'.[37] This led to a new kind of societal stratification, one supported by economic policy rather than explicitly by law, in which racial segregation was gradually transformed into a

---

32 Seekings and Nattrass, *Class, Race, and Inequality*, p. 102.
33 Ian Goldin, *Making Race: The Politics and Economics of Coloured Identity in South Africa* (Cape Town: Maskew Miller Longman, 1987), pp. 178–89.
34 Seekings and Nattrass, *Class, Race, and Inequality*, pp. 101–02.
35 Richard Rive, *Emergency: A Novel* (Cape Town: David Philip, 1988), p. 75.
36 Seekings and Nattrass, *Class, Race, and Inequality*, p. 6.
37 Ibid., p. 6.

striated and increasingly calcified class structure that largely reproduced the racial categories of the apartheid era. Economist Patrick Bond has gone so far as to call this new societal formation 'class apartheid'.[38] In this new model, some 'black South Africans', here signifying 'African, coloured, and Indian people collectively', could become 'insiders while others remained largely excluded from the benefits of prosperity'.[39] A small number of insiders have gained access to skilled jobs and better pay, while a majority of outsiders have been left bereft both of employment and of the skills necessary to find it.

The coloured population came to occupy a difficult societal position in this structure. Their shared history of disenfranchisement sometimes led to political allegiance with those classified as black, yet their relative privilege and often distinct cultural practices troubled this affiliation. Wicomb, for one, defiantly 'define[d] herself as black, in solidarity with all those oppressed by virtue of their "race"', although much of the experience she describes in her writing would have been unfamiliar to most of those classified as black.[40] Wicomb's 'education in a city school, her parents' use of languages with European origins, and their affinity for the dominant cultures' were the result of both different cultural roots and apartheid's construction of coloured identity as distinct from (and superior to) that of blacks.[41] Societally, coloured people were 'permitted to occupy a sort of middle ground [...] that shift[ed] according to gender, education, and class', a privileged though precarious position that left them, in Mohamed Adhikari's words, 'not white enough, not black enough'.[42]

This interstitial identity takes on a particular inflection for intellectuals such as Wicomb. As Grant Farred describes:

> [t]he relationship radical intellectuals have with the disenfranchised community they belong to is complex. Characterised by a tension between belonging and apartness, intellectuals are ambivalently

---

38 Patrick Bond, 'The Mandela Years in Power: Did He Jump or Was He Pushed?', *Counterpunch*, 6 December 2013, <http://www.counterpunch.org/2013/12/06/the-mandela-years-in-power/> (accessed 12 October 2022).
39 Seekings and Nattrass, *Class, Race, and Inequality*, pp. 6, ix.
40 Hunter and MacKenzie (eds), *Between the Lines II*, p. 14.
41 Ibid., p. 14.
42 Ibid., p. 91; Adhikari, *Not White Enough, Not Black Enough*.

situated: They shift, some more than others, between a transient integration and a momentary but intense alienation.[43]

This shift comes about, in large part, through education and the class mobility that it allows. This mobility was outlined by Rive: 'Because of my education, I was able to take my first shaky steps into the ranks of the "Coloured" middle class.'[44] Although Farred claims that Rive was '[a]utomatically propelled into a higher social class by his diplomas and degrees', the 'shaky steps' Rive describes sound much less confident.[45] He gets closer to the truth in stating that '[Rive's] education substantively altered his ability to align himself ideologically with District Six [the economically poor but culturally rich area from which he came]'.[46] This gives a more nuanced depiction of the contested nature of such changes. It is not so much that education provides unquestioned entry into another social class, as that it allows movement between classes, and that this movement may create problems as well as solve them. For Wicomb, as for Rive, an analysis of class must take into account the contradictory effects of education, and how it interacts with, among other things, the 'nettlesome' question of coloured identity, a question further complicated by Wicomb's position as a diasporic intellectual.[47] Such concerns of race, class, empire, geographical mobility, and education crosshatch *The One That Got Away*.

Each of the twelve stories in the collection can be read independently of the others, but they are bound together by recurring characters, places, and patterns of imagery, encouraging the reader to read across as well as within stories, giving the volume the character of a short story cycle. This amalgamated form provides Wicomb with a suitably contradictory framework around which to structure narratives that engage with the complexities of belonging, the politics of classification, and the subtleties of class. The short story cycle challenges attempts at

---

43 Grant Farred, *Midfielder's Moment: Coloured Literature and Culture in Contemporary South Africa* (Boulder, CO: Westview Press, 2001), p. 31.
44 Richard Rive, *Writing Black* (Cape Town: David Philip, 1981), p. 10, cited in Farred, *Midfielder's Moment*, p. 33.
45 Farred, *Midfielder's Moment*, p. 33.
46 Ibid., p. 33.
47 Étienne Balibar, 'Racism and Nationalism', in Étienne Balibar and Immanuel Maurice Wallerstein, *Race, Nation, Class: Ambiguous Identities* (London: Verso, 1991), pp. 37–85 (p. 72).

classification. In Julika Griem's words, it is 'a generic hybrid operating between the novelistic claim for totality and the short story's more fragmented outlook; a combination of continuous and discontinuous reading experiences'.[48] While the single short story thrives on moments of great personal intensity, it is less likely to represent longer timespans, or offer a broader picture of society. The world and the characters outside its immediate focus tend to become 'elements in a central character's emotional landscape', and although this can be very powerful, it can lead to an inwardness that de-emphasises an individual's position in a societal structure.[49] The problem the short story has with class is, in this respect, one of how to articulate the workings of class in a form that often prioritises isolated experience. The short story might show how class is experienced subjectively and affectively, but it less often elaborates on the societal logics that lie behind this. The short story sequence gets around this awkwardness to some extent by maintaining tension between the isolation of the single story and the integration a novel might offer, gesturing towards wholeness while retaining the fractured and riven quality of isolated experience.

The Elliptical Stylus: 'In the Botanic Gardens'

The contest over what class of thing an artwork might be, the co-production of race and class, and the place of art in the political sphere are central concerns in Wicomb's writing. 'In the Botanic Gardens' not only presents readers with ways to think through these ideas, it also offers an opportunity to see how these questions are shaped by the material conditions of a text's publication. The very shortness of the short story makes it amenable to being published in multiple contexts, and the publication history of this particular story brings out the very different resonances of a text depending on its paratextual features. The story was originally published in 1990, and some knowledge of its publishing history introduces a historical depth which textures its appearance in *The One That Got Away*, and brings

---

48 Julika Griem, '"The Trick Lies in Repetitions": The Politics of Genre in Zoë Wicomb's *The One That Got Away*', *Safundi*, 12.3–4 (2011), 389–406 (p. 393).

49 Raymond Williams, 'Realism and the Contemporary Novel', *Universities & Left Review*, 4 (1958), 23–25 (p. 24).

1. Cover of *Landfall: A New Zealand Quarterly*, 176. Reproduced by kind permission of *Landfall*. Photo of graffiti in the Cape Town area by Rene Weideman.

with it the political concerns of a very different historical moment from those of its later publication.

'In the Botanic Gardens' first came out in the New Zealand quarterly *Landfall* in 1990, and then appeared in 1991 in the Aberdeen-published collection *The End of a Regime? An Anthology: Scottish–South African Writing against Apartheid*.[50] The cover of the *Landfall* edition in which it first appeared shows a Cape Town graffito reading 'You ANC nothing yet' (fig. 1), and the issue was devoted to pieces of current African writing in English that 'address in different ways Africa's relation to

---

50 Zoë Wicomb, 'In the Botanic Gardens', *Landfall*, 44.4 (1990), 484–92; Brian Filling and Susan Stuart (eds), *The End of a Regime? An Anthology: Scottish–South African Writing Against Apartheid* (Aberdeen: Aberdeen University Press, 1991).

2. Cover of *The End of a Regime? An Anthology – Scottish/South African Writing Against Apartheid*, edited by Brian Filling and Susan Stuart, 1991. Cover art by Bhekisani Manyoni.

Europe and the West'.⁵¹ *The End of a Regime?* (fig. 2) contains texts that are 'either [...] overtly about South Africa or Scottish–South African connections, or which would show Scottish writers engaging with some of the range of issues which exist on a continuum with apartheid'.⁵² In both of these publications, the story's role in explicit political struggle is foregrounded. The *Landfall* cover's graffito suggests clandestine resistance and the punning message promises a very different political future. *The End of a Regime?* bears a linocut by Bhekisani Manyoni showing African musicians weeping tears of joy or sorrow.

When the story appeared in *The One That Got Away* in 2008, however, such 'engaged' paratextual features were largely absent (fig. 3).

51 Hugh Lauder, 'Introduction', *Landfall*, 44.4 (1990), 395–96 (p. 395).
52 Filling and Stuart (eds), *The End of a Regime?*, p. xxii.

3. Cover of *The One That Got Away* by Zoë Wicomb, 2008 © UMUZI, an imprint of Penguin Random House South Africa.

Rather, the cover invites a reading more weighted towards the ludic and literary than the committedly political. The Umuzi edition bears a playful image of an ostrich running from sea to land, suggesting the contact zone of the beach as a site for playful individuality, fluxional identities, and the jouissance of untethered signification. Any notion of the group struggle implied by the political slogans and other paratextual features of the previous editions is downplayed in favour of an emphasis on individuality and creative whimsy. In short, there has been a shift in how the role of the artwork is presented, from one of overt political engagement to one in which this is less of an immediate concern. That Wicomb's story could be published in both contexts suggests its amenability to being read from both sides of the 'struggle over the sign', that is, for its historical situatedness as well as its shucking of that contextual yoke. As I go on to describe below, one feature of this story that allows such plural meanings is its use of ellipsis, a formal feature that invites political readings, but that also stymies any attempt at a strong political interpretation.

'In the Botanic Gardens' describes the experience of Dorothy Brink, a middle-aged coloured woman who has travelled from South Africa to Scotland following the disappearance of her son, Arthur, who has become involved in politics.[53] She speaks with Mr MacPherson, a representative of the British Council, which provided Arthur's scholarship to study at Glasgow University. Dorothy becomes increasingly frustrated by Mr MacPherson's inability or unwillingness to make the circumstances of her son's disappearance clear, and finds little solace in his patronising, formal manner, and his efforts to 'steady her with practical advice'.[54] Later that day she takes a taxi to Glasgow's Botanic Gardens, and on the way has a brief altercation with her short-tempered driver over what she mistakenly takes to be a forged banknote. She then spends time in a hothouse in the gardens, among the flora of South Africa. Becoming increasingly paranoid that coded messages about her son and his involvement in politics are eluding her, she collapses on the floor in a state of bewilderment and fatigue.

In this story, the 'problem of class' plays out specifically in the areas of linguistic competence, and the double political affordances of the ellipses that permeate the story. The former is evident in Dorothy's meeting with the tasselled, kilted Mr MacPherson, a scene notable for the shifting class dynamic between the two, established primarily through their varying facility with English. Mr MacPherson's 'English was very smart [...] quite different even from the English of the SABC newsreader', and causes Dorothy to doubt her own abilities: 'He spoke very fast, so it was difficult to follow him, but perhaps she would not have understood anyway' (161). She thinks that Mr MacPherson

[53] Dorothy's surname, 'Brink', not only illustrates her psychological condition 'on the brink', her liminal economic position, and her rural positioning *vis-à-vis* the urban setting in which she finds herself ('brink' means 'a grassland area' in Afrikaans), but it also recalls the author André Brink, whose *Kennis van die Aand* [*Looking on Darkness*] (Cape Town: Buren, 1973) was the first novel in Afrikaans to be banned by the apartheid government, a silencing of voice that resonates with Wicomb's story. Her first name, of course, points to her sudden transportation into another world.

[54] Zoë Wicomb, 'In the Botanic Gardens', in *The One That Got Away* (Nottingham: Five Leaves, 2011), pp. 161–72. All further references to this work are given parenthetically in the text until the end of this section.

'might as well have been speaking a special language understood only by those in national costume' (161), creating an association between linguistic competence and national identity that takes on an overt class dimension when she 'd[oes] not quite catch his name but decide[s] that Sir would be an appropriate form of address' (161). This deference to a class structure intuited through linguistic proficiency might reveal Dorothy's self-consciousness about her position, but it nevertheless encodes a gently mocking depersonalisation of the man before her, as his distinctively Scottish name is flattened into a generic title: 'Sir'. Wicomb also maintains a certain ironic distance from him, referring to him throughout as 'Mr MacPherson', in contrast with the more familiar 'Dorothy'.

When she speaks, Dorothy finds she has 'no control over the thickening of her tongue' (162), suggesting coarseness and a lack of fluency that manifests itself at the level of the body, a key site of class and racial signification. She fears that 'here in Glasgow her English would squeak like crickets in a thorn-bush' (161), the rural image standing out both for its humour and for its opposition to the richly furnished room in which they sit. Wicomb explains in an interview that 'in racist literature rural people are associated with animals', but that her use of such figures is catachrestic, as the old trope is given 'a new slant, a new accent, where it's not degrading or denigrating, but [serves] instead to show a closeness of people with the land'.[55] In the over-stuffed British Council reception room, '[a] room of muted colours in which to speak about death' (162), the squeak of crickets provides a breath of life, and a moment of humour that troubles the hierarchy between Dorothy and her more professionally fluent interlocutor.

Overarching both Mr MacPherson's and Dorothy's command of English is, of course, Wicomb's own, and her implicit mastery of both registers, as well as of the shifting modes of narration, provides an ironic meta-commentary on their exchange. This is perhaps not as obvious a point as it might seem: Wicomb describes English as 'both my first and my second language', having grown up in both Afrikaans- and English-speaking environments.[56] Further, if this story is in part to do with the difficulties of comprehension, this happens both in the content and in the style, via an aesthetic characteristic that has been intensified across the story's publication history. On its first publication

55 Hunter and MacKenzie (eds), *Between the Lines II*, p. 88.
56 Wicomb and Attridge, 'Zoë Wicomb in Conversation', p. 211.

in *Landfall*, Wicomb put direct speech in separate paragraphs, but by the time the story appeared in *The One That Got Away*, the direct speech was fully integrated into the body of the text, with no quotation marks to distinguish it from the narration. As I argued was the case in Gordimer's writing in Chapter 1, the omission of quotation marks in reporting speech, and the de-differentiated segueing between interior monologue and exterior dialogue, has a disorienting effect and demands considerable effort to decipher what is happening. Dorothy's difficulties of comprehension are then also experienced by the reader, and her suspicion that there is a hidden meaning in what she is being told pushes the reader towards a suspicious mode of reading, while also ironising it.

The possibility of reading Wicomb's story for what it does not say is further encouraged by her increasing use of ellipses, a quality of her style that opens a space in which a critic might decide to read between the lines. Mr MacPherson's comfortable surroundings of 'chintz chairs', elaborately moulded cornicing, a 'glass [coffee] pot with a plunger', and a 'plush carpet' (162) suggest stability and the shoring up of a stable sense of self through what Julia Prewitt Brown calls the 'protective material expressions of bourgeois life'.[57] However, as the conversation progresses, his speech begins to 'falter'. It becomes strewn with elliptical pauses at telling moments, drawing attention to the instability of his otherwise unflappable 'bourgeois interior':

> Very important to have these records [of Scottish labour movements]. Of the struggle ... eh ... you'll understand how here in Scotland ... but remembering the people of the city, eh, that's what being human is all about. (164)

His discomfort is evident in his halting speech, although it is unclear whether this is rooted in the general awkwardness of the situation, or in an awareness of his own evasions. His euphemistic reference to the 'people of the city', which in this case presumably does not include employees of the British Council, distances him from the working classes he professes to valorise. Further, the humanist platitude on which he finishes flattens material differences between the various people who live in Glasgow, and transposes any obligation to address

---

57 Julia Prewitt Brown, *The Bourgeois Interior: How the Middle Class Imagines Itself in Literature and Film* (Charlottesville: University of Virginia Press, 2008), p. xii.

inequality in the present into a general debt to memory, 'remembering the people of the city'. While Mr MacPherson uses the word 'struggle' to describe the Scottish workers' struggle, in a South African context 'the struggle' refers specifically to the fight against apartheid, particularly in its intensified form in the wake of the 1960 Sharpeville Massacre. As soon as he pronounces the word, Mr MacPherson seems to realise the political direction the conversation is taking, and leaves a telling pause.

The kind of political work done, or not done, by ellipsis is central to understanding the double political voicing of Wicomb's story. For Anne Toner, ellipsis marks in literature 'have long served as a means of promoting access to emotional or psychological states',[58] and the extended pause after the word 'struggle' here suggests Mr MacPherson's discomfort when approaching topics related to the politics that might lie behind Arthur's disappearance.[59] That such ellipsis happens specifically when he is talking about class points to the wider consequences that the elliptic aesthetics of Wicomb's short stories have for political interpretation. In one reading of these ellipses, the political work of the story would mainly come about through the critic recognising a formal manifestation of societal fracture and reading the telling silences of elided content. Clare Hanson asks whether, in short fiction, typographical ellipses, and elliptical content more broadly, offer an invitation to allow the 'reader's desire [...] to enter the text?'[60] Ellipsis could then hold within it a political kernel, as, in Michael Chapman's words, to 'elicit forms of desire [...] can motivate efforts to produce social change'.[61] If the text offers a blank space, the reader can project onto that space what they want it to contain, and this might be the manifestation of a political desire. The idea that a critic can most clearly find 'the presence of ideology' in 'the significant silences of a text' – here described by Terry Eagleton – and further, that it is their role to make

---

58 Anne Toner, *Ellipsis in English Literature: Signs of Omission* (Cambridge: Cambridge University Press, 2015), p. 1.
59 In the version published in *The End of a Regime?*, this '... eh ...' after the words 'the struggle' was replaced by a three-dot ellipsis, although the 'eh' was present in the earlier *Landfall* printing. Although possibly editorial, it is as if Wicomb was weighing up how much to leave to implication, how much to make explicit.
60 Clare Hanson, 'A Poetics of Short Fiction', in *Re-reading the Short Story* (London: Macmillan, 1989), 22–33 (p. 25).
61 Michael Chapman, 'Storyteller and Journalist: Can Themba in Sophiatown', in *Art Talk, Politics Talk: A Consideration of Categories* (Scottsville: University of KwaZulu-Natal Press, 2006), pp. 47–57 (p. 56).

those 'silences [...] "speak"' has had considerable critical purchase, from the work of Pierre Macherey to the 'hermeneutics of suspicion' critiqued by Eve Kosofsky Sedgwick, Stephen Best and Sharon Marcus, and Rita Felski, among others.[62]

The model of making silences speak brings with it at least three consequences. First, there is the very real risk that rather than offering a window onto the hidden ideology behind the text, gaps and absences might rather serve as mirrors in which the ideology of the critic is reflected. Whatever the gap, and whatever the text, the hidden component might then always look the same. Secondly, by filling in the gaps in a text, there is a risk of closing down a text's political potential rather than realising it fully. This is best put by Dominic Head, who notes that by filling in the cracks in short stories, there is a risk of completing a 'dot-to-dot exercise [that] re-estabish[es] order at the expense of devaluing, and hence *misrepresenting*, the element of disorder'.[63] In other words, by flooding those gaps with readerly desire, the texts' radical instability might be neutralised into one coherent reading. Thirdly, prioritising an aesthetics of absence precludes, in Sarah Brouillette's words, an 'unambiguous commitment to the truth of a particular point of view about an identifiable problem that could be redressed by human actions'.[64] While a clear expression of political commitment is not required of any author, it is the case that the more a text tends towards not stating its commitments, the more it relies on often unreliable acts of reading for its political potential to be fulfilled. If Wicomb's work is indeed torn, as Driver suggests, between art's ability to break free of its historical embeddedness and its inescapable locatedness in history, then it is important also to recognise the fine line it treads between the resonance of significant absence and an inability to voice an unambiguous political position.

The troubled role of absence in the story's literary politics is further emphasised when Dorothy asks about her missing son. She asks if

---

62 Terry Eagleton, *Marxism and Literary Criticism* (Berkeley: University of California Press, 1976), pp. 34–35. See Sedgwick, *Touching Feeling*; Best and Marcus, 'Surface Reading'; Felski, *The Limits of Critique*; Felski, *Hooked*.

63 Dominic Head, *The Modernist Short Story: A Study in Theory and Practice* (Cambridge: Cambridge University Press, 2009), p. 24.

64 Sarah Brouillette, 'Literature is Liberalism', *Jacobin Magazine*, 2014, <https://www.jacobinmag.com/2014/10/literature-is-liberalism/> (accessed 22 October 2014).

Arthur has become 'Just a name? A missing person? An absence? A nothing?' (167). This process of lexical reduction, following Hanson and Chapman, might at each stage incite in the reader a greater sense of injustice at her loss, and a desire for Arthur's reinstatement to full signification. In what amounts to a textual performance of Driver's 'struggle over the sign', the sign moves increasingly further from the referent, as what remains of Dorothy's son in her series of questions moves step by step from the relative presence of 'a name', through the generic 'missing person' and the haunting presence of an 'absence', to 'a nothing', complete non-presence. Arthur's absent presence in this interpretation acts as the fulcrum on which the story pivots, with his disappearance representing both the occlusion of politics in the text and its irrepressible presence there. Arthur's missing body becomes what Graham Huggan, discussing Gordimer's short stories, calls an 'invisible node [...] around which the story coheres'.[65] While this allows for considerable interpretational freedom, as Dorothy's missing son haunts the text, the political charge his presence could carry is left unarticulated. This paradox is central to Wicomb's practice as a writer, and her short stories offer a means through which its complexities can be staged and so thought through.

Reading 'In the Botanic Gardens' in the light of class concerns reveals, first, the unspoken class codes that structure societal interaction. Further, it allows an elucidation of the conflict in Wicomb's writing between the aesthetic demands of a short story form that has increasingly privileged ambiguity and aporia, and the difficulties this presents for political writing. On the one hand, the short story's tendency towards elliptic content and its use of literary effects that render the world distant and strange feed a desire in the reader for more, a utopian possibility that exceeds the present. The short story, in this understanding, is productively dissatisfying, as the reader is left feeling frustrated, short-changed, and so desirous of new logics, new forms of organisation. However, by the same token, these moments are politically recalcitrant, shying away from the articulation of politics, while gesturing towards it. As the elliptical character of Wicomb's texts intensifies, this enables and disables modes of political writing.

---

65 Huggan, 'Echoes from Elsewhere', p. 71.

'There's the Bird that Never Flew': The Fountain and the Factory

If 'In the Botanic Gardens' allows a critical analysis of how social class and the political affordances of aesthetics intersect with one another, 'There's the Bird that Never Flew' goes one step further, in making the question central to both the plot and the form of the story. The story opens with Jane, the story's university-educated coloured protagonist, on honeymoon in Glasgow with her aptly named artist husband, Drew. As Jane's mother Grace, 'an old Griqua charlady', puts it: 'What kind of a name was that? If he was in the drawing business, then it was no good having a name that announced that his career was all in the past, all finished and *klaar*.'[66] Like Dorothy in 'In the Botanic Gardens', Jane feels alienated in her unfamiliar surroundings, and is further embarrassed about her patchy knowledge of art. She sets out to hone her analytical skills by performing an extended ekphrasis on a colonial-era fountain, an exercise that leads to a consideration of the relationship between reality and representation, art and politics, class and cultural capital. In particular, 'fearful, tottering' (70) Jane's attention is drawn to the terracotta figure of a coloured girl, whose quiet confidence inspires her. The next day on the way out of her hotel, she talks with Margaret, a Glaswegian cleaner, who speaks about her family, the fountain, and the factory that stands next to it.

Jane's understanding of how class operates, and of her own class position, is rooted in her experience of education and her family's ideas about what constitutes civilised behaviour. Unlike her other family members, Jane has been to university, and this has created distance between her and her mother, her father, and other relatives. Jane occupies an unstable societal position at home in South Africa, where both her class and racial identities are contested. Her socially aspirational in-laws sip tea from 'Royal Doulton Bone China', 'cups that were introduced as if they were posh cousins with double-barrelled names' (64).[67] Meanwhile, Drew's Aunt Trudie checks the nape of Jane's neck

---

66 Zoë Wicomb, 'There's the Bird that Never Flew', in *The One That Got Away* (Nottingham: Five Leaves, 2011), pp. 61–74 (p. 62). All further references to this work are given parenthetically in the text until the end of this section.

67 This is the same Doulton company that made the fountain that Jane analyses in Glasgow, showing the semiotic power that inheres in both bombastic and subtle forms of 'soft power'. As Mariangela Palladino and John Miller note, Doulton were also the 'nineteenth century's lavatory makers par excellence',

for tell-tale frizz. The in-laws' attempts to use the straightness of Jane's hair to police the boundaries of racial classification are matched by their demarcation of class identity through the performative presentation of upmarket crockery. Jane is 'outraged' by the reinscription of apartheid practices in Trudie's hair-checking, and by Drew's lack of protest, but she does nothing. Instead, she imagines a snappy response to Trudie, and pictures the flustered aunt 'smooth[ing] her own thin strands nervously [...] and remember[ing] that no one in her family had cleaned for white people' (64). This final exchange in Jane's imagination is, on the one hand, a retaliation against her overly intrusive aunties, but on the other suggests her insecurity over her mother's job as a cleaner, even as she seems to downplay its importance.

The intersection of class and racial propriety, evident in the aunts' dainty crockery and policing of errant curls, shows systems of class and classification to be coded, and often internally policed. V.A. February observes that with the premium placed on race by the apartheid government, it is 'hardly surprising' that the coloured community 'suffer[s] from what Freud calls, "the narcissism of small differences", that is, they distinguish expertly between subtle shades of brown or light which is normally not so overtly apparent to the non half-caste'.[68] This heightened sensitivity to colour intersects with a close attention to the minutiae of class distinctions, encoded in the scene described above through notions of genteel propriety and civility, rather than in strictly economic terms. Jane's mother describes Drew's family as *'khoity-toity* [...] no matter how toity, there's no getting away from the Hotnot, or Khoi' (62), revealing both her reservations about social climbing, and the extent to which she has absorbed apartheid's discourse of essentialist racial classification and the class identities that accompany it.

Grace sees education as a means to class mobility that would place her daughter Jane in higher stead than her genteel in-laws. Grace assures

---

and supplied the necessary facilities to Glasgow's Empire Exhibition. See John Miller and Mariangela Palladino, 'Glasgow's Empire Exhibition and the Interspatial Imagination in "There's the Bird That Never Flew"', in *Zoë Wicomb & the Translocal: Writing Scotland and South Africa*, ed. Kai Easton and Derek Attridge (Abingdon: Routledge, 2017), pp. 148–65 (p. 160).

68 Here, as elsewhere in his book, it is unclear to what extent February uses terms such as 'half-caste' ironically. V.A. February, *Mind Your Colour: The 'Coloured' Stereotype in South African Literature* (London: Kegan Paul International, 1981), p. 54.

Jane that 'with your B.A. you can just ignore [your in-laws'] airs and graces' (62), but Jane's social mobility comes at the cost of distancing her from her family. Jane's father is portrayed as a man who spoke little English, yet she remembers the 'pride of place [the word 'uncultured'] took on the rough edge of his tongue' (63). This recalls the 'thickening' of the tongue in 'In the Botanic Gardens', and again invokes the body, and specifically the organ of language, as revelatory of class identity. For Jane's father, 'cultured' meant 'respectable, and [was] somehow tied up with the incomplete set of *Encyclopaedia Britannica* he had bought on the parade' (63). The *Encyclopaedia Britannica* was always tantalisingly out of Jane's father's reach, both linguistically due to the 'rough edge of his tongue', and materially, as suggested by his incomplete set. In Jane's father's eyes, culture is associated with propriety and the knowledge systems of the West, while the uncultured are described as 'beyond the pale' (63), a punning conflation of historical acts of classification – the expression originates in England's colonial presence in Ireland – and South Africa's melanocracy. The *Encyclopaedia* establishes a clear affiliation between the Victorian mania for classification,[69] the 'scientific racism' that arose around the same time, and the apartheid system of discrimination that made use of it.[70]

Jane's class anxiety is visible in her embarrassment about her unfamiliarity with the codes of the middle-class *habitus*, and particularly her knowledge of art.[71] Like her father, the fear of being branded 'uncultured' still 'instils dread' in Jane, even though she now thinks it means something 'quite different from what she thought it meant' (63). While once she thought 'uncultured' meant fighting in the street, she now understands it as meaning lacking knowledge of art's social codes. Although their benchmarks differ, both Jane and her father understand the demarcation of class boundaries as emerging through social practices,

---

69 The *Encyclopaedia* was originally published in Edinburgh, including a landmark ninth edition in 1889, one year after the construction of the Doulton Fountain featured in this story, and the book's appearance in South Africa knits together the cycle's patterning between the two countries.

70 See Saul Dubow, *Scientific Racism in Modern South Africa* (Cambridge: Cambridge University Press, 1995).

71 I use the term 'habitus', following Bourdieu, to mean a set of schemata, sensibilities, dispositions, and tastes that are implicitly acquired and unconscious in operation. See Pierre Bourdieu, *The Logic of Practice*, trans. Richard Nice (Palo Alto, CA: Stanford University Press, 1990), p. 53.

and for Jane the possibility of revealing her social position is a source of anxiety. At exhibition openings, her husband Drew gets her to admit: 'I don't know anything about art [...] and what's more, I don't even know what I like', with the narrator adding: 'It embarrasses her' (61). Lacking the cultural capital to form such opinions, she worries when 'Drew is not there to consult' (61) about artistic matters. While 'In the Botanic Gardens' offers a way to think through the role of elliptical language in the short story's mediation of class, 'There's the Bird that Never Flew' more explicitly points to the role artworks play in the construction and projection of class identity. This introduces a subtle interaction between the characters in the story and the reader who reads it, both of whom are involved in an experience of art that is at once a source of aesthetic experience, a route to understanding the social, and an expression of class identity.

While Jane worries about whether her taste is sufficiently refined, Grace worries about Drew's solvency: 'You in love with an artist! [...] after all I've spent on your education? How could you sink so low [...] Miss High-and-Mighty?' (61). Drew's 'career' as an artist is of primary importance to Grace, rather than his creative practice, and she sees his artistic endeavours only in financial terms, calling his work 'the drawing business' (62). In contrast with this commodity-based understanding of art, Jane seeks both the cultural capital that comes with knowledge of the rules of art, and a greater sensitivity to the kinds of sensory experience art can offer. She decides to spend her time in Glasgow trying to learn, with Drew's guidance, how art should be appreciated, and uses a colonial-era fountain as her chosen object of analysis. These various strands lead to a knot of overlapping interpretations over where art's value lies – as a product, in its capacity to mediate historical conditions, in its role as a marker of societal status, or as a route to various kinds of aesthetic experience – and so Jane's actions in the story draw attention to the contested class of the artwork, and sensitise the reader to their own navigation of these competing regimes of value.

Jane comes across the Doulton Fountain outside the People's Palace in Glasgow (fig. 4) and decides to use its sculpted figures as a way of learning how to appreciate art: 'There's nothing to it', Drew insists, 'it's just about giving time, attention, looking carefully' (65). A monument such as this one, however, is an unusual choice for learning about art, although in a story so concerned with art's contested role, it is apt. As I discussed in Chapter 2, monuments are more explicitly world-oriented than many artworks, yet they still use art's formal techniques to achieve

4. The Doulton Fountain and Templeton carpet factory, Glasgow ©
MSeses / Wikimedia Commons / CC BY-SA 4.0.

their effects. The Doulton Fountain is the world's largest terracotta fountain, at 46 feet in height and 70 feet across the base. Erected in 1888 as part of the Empire Exhibition held at Glasgow's Kelvingrove Park, the fountain was intended to commemorate Queen Victoria's 1887 Golden Jubilee by celebrating the achievements of empire. The fountain has four panels, showing figures from Australia, Canada, India, and South Africa. Each panel portrays a man and a woman who bear the produce of their land. Jane is quick to note that the South African panel 'does not speak of the gold in the colony, of the rich Witwatersrand seams that lure settlers and investors, or of the war that looms' (66). Although colonialism was a large-scale act of racialised dispossession that laid the foundations of world capitalism, the depiction of brute economic interest, the gold, has been suppressed in favour of a pastoral portrayal of harvests and crops. Looking at the moustachioed men and subservient women, Jane 'fingers her ring of plain white gold nervously' (71), drawing symbolic parallels between the power relationships created by imperial capitalism, the family, and her own marriage. Like Dorothy in 'In the Botanic Gardens', as an African exploring Britain, Jane reverses the trope of colonial expedition, and her physical position between the

Doulton Fountain and the People's Palace – built at the height of the British Empire in 1898, and a somewhat grandiose gesture to Glasgow's urban poor – leaves her symbolically placed between concerns of empire and those of class.[72]

As a relatively well-off coloured South African halfway between the People's Palace and the Doulton Fountain, Jane stands in an eddy where empire and class meet. Her analysis of the fountain is informed by this positioning, and further brings the interrelation of aesthetic and political concerns in artworks to the fore. She looks closely at the South African panel (fig. 5), seeing a 'boer with bandolier', before her attention follows the 'phallic neck' (72) of an ostrich down to a figure 'sitting cool as a cucumber in the Glasgow chill […] a young woman, no more than a girl, but unmistakably coloured' (67). The slippage between the ostrich and the girl, echoed when 'the plumage of the ostrich' is 'repeated, refashioned in [the girl's] crown of tight curls' (71), harks back to an earlier story in which the fountain appears: 'Boy in a Jute-Sack Hood'. In it, Grant Fotheringay likes 'best of all the ostrich with a long snake-like neck and full, soft feathers like the girl's bosom, an image that guided his hand at night under the blanket and brought wet dreams of copulating with a continent'.[73] This ambivalent portrayal of sex, race, and power comments on, while participating in, long-standing

---

[72] Once a cultural hub for Glasgow's underprivileged East End, the People's Palace is now a museum to the history of Glasgow's workers. It contains Ken Currie's eight-panel mural of 'scenes from Scottish labour history', ranging from the 1787 Calton Weavers Massacre through the Red Clyde movement, to the miners' strike and beyond, the very history of Scottish workers to which Mr MacPherson elliptically alludes in the story discussed above. Ray McKenzie and Gary Nisbet, *Public Sculpture of Glasgow* (Liverpool: Liverpool University Press, 2001), p. 172. After the palace's construction, a large glasshouse packed with tropical plants, a space that features prominently in Wicomb's novel *David's Story*, was added to the rear. The recurring appearance of glasshouses in *The One That Got Away* – Dorothy visits the Botanic Gardens after her meeting with Mr MacPherson – adds a cohesive patterning to the collection, while serving as an ongoing reminder of the historical parallels between the high Victorian classification mania and the racial and class categories that it helped produce. McKenzie and Nisbet, *Public Sculpture of Glasgow*, p. 172; Zoë Wicomb, *David's Story* (Cape Town: Kwela, 2000).

[73] Zoë Wicomb, 'Boy in a Jute-Sack Hood', in *The One That Got Away* (Nottingham: Five Leaves, 2011), pp. 7–18 (p. 9).

5. The South Africa panel of the Doulton Fountain, author's photograph.

representations in South African literature of the relationship between Boer and coloured, in which '[o]ne is confronted with a picture ranging from ambiguity and almost near-kinship to total rejection and hatred'.[74]

While this reading of the fountain suggests contextual knowledge as one possible route to interpreting an artwork, Jane's method does not rely on this alone. She combines it with a formalist approach, by reading the pairing on the fountain as a public depiction of miscegenation in the colonial centre, and justifying her reading by interpreting 'the repeated verticals of spade and rifle in contact with each left hand' as 'metonymies of matter-of-fact intimacy' (72). In so doing, she draws attention to what formalist and historicist forms of criticism allow and disallow. Reading the monument formally allows Jane to make a conceptual leap that might otherwise have eluded her, but there is a lingering sense that

---

74 February, *Mind Your Colour*, p. vii. For more on this, see pp. 1–40 and *passim*.

she has overreached form's ability to carry meaning, or perhaps even committed a kind of category error by formally analysing an object that is meant to communicate its historical message in less abstract terms. Furthermore, given the girl's bared breast, this same patterning could as easily be interpreted as depicting the coloured girl's sexual subservience and coerced manual labour in the face of the Boer's military might, in a concentrated figuring of race, class, and gender iniquity. Further, the representation of an Afrikaner and a coloured girl in a sexual relationship on a British fountain completed just one year before the outbreak of the second Anglo-Boer War might have been politically motivated. In a historical context in which *Boerehaat*, literally 'hatred of Boers', was reaching a crescendo in Britain, the depiction of miscegeny may have sought to portray the Boers as racially degenerate, rather than the coloured girl as defiantly self-confident. However, none of this historical knowledge explains away form's role in shaping Jane's experience of the fountain, and how formal characteristics can generate ways of knowing that exceed, or even contradict, an understanding of art as strongly determined by contextual knowledge.

Jane's interpretative leap might be thought somewhat solipsistic, a projection of her own desires onto the statue before her. The figure's 'slanted Khoisan eyes gaze out brightly at the world, with neither arrogance nor humility, rather, with calm curiosity' (72), and Jane sees the figure as a model of how she would like to be, someone for whom 'difference is not a burden', a 'sculpted figure who will not be an image; she cannot be subjected to anyone's gaze' (72). Sue Kossew asserts that Jane's 'deconstructive reading' constitutes 'a resistant reading of history that undoes [the fountain's] power to control through representation of otherness and difference'.[75] While it may be true that such readings provide alternative narratives, it is overstating the case to claim that they can undo the power of those already in place, particularly when a gross imbalance of power pervades the relationship. In Anne McClintock's words, 'it seems crucial to recognise that what has been vaunted by some as the permanent undecidability of cultural signs can also be violently and decisively foreclosed by superior military power or hegemonic dominion'.[76] A large public sculpture will be seen by more

---

75 Sue Kossew, 'Re-Reading the Past: Monuments, History and Representation in Short Stories by Ivan Vladislavić and Zoë Wicomb', *Journal of Southern African Studies*, 36.3 (2010), 571–82 (p. 581).
76 McClintock, *Imperial Leather*, p. 226.

people and carries considerably more semiotic clout than Jane's highly personal interpretation, or indeed Wicomb's description of it. Although doubts remain over the breadth of their political import, such acts of interpretation nevertheless draw attention to the routes towards social thinking that Wicomb's stories offer. Her project is not, for the most part, to show overt political resistance or to disparage those who do not partake in it. Rather, as Judith L. Raiskin argues, Wicomb 'refocuses the concept of the "political" to include the psychological experiences of living in [...] society'.[77] She shows the ways 'rituals and scripts become internalised and re-enacted in daily life', and how individuals live with and respond to that internalisation.[78] In Wicomb's own words, '[a]ll writing is political, whether you think it or not. Because all human relations are political.'[79] This broad conception of the political has been prominent in the short story since apartheid's end, and constitutes, in part, a literary processing of the growing individualisation of politics during that period. Although this is a conception of the political on a much smaller scale than the larger-scale politics that preoccupied writers of previous decades, Wicomb's portrayal of Jane does speak to a moment in which analysis of the group dynamics of class have often been secondary to those of individual emancipation.

This somewhat insular perspective is, however, challenged when Jane speaks with Margaret, the hotel cleaner. The meeting between the two recalls moments in stories such as those by Njabulo Ndebele, in which, as Michael Vaughan argues, 'the nascent middle-class intellectual is confronted [...] by the powerful presence of working-class [...] cultures', and '[t]he inner growth of the protagonist [...] involves a dramatic and challenging encounter with personalities in the [...] "non-intellectual" culture [...] an encounter which may lead to self-criticism, and an altered self-perception'.[80] Margaret looks at Jane with 'friendly contempt' (70), and says 'cryptically': 'See yous [...] yous get to see everything, but yous

---

77 Judith L. Raiskin, *Snow on the Cane Fields: Women's Writing and Creole Subjectivity* (Minneapolis: University of Minnesota Press, 1996), p. 222.
78 Ibid., p. 222.
79 Patricia Glyn and Zoë Wicomb, 'Interview', *Patricia's People* (2001), transcript held at the National English Literary Museum, Grahamstown, South Africa.
80 Such encounters are something of a trope in the South African short story, appearing in early Gordimer stories such as 'Is There Nowhere Else We Can Meet?' through to Henrietta Rose-Innes's 'Falling', which I discuss in Chapter 5. Vaughan, 'Storytelling and Politics in Fiction', pp. 189, 197.

dinnae know a thing about the real Glasgow' (64). Earlier in the story, Jane hears Margaret's use of the plural 'yous', and is drawn in, made to feel included by the linguistic similarity to Afrikaans: 'In Glasgow the familiar "yous" was comforting' (64). Derek Attridge points out that this similarity could be thought uncanny, with any comfort haunted by the alienating distance the coincidence emphasises.[81] This takes on an additional resonance when it is acknowledged that in Glasgow the use of 'yous' is strongly indicative of class identity. In Joan Beal's words, '[one] of the "shibboleths" of urban working-class Scots [...] is the use of yous as the second person plural pronoun'.[82] Wicomb herself has observed that '[i]deology is inscribed in the very grammatical choices we make in expressing ourselves in any language', and Margaret's 'yous' excludes Jane while affirming her own place in a Scottish working-class speech community.[83] In contrast with 'In the Botanic Gardens', in which Dorothy feels intimidated by Mr MacPherson's 'smart' English, here Jane is subtly excluded by Margaret's typically working-class speech.

While Jane reads the fountain as an artwork, in an effort to accrue cultural capital, Margaret takes a different view. She has not been to see it in its current location, but remembers visiting it as a girl in its old location, when 'the monument [was] a dump, all in a mess, the fountain dead, statues without noses, the Queen's head lopped off [...] and the dogs shat in the dry moat' (69).[84] With the monarch symbolically decapitated, and the liquidity provided by the colonies run dry, the fountain in an advanced state of decrepitude perhaps best illustrated the rot at the heart of the imperial project. The fountain as Jane describes it in the story, however, is how it looked after a 4-million-pound redevelopment project intended to reinvigorate the underprivileged East End. Margaret cares little about the fountain's refurbishment, her attention being drawn rather to the flamboyant, glazed brick, vitreous enamel

---

81 Derek Attridge, '"No Escape from Home": History, Affect and Art in Zoë Wicomb's Translocal Coincidences', in *Zoë Wicomb & the Translocal: Writing Scotland & South Africa*, ed. Kai Easton and Derek Attridge (Abingdon: Routledge, 2017), pp. 49–63 (pp. 63–64).

82 Joan Beal, 'Syntax and Morphology', in *The Edinburgh History of the Scots Language*, ed. Charles Jones (Edinburgh: Edinburgh University Press, 1997), pp. 335–77 (p. 344).

83 Zoë Wicomb, cited in 'South African Writers and the Problem of Languages...', *Commonwealth Essays and Studies*, 16.1 (1993), 96–103 (p. 102).

84 The fountain was moved from outside Glasgow's judiciary court to its present location in 2004.

tile, and terracotta façade of the nearby Templeton carpet factory (fig. 4). Margaret explains how her grandmother, a weaver, was trapped inside the factory when it caught fire:

> So busy were they [the factory's owners] making the grand façade, making money out of working folk, that they clean forgot about Health and Safety, and a blazing fire broke out in the factory killing so many weavers. Another tourist attraction now, but did Jane think that was a place she, Margaret, wanted to ooh and ah about? (70)

The majestic 'façade' of imperial industrialism obscures such narratives from view, and the attention Margaret pays to the factory's weavers, an economically underprivileged section of society, shows why Jane still knows little of the 'real Glasgow', despite her moment of partial epiphany on a honeymoon tour.[85] The turn from the fountain to the factory complicates Jane's subjective emancipation through the cultural capital accrued by learning to appreciate art, by focusing on the material history that striates the space in which the fountain sits.

While Jane's reading of the fountain tends towards an affirmation of the individual that incorporates a resistant reading of colonialism's representational practices, Margaret's view beyond the fountain troubles both Jane's search for psychological affirmation and the reader's response to it, with a depiction of the violence perpetuated on one class by another. This distinction might equally be understood as that between a broadly Weberian or Bourdieusian way of understanding class that holds symbolic status, political power, and cultural capital as central, and a Marxist, materialist perspective in which it is one's relation to the means of production that is paramount. Jane's efforts to forge her identity amid the shifting class and racial dynamics of the post-apartheid period take place in a global system of economic asymmetry, and her subjective emancipation through learning about art is complicated by its interaction with the economic system in which that knowledge comes to hold value. The 'struggle over the sign' that Dorothy Driver describes in Wicomb's writing is here present in the space between the fountain and the factory, a physical space that comes to signify the gap between

---

85 In fact, Wicomb synthesises two stories about the factory. The fire took place in 1900, but during construction in 1889, almost coterminous with the fountain's completion, the façade of the factory toppled, killing 29 weavers.

art's transcendence of its conditions of production and its inevitable situatedness within them.

Both 'In the Botanic Gardens' and 'There's the Bird that Never Flew' depict characters whose experience is strongly influenced by their class identity. The contested class position of coloured South Africans, which I described in the opening of this chapter, is further complicated when Dorothy and Jane travel to Scotland and have ambivalent experiences with those they meet there. Dorothy is tongue-tied by Mr MacPherson's English, to the extent that she can get little information about her missing son, while Jane's awkward interaction with Margaret draws into focus the differing forms of capital – economic and cultural – that shape class identity. However, it is not only Wicomb's characters who have a problem of class. The intricacies of class are 'discernible to natives alone who talk about these things in code' (126), and the same is true of politics in Wicomb's stories. Dorothy and Jane's experience is described using aesthetic strategies that allow the reader to partake of her characters' unease and confusion. This allows Wicomb considerable scope for literary experiment and political suggestion, but also impedes the articulation of an identifiable political stance. Rather than choose between these demands, Wicomb opts to foreground the very constraints under which she writes, making them integral to her work. Form here structures our perception of the social and in so doing provides a way for readers to think with the text. In Wicomb's words, 'we are of course shaped by what we read. The equivocal teaches to think carefully, and so slowly, over time, perhaps those who read come to a more ethical understanding of the world.'[86] Whether every reader will come to such an understanding or not, it is the case that her short stories offer the kind of interlocutor to thought that might allow this to come about. As Wicomb navigates the changing political determinations of post-apartheid authorship, her short stories offer ambivalent, equivocal aesthetic experiences that can help make the kinds of reader they require.

Ellipsis, and the lure it offers to suspicious reading, is one route by which the short story allows us to think about the social through an experience of reading. It works, as is the case in some of Ivan Vladislavić's apophatic fictions, through omission that brings a subject into view, or though coded utterances that speak around a subject, and so attest to the insufficiency of language to discuss it. This mode of writing gains its

---

86 Phiri and Wicomb, 'Black, White and Everything In-between', p. 125.

political traction by inviting the reader to complete these missing parts but denying them the means with which to do so, or rather, by insisting that to do so would be to oversimplify, or to miss the point entirely. This writing offers a conceptual apparatus that requires holding contradictory thoughts in mind and uses the tension between the said and the unsaid to animate social thought. In the following chapter, I turn to the work of Phaswane Mpe, whose writing's most apparent trait is not absence but excess. This takes the form of melodramatic and tragic plots, looping sentences, obsessive reiterations, compulsive returns, and a brooding consciousness that dwells on a social compound of disenfranchisement.

CHAPTER FOUR

Phaswane Mpe's Aesthetics of Brooding

I am saturated with violence. It was, and is, the expression and clarification of our society.[1]

Bloke Modisane

The previous three chapters have explored how post-apartheid short stories might help us think differently about the world. This pathway – from aesthetic encounter to social thought – is indirect and unreliable. Yet, in its small way, the short story can give readers a better understanding of the variegated texture of post-apartheid life, perhaps even causing them to experience it quite differently from how they did before. It has been my contention that the kinds of experiences these short stories allow are tightly bound up with their formal characteristics. These chapters have argued that short stories can serve as interlocutors to social thought, but we might look at this slightly differently, and say that each author's work also offers a theorisation of art's mediated relation to the social. For Gordimer, her recursive aesthetics and tacking between realist and allegorical modes pose a challenge to post-apartheid political writing. Vladislavić's short stories question monumental forms of public memory, and in so doing they draw into focus the social affordances of literature, sculpture, illustration, and performance art. For Wicomb, it is the use of ellipsis that allows her to stage how the short story allows and disallows political thought.

This chapter examines how Phaswane Mpe's posthumously published short story collection *Brooding Clouds* (2008) offers a formal

---

[1] Bloke Modisane, *Blame Me on History* (London: Thames and Hudson, 1963), p. 57.

negotiation of the types of violence, both structural and spectacular, that still disproportionally affect black South Africans. This violence appears in shocking individual acts – murders, suicides, and robberies – but is also a cumulative and crushing accretion of poverty, racism, curtailed education, stifled opportunity, disappointed hope, and the psychological harms that these factors cause. Mpe finds in the short story a form through which to express a political consciousness that comprehends singular acts of oppression as part of a distributed climate of disenfranchisement. In this regard, Mpe's writing can usefully be understood in relation to earlier generations of short story writers such as Bloke Modisane, Can Themba, Mtutuzeli Matshoba, and Mothobi Mutloatse, in whose work, as Martin Trump argues, it is 'often difficult to disentangle the violence which takes place within the black [...] townships from the violence of the social system [...] which subordinates black people'.[2] Mpe's work differs, however, first in that it is stylistically quite distinct from these authors, evincing greater formal experimentalism than these precursors, and drawing on cosmologies that refuse the terms of the necropolitical state. The influences he cites for himself include Herman Charles Bosman, Oliver Matsepe, J.M. Coetzee, Zakes Mda, Bessie Head, and William Blake.[3] This list offers tempting routes of enquiry through Mpe's work – Bosman's narratorial framing, global modernism in the Sepedi literary tradition via Matsepe, Blake's visionary social conscience, and so on – but it equally testifies to the eclecticism of Mpe's reading, and the risk of categorising his writing too narrowly. His work also differs from the earlier generation of black short story writers, however, because the political present he addresses, the late 1990s and early 2000s, is no longer immediately determined by the oppressive force of apartheid, but rather by the structural perpetuation of the societal inequalities it put in place.

Mpe's short fiction articulates this condition through what he calls 'brooding', a state which is sometimes a cast of mind, sometimes an orientation towards the world, sometimes a threatening or melancholy atmosphere in which life plays out. While in the previous chapters my focus was largely on one aesthetic characteristic in each author, Mpe's aesthetics of brooding – appropriately for something which is closer in

---

2 Trump, 'South African Short Fiction', p. 434.
3 Phaswane Mpe and Lizzy Attree, 'Healing with Words: Phaswane Mpe Interviewed by Lizzy Attree', *The Journal of Commonwealth Literature*, 40.3 (2005), 139–48 (p. 143).

character to an atmosphere or mood than an object or event – comes about through plural means. *Brooding Clouds* creates an atmosphere of brooding by dwelling on recurring ideas, depicting obsessive states, and retelling the same event from multiple perspectives. It is precisely the difficulty of disentangling the multiple vectors of brooding that creates its formal effect, and this in turn constitutes the heuristic device it offers: a model of complexity that shuns monocausal explanations.

Before turning to a theorisation of brooding and a discussion of how it informs my reading of this collection, it is helpful to understand something of Mpe's proximity to the precarious life the collection describes, and how this informed the book's unusual genesis and publication. Mpe's life was often lived in close contact with the forms of immediate and structural violence that his collection engages. He was born in 1970 in Ga-Mogano, a village near what was then Pietersburg, Northern Transvaal, and is now Polokwane, Limpopo, one of the poorest provinces of South Africa. During the years of his schooling, per capita spending on education for black students was one tenth that for whites, with teacher–pupil ratios at 1:18 for white students and 1:39 in black schools, and with only 15% of teachers in black schools holding teaching certificates.[4] The deficiencies of apartheid-era schooling led many students in the 1980s to strike, destroy school property, and otherwise undermine schools' ability to function.

The 1980s were the most violent years of apartheid, with government suppression reaching a crescendo and a series of states of emergency beginning in 1985. Mpe left a life of 'crushing early poverty' at 19 for Johannesburg, where he would study African Literature at the University of the Witwatersrand.[5] The early 1990s were in some ways an optimistic time, with the transfer of power to the ANC in progress, but these years also saw government financial scandals, allegations of police brutality, and escalating violence, particularly around Johannesburg where Mpe was studying. Elana Bregin notes that Mpe found his experience at university alienating, as there was a 'lack of tangible support for those carrying the weight of their disadvantaged backgrounds, hamstrung as they were by the twin legacies of poverty

---

4 Rita M. Byrnes, *South Africa: A Country Study*, 3rd edn (Washington, DC: Library of Congress Federal Research Division, 1997), p. 156.
5 Elana Bregin, 'Editor's Preface', in *Brooding Clouds* (Scottsville: University of KwaZulu-Natal Press, 2008), p. xiii.

and Bantu Education'.[6] He nevertheless overcame these difficulties, and went on to complete a master's degree in African Literature at Wits in 1996, then a diploma in publishing at Oxford Brookes University in the UK in 1997. In 2001 he published his only novel, *Welcome to Our Hillbrow*, which was met with local and international acclaim. While teaching at the University of the Witwatersrand in 2003 he began a doctorate, but began to suffer from an undiagnosed illness. After a consultation with an ngaka, Mpe decided to leave academia to become a traditional healer himself, but he died in 2004 at the age of 34, soon after beginning his apprenticeship.

Four years later *Brooding Clouds* appeared, and the genesis of this collection is fascinating both for what it can tell us about Mpe's process as a writer and as a form of material witness to the precarity of black life to which it attests. Most of the collection was written while Mpe was studying at Oxford Brookes in 1997, and the collection as Mpe had conceived of it contained poems, mostly written in parallel with the stories.[7] Mpe self-translated the collection into Sepedi under the title *Maru a Maso*, but neither the original collection nor the translation was published in its complete form at the time, due to disagreements with the publisher in the case of the translation, and uncompleted revisions in the case of the English-language version.[8] Some stories did, however, appear in other places, particularly in the anthology *Unity in Flight*. The published version of *Brooding Clouds* exists in large part thanks to Elana Bregin, who edited the collection after Mpe's death. She was also an important actor in *Welcome to Our Hillbrow*'s publication, both in that she persuaded UKZN Press to publish the book, and in that she edited it.[9] The decision to publish *Brooding Clouds* was taken in part to offer a 'lifework collection' that would allow readers to see the development of Mpe's writing.[10] The volume's bookending preface

6 Ibid., p. xiii.
7 I do not analyse the poems in this chapter, but there is certainly something to say about how lyric poetry and the short story overlap in their tension between syntagmatic and paradigmatic forms of sense-making.
8 Mpe and Attree, 'Healing with Words', p. 142.
9 In the copy of the novel that Mpe signed for Bregin, he thanks her for 'combing through the jungle in search of an elusive story and thanks for discovering something'. Percy Zvomuya, 'Sharp Read: Phaswane Mpe's One Great Novel', *New Frame*, 2021, <https://www.newframe.com/sharp-read-phaswane-mpes-one-great-novel/> (accessed 15 April 2022).
10 Bregin, 'Editor's Preface', p. xvi.

and final interview, as well as its sombre cover showing a threatening sky, give it the character of a memorial, a painfully apt framing for the stories and poems it contains, which themselves turn around questions of mortality and finitude.[11]

If the texts in Mpe's collection are, in part, a means of finding a form fit for depicting precarious life, then the volume in which they are contained constitutes a material token of that precarity. There is even a direct link between Mpe's practice as a writer and these concerns: Mpe was prone to depression, caused by what he describes as 'very personal stuff', and the bulk of *Welcome to Our Hillbrow* was drafted in one 24-hour period as an 'alternative to suicide' during one of these low ebbs.[12] Sarah Nuttall goes so far as to call the book an 'extended suicide note that also comes to save his life'.[13] Writing for Mpe was, then, both a means of being present to the fragility of life he saw around him and, at times, a means of negotiating his own suicidal ideation.

While *Welcome to Our Hillbrow* is considered a key text of post-apartheid literature, *Brooding Clouds* has attracted only scattered attention. This is despite Bregin's description of it as the 'prequel manuscript' to *Hillbrow* and despite the two texts appearing, in Annika McPherson's words, to be 'thematic and stylistic versionings of each other'.[14] This 'versioning', to which we might add 'generic versioning',

---

11 A few years before *Brooding Clouds* was published, a collection of tributes, poems, stories, and interviews was published that also memorialised Mpe's life, along with that of K. Sello Duiker, who gave a eulogy at Mpe's funeral just a month before taking his own life in early 2005. See Mbulelo Visikhungo Mzamane (ed.), *Words Gone Two Soon: A Tribute to Phaswane Mpe & K. Sello Duiker* (Pretoria: Umgangatho Media & Communications, 2005).

12 Emily S. Davis, 'Contagion, Cosmopolitanism, and Human Rights in Phaswane Mpe's *Welcome to Our Hillbrow*', *College Literature*, 40.3 (2013), 99–112 (p. 9); Mpe and Attree, 'Healing with Words', pp. 140, 141.

13 Sarah Nuttall, 'Literary City', in *Johannesburg: The Elusive Metropolis*, ed. Sarah Nuttall and Achille Mbembe (Durham, NC: Duke University Press, 2008), pp. 195–218 (p. 203).

14 Bregin, 'Editor's Preface', p. xi; Annika McPherson, 'Tracing the Rural in the Urban: Re-Reading Phaswane Mpe's *Welcome to Our Hillbrow* through *Brooding Clouds*', in *Re-Inventing the Postcolonial (in the) Metropolis*, ed. Cecile Sandten and Annika Bauer (Leiden: Brill, 2016), pp. 55–69 (p. 61); For other articles on *Brooding Clouds*, see Benjamin H. Ogden, 'The Palimpsest of Process and the Search for Truth in South Africa: How Phaswane Mpe Wrote *Welcome to Our Hillbrow*', *Safundi*, 14.2 (2013), 191–208; Estelle Trengove,

offers a useful starting point to consider how Mpe's short stories might offer readers a way to read, think, and imagine differently than his novel. Readers familiar with *Welcome* will recognise many of the characters, locations, and events in *Brooding Clouds*. Both *Brooding* and *Welcome* span urban Hillbrow and rural Tiragalong, two places tied by threads of filial duty; the collection begins with Tshepo's death by lightning, which also triggers the events of *Welcome*; we find Refentše and Lerato, lovers torn apart by infidelity and driven to suicide, and a whole cast of other familiar characters – Sammy, Refilwe, Terror – whose back stories are fleshed out. In Sam Durrant's words, *Welcome* is 'saturated with death', and likewise, nearly every major character in *Brooding Clouds* is murdered, commits suicide, or suffers from the degrading structural violence caused by poverty, what Mpe calls 'liv[ing] on lice'.[15] Striking in this collection are not just the deaths that occupy the foreground of the text but also those deaths and acts of violence that make up the background fabric against which these events occur. There are the 'Robbers. Murderers. Rapists' Lerato is warned about, the friend who is 'gang-raped at gunpoint' (73), the murder of Lerato's father Piet, who is forced to find work in the city when his parents' meagre livestock die and is stabbed to death for 'as yet unknown reasons' (78). But there are also what Lauren Berlant calls 'slow deaths', the accretive deaths that occur when populations are 'marked for wearing out'.[16] The collection is, in other words, deeply enmeshed with the modalities of what Christina Sharpe describes as 'Black life lived in, as, under, and despite Black death'.[17]

In formal terms, *Welcome* has often been discussed in terms of its innovative use of the second-person address, which has been seen to encourage and inhibit forms of community.[18] *Brooding Clouds* has no

'Lightning and Fiction: An Engineer Reads Phaswane Mpe's *Brooding Clouds*', *Current Writing: Text and Reception in Southern Africa*, 27.1 (2015), 38–49.

15 Sam Durrant, 'The Invention of Mourning in Post-Apartheid Literature', *Third World Quarterly*, 26.3 (2005), 441–50 (p. 448); Phaswane Mpe, *Brooding Clouds* (Scottsville: University of KwaZulu-Natal Press, 2008), p. 4. All further references to this work are given parenthetically in the text until the end of this section.
16 Lauren Berlant, 'Slow Death (Sovereignty, Obesity, Lateral Agency)', *Critical Inquiry*, 33.4 (2007), 754–80 (p. 761).
17 Christina Sharpe, *In the Wake: On Blackness and Being* (Durham, NC: Duke University Press, 2016), p. 20.
18 Davis, 'Contagion, Cosmopolitanism, and Human Rights', p. 102; María J. López, 'Communities of Mourning and Vulnerability: Zakes Mda's "Ways

such communal narrative voice binding the text together, rather being held together by thematic and formal threads that weave through the collection. Chris Dunton describes the stories as 'relat[ing] to each other on an elastic principle, with strands of subject matter (witchcraft, suicide) dispersing and then consolidating again'.[19] And yet despite the recurring themes, characters, and locations, the collection retains something of what Elizabeth Bowen argues to be characteristic of the short story: unlike the novel, the short story tends to 'measure man' not by his relation to society, but rather 'by his aspirations and dreads and place him alone on that stage which, inwardly, every man is conscious of occupying alone'.[20] Similarly, Michael Trussler suggests that the short story form gives us the '"scandal" of irrevocable isolation and radical discontinuity in reply to those cultural and social forces that would comfort (if not redeem) individual anguish by rendering human experience into shared communal narratives'.[21] For Trussler, the short story in some measure eschews the consolation of narrative community in favour of showing us perhaps the most disturbing side of human experience: the ever-present horizon of our death. As Susan Lohafer observes, '[s]hort fiction [...] is the most "end-conscious" of forms [... and] [r]eaders of short fiction are the most "end-conscious" of readers', and this pervasive end-consciousness gives us tools for understanding our relationship to mortal closure.[22] It is worth noting the assumption here of an essentially individualist worldview and a cosmology in which there is no communion between the living and the dead, an assumption that many South African belief systems do not share; nonetheless, these comments remain useful for analysing Mpe's collection, which stages

---

of Dying" and Phaswane Mpe's "Welcome to Our Hillbrow"', *English in Africa*, 40.1 (2013), 99–117 (p. 112); Michael Green, 'Translating the Nation: From Plaatje to Mpe', *Journal of Southern African Studies*, 34.2 (2008), 325–42 (pp. 340–41); Carrol Clarkson, 'Locating Identity in Phaswane Mpe's *Welcome to Our Hillbrow*', *Third World Quarterly*, 26.3 (2005), 451–59.

19 Chris Dunton, 'Between Rural Roots and Urban Possibility', *The Sunday Independent*, 11 May 2008, p. 17.
20 Elizabeth Bowen, 'The Faber Book of Modern Short Stories', in *The New Short Story Theories*, ed. Charles E. May (Athens, OH: Ohio University Press, 1994), pp. 256–62 (p. 262).
21 Michael Trussler, 'Michael Trussler on Hayden White, Paul Ricoeur, and Others', *Narrative*, 20.2 (2012), 163–64.
22 Susan Lohafer, *Coming to Terms with the Short Story* (Baton Rouge: Louisiana State University Press, 1983), p. 94.

the conflict between a traditional conception of selfhood as a network of social relations and a modern one marked by that model's dissolution.[23]

Furthermore, in combining several isolated stories while never wholly integrating them, readers are forced to mediate between the solitary and the communal, to shift between the certainty of death and community's mitigation of that burden. If the 'we' perspective of *Welcome to Our Hillbrow* emphasises the communal dimension of this dynamic, then we might say that *Brooding Clouds* combines an implied community with the radical isolation and proximity to death the short story can afford. *Brooding Clouds* offers a form in which private torments are seen to both shape and be shaped by the societal context in which they occur. In refusing to disambiguate larger-scale societal forces from their individual consequences, Mpe offers neither individual characters who are allegories for some wider societal ill, nor monadic entities whose suffering has no wider resonance. Rather, they are the individuals through which structural conditions are expressed, and by virtue of that individuated expression those conditions take on particularised forms.

The relationship between short stories, end-consciousness, and the horizon of our deaths is significant in a general sense, but the immanence and unpredictability of death in Mpe's collection grants it a particular urgency and significance. As Andrew van der Vlies persuasively argues, readers seek in narrative ways of understanding their temporal existence, so 'if readers anticipate an ending to a narrative, a degree of anxiety is inevitable if it does not come or arrives precipitously or in uncertain fashion'.[24] What particular affordances, then, might short stories offer readers in structuring an understanding of such precarious life? Short stories are known for their foreshortened and ambiguous endings, and so offer focused examples of the 'disappointment of [...] anticipation' that van der Vlies identifies as characteristic of much post-apartheid literature.[25] Mpe's collection provides curtailed experiences of curtailed lives, and so offers a formal apparatus through which to perceive life in sight of immanent death rather than a narrative mode through which to overcome it. However, this is counterbalanced in *Brooding*

---

23 Carrol Clarkson perceptively reads the 'we' narration of *Welcome to Our Hillbrow* as the elegiac figuring of a waning social conception of selfhood. Clarkson, 'Locating Identity', pp. 453, 455.
24 Van der Vlies, *Present Imperfect*, p. 20.
25 Ibid., p. 20.

Clouds, as the stories in this collection disrupt the 'end-consciousness' of the short story form by replaying events from multiple perspectives. Neither of these perspectives – the immanence of death and the fluidity of mortality – overwhelms the other, but it is rather in the restless pull between them that Mpe articulates the paradox of life in death and death in life.

Brooding and Mourning

The 'brooding clouds' alluded to in the collection's title are, on the one hand, an indication of the book's content, which features descriptions of immanent societal threat and characters who dwell in ruminative mental states. On the other hand, Mpe's short stories create what I call an 'aesthetics of brooding', a mode of writing that reiterates and revisits formulations and patterns of thought, and that retells single events from multiple perspectives. The aesthetics of brooding inheres in sentences and paragraphs but is also perceptible in the structures of stories that turn obsessively around a single event, and even across the whole collection, which is constantly pulled back to its recurring concerns. Mpe's writing, while quite busy in its surface proliferation of images and figures of speech, structurally turns in circles around its central axis, suggesting perpetual repetition in the present. A version of what I am describing is identified by Bregin, who perceptively notes that Mpe's writing 'challenges the reader's perpetual frame with its allusive – and elusive – unfolding', and that his body of writing as a whole has a 'prismatic effect', in that separate texts in Mpe's oeuvre do not 'follow one another in a linear sequence, so much as erupt together' as 'tangential strands'; or, put otherwise, that his writing has 'the spatial configuration of a musical score, with all the different segments [...] resonating – and reflecting – off the others, adding new facets to the whole'.[26] Bregin's descriptions reveal the aspect of Mpe's writing that, in returning to and worrying away at a central set of concerns, events, and structures, creates a mood or atmosphere of brooding that saturates nearly every aspect of the text. This atmosphere is in part caused by the events the stories describe, but it also embodies an orientation towards the world, and one that shapes how readers might experience it. The feeling created is one of an overwhelming 'at-onceness' or

---

26 Bregin, 'Editor's Preface', pp. xv, xiii.

simultaneity, in which multiple times, pressures, ontologies, and epistemologies threaten to engulf or subsume everything that falls within the aesthetic's orbit. In Jonathan Flatley's words, '[i]n an important sense, a mood creates our world at a given moment', and by sensitising readers to the absolute character of that mood, Mpe's short stories suggest an understanding of the world that is conceptually irreducible.[27]

Mpe's aesthetics of brooding can productively be understood in dialogue with several existing theorisations of art's mediation of mortal precarity. Christina Sharpe uses the concept of 'the wake' to conceptualise the perpetuation in the present of structures of violence instigated by chattel slavery.[28] Her work theorises the past's immanence in the present, and this same structure can be adapted to better understand Mpe's post-apartheid writing. The wake, for Sharpe, is a dense and polysemous concept that includes ways of 'think[ing] about the dead and about our relations to them', including 'rituals through which to enact grief and memory'.[29] A wake is also the track or trace of a moving object, such as 'the air currents behind a body in flight' – we might think here of Refentše's tragic suicide from a Hillbrow balcony – or metaphorically the disturbance caused by a momentous event.[30] Along with these meanings, there is also the sense of being awake, that is, conscious and alert. The absolute character of the wake is in places described as a 'weather' or 'climate' that makes up 'the totality of our environments [...] the total climate; and the climate is antiblack'.[31] Sharpe's examples are mostly drawn from America and the Caribbean, but she hopes that 'the praxis of the wake and wake work might have enough capaciousness to travel and do work that I have not here been able to imagine or anticipate'.[32]

The apartheid period cannot be mapped onto the context that is

27 Jonathan Flatley, 'How a Revolutionary Counter-Mood is Made', *New Literary History*, 43.3 (2012), 503–25 (pp. 503–04).
28 While my focus is on the more immediate wake of apartheid, the history of slavery in South Africa is an essential component in understanding apartheid's structures of violence and oppression. Historical slavery in South Africa existed officially from 1653 to 1834 – in practice this final date is muddied by a four-year transition period – and this composes part of the long historical arc under which apartheid falls.
29 Sharpe, *In the Wake*, p. 21.
30 Ibid., p. 21.
31 Ibid., p. 104.
32 Ibid., p. 22.

Sharpe's concern in any one-to-one way, but the scale of apartheid's violence – both immediate and structural – also requires 'a method of encountering a past that is not past' and that might watch over and give heed to the ongoing 'specific and cumulative deaths' it caused and continues to cause in new forms.[33] Apartheid as a system of governance may have ended, but it continues to shape contemporary lives, and cause contemporary deaths, and Mpe's 'brooding' is an attempt to find a form fit to articulate this condition, described by Achille Mbembe as a form of 'social existence in which vast populations are subjected to living conditions that confer upon them the status of the living dead'.[34] Mpe's collection explores the same paradox of living in a society that is structured around the precarity of black lives that interests Sharpe: it is a form of 'Black expressive culture' that 'depict[s] aesthetically the impossibility' of resolving societal exclusion through 'assimilation, inclusion, or civil or human rights'.[35]

The symbolic centre of Mpe's collection is provided by the 'brooding clouds' that give the volume its title. It is through this dense metaphorical knot that Mpe engages with the 'weather' of anti-blackness. These clouds mediate between internal and external states, and so suggest how external conditions affect one's state of mind, but also how a mental state can in some measure alter the way the external world is understood. The meaning of these clouds modulates between a literal weather phenomenon and a range of metaphoric resonances, which for Bregin include:

> the thirsty land of physical and psychic drought [...] The sinister subtext of violence that runs through the narratives [...] and depressive emotional states that hover like engulfing miasma over the afflicted ones. But most of all, the image conjured up for [Mpe] the overhanging balconies of Hillbrow high-rises that loom overhead with menacing portent as one looks up from below them.[36]

These clouds are, then, at once meteorological, architectural, and symbolic of societal threat, but they also indicate a cast of mind that filters everything through its depressive gloom. To brood is to dwell on

---

33 Ibid., pp. 62, 7.
34 Achille Mbembé, 'Necropolitics', trans. Libby Meintjes, *Public Culture*, 15.1 (2003), 11–40 (p. 40).
35 Sharpe, *In the Wake*, p. 14.
36 Bregin, 'Editor's Preface', p. xiii.

a thought in a morbid or meditative way, or here to overhang threateningly. But if 'brooding' has this range of darker associations, it is also to meditate upon, to sit with, or to incubate. Mpe creates in this collection an aesthetics of brooding that ruminates on the past, and recognises its continuing shaping of the present, and while remaining weighted towards this impasse, it still ends by offering an orientation to the future, albeit one that does not suggest overcoming the past.

Mpe's best-known work, *Welcome to Our Hillbrow*, has been read by several critics in terms of mourning, perhaps most interestingly by Emily Davis, who notes that the novel challenges 'the Eurocentric divide between melancholia and mourning', as in some South African belief systems, 'the dead stay with us', drawing us into a 'more complex sense of how and what we might draw from the ongoing presence of the dead among us'.[37] This is persuasive, but in my reading, *Brooding Clouds* is concerned not only with the ongoing presence of the dead among the living, but also the immanence of death in black South African life. This has been theorised in a South African context by Bhekizizwe Peterson, who describes the 'regular encounter with forms of violence and alienation as well as unresolved grief' that leaves individuals and families in '"a permanent wake"'.[38] Peterson's model, like Davis's, is sensitive to an 'experience of loss' that is 'broached from ontological, subjective and temporal senses that are drawn from African culture', namely in that when a culture upholds 'ancestral veneration', then '[d]eath [...] is only one phase in a complex and continuing relation between those who have passed on and those who continue to inhabit the earthly realm'.[39] However, Peterson's model is also alert to how artworks might engage 'existential crises embedded in the tropes of homelessness, poverty and disaffection [...] [of black lives] stuck in different kinds of living, displacement and death'.[40]

Clearly, the past's occupation of the present is one source of what Peterson calls 'melancholia', Sharpe calls 'the wake', and Mpe calls

---

37 Davis, 'Contagion, Cosmopolitanism, and Human Rights', p. 109. See also Neville Hoad, 'An Elegy for African Cosmopolitanism: Phaswane Mpe's *Welcome to Our Hillbrow*', in *African Intimacies: Race, Homosexuality, and Globalization* (Minneapolis: University of Minnesota Press, 2007), pp. 113–26.
38 Bhekizizwe Peterson, 'Spectrality and Inter-Generational Black Narratives in South Africa', *Social Dynamics*, 45.3 (2019), 345–64 (p. 346).
39 Ibid., p. 353.
40 Ibid., pp. 354–55.

'brooding', but equally important is the accretive slow death of structural violence that continues to cause suffering in the present. Sharpe's theory of the wake includes aspects of mourning and melancholia, and attests to how the past not only disturbs the present, but continues to be reproduced in it. Peterson's and Davis's models add to this the more visible presence of a cosmology that allows for the ongoing relation between the living and the dead. Mpe's brooding offers an aesthetic form through which to articulate this compound, paradoxical state. While apartheid as a system of government may have come to an end, the slow violence of its structural consequences continues to shape 'the modalities of Black life lived in, as, under, and despite Black death'.[41] How might a writer engage the melancholic and mourning dimensions of addressing the dead, and what Saidiya Hartman describes as the 'skewed life chances, limited access to health and education, premature death, incarceration, and impoverishment', without succumbing to the hopelessness this condition suggests?[42]

The Experience of Brooding

The first component of Mpe's aesthetics of brooding takes the form of the constant presence of brooding threat in the collection. This threat permeates every part of the characters' daily lives in the form of precarious structural disenfranchisement, and sometimes erupts in spectacular acts of violence. The dynamic between these two kinds of violence is evident from the first story, 'Brooding Clouds', in which the village of Tiragalong is suffering from a drought that has left the crops 'grey like ash' and the livestock 'merely collections of bones in the shapes of cattle, sheep and goats' (3). When the crops here fail, the people, living in 'raving poverty' (37), go hungry. In the village, a promising young man, Tshepo, is struck by lightning and killed, and in response an old woman, Makgolo, is accused of witchcraft and necklaced by some 'comrades' (8), here referring to young male ANC activists who were spurred to radicalism by the lack of education and widespread unemployment.[43] What emerges from this description is

---

41 Sharpe, *In the Wake*, p. 20.
42 Saidiya V. Hartman, *Lose Your Mother: A Journey Along the Atlantic Slave Route* (New York: Farrar, Straus, and Giroux, 2007), p. 6.
43 Isak Niehaus, 'Witches and Zombies of the South African Lowveld: Discourse,

an all-encompassing mood of mortal risk which is instantiated in immediate acts of violence but made possible by the slow violence of structural neglect.

The link between these two kinds of violence – spectacular and structural – is made clear in that the sudden cruelty of necklacing Makgolo is immediately tied to the confidence invested in Tshepo to go to university and then return to the village and teach. Tshepo and his mother faced multiple challenges in their lives: they 'lived on lice' (4) in poverty, and his father was killed in Alexandria for unknown reasons (78), but his academic promise allowed him to go to university and complete a degree. However, on the day of his receiving his results, disaster strikes:

> It was on the day he received his sparkling results that the fatal lightning struck him. There was nothing one could really call rain. Just black clouds, brooding for a long time over the village. The people, seeing such ugly clouds, feared a devilish storm after the drought that had done enough damage already. Blinding lightning tore the black clouds mercilessly, and rumbling thunder backed it up. But rain, no! Only a few drops left the land as dry as a bleached bone. The clouds dragged their feet away when the blowing horn mournfully announced Tshepo's death. (5)

Mpe here juxtaposes Tshepo getting his degree with his death by lightning, a product of the 'brooding clouds'. The suggestion is that despite nearly escaping the impediments of his upbringing, Tshepo has been hampered by the total inertial force that society exerts upon him, for which the brooding clouds offer a symbolic correlate. The sudden violence they exert does not even offer cathartic release, but rather 'drag[] their feet', leaving only a few sparse drops of rain on the parched ground.

The link between structural disenfranchisement and an early death recurs in 'Occasion for Brooding', a story focalised through Refentše, who sits and drinks while brooding on Tshepo's death and his girlfriend Lerato's infidelity with his best friend Sammy. Like Tshepo, Refentše is a rare university graduate, who 'was going to bring advancement to the whole village', and so '[h]is death was in many ways the death of

Accusations and Subjective Reality', *The Journal of the Royal Anthropological Institute*, 11.2 (2005), 191–210 (p. 191).

this advancement' (35). As the narrator notes, it would be a big change to have 'a teacher whose education transcended Verwoerdian food for thought' (35) or the 'product of [...] "Bantu Education"' (37). The story also makes clear the amount of pressure on Refentše to help his family out of poverty. Despite his ill-treatment at the hands of some of the lecturers – he calls the university an 'institution of higher alienation' (36) – he cannot quit, as he remembers 'his mother ... the poverty... [...] The possibility that he might not be able to return to the university due to financial difficulties haunted him constantly' (39). Despite eventually getting a job at the university, he finds the structural pressures of the system in which he works too much. His contracts are 'not explained to him in the way that he now knew they should have been. His limited English vocabulary and innocence as to how contracts worked did not stand him in good stead' (40), and so his salary soon disappears in repaying student loans, taxes, rent, and furniture payments. The strains that this situation puts on his finances cause a falling-out with his mother, who feels that she is being neglected in favour of Refentše's girlfriend in Johannesburg. The compounded problems that Refentše faces create a feeling of inescapable hopelessness, a total atmosphere in which every possible option leads to defeat.

We might call this mood elegiac, or melancholic, but this does not fully capture the present unfolding of the cause of the mood. If both elegy and melancholy construct their cause as anterior, albeit by reactivating the past in the present, Mpe's brooding refuses to bracket off the anteriority of the cause. There are problems largely caused by an apartheid past, and their influence shapes the collection's present as people live with the consequences of their partial education. However, these problems are kept alive in the present by structures that exploit those difficulties. Mpe's decision to depict the same arc of rise and abrupt fall in Tshepo's and Refentše's stories creates a formal pattern across the collection that again recurs in a changed form in the final story, which I discuss below. This formal patterning, repeated in close proximity, recalls Gordimer's use of structural repetition in 'Karma' and 'Alternative Endings', in which archetypal experience suggests the essential substitutability of the characters concerned. However, like Gordimer, Mpe tempers this by particularising each character's experience, and so impeding their ready association with existing social categories.

Styles of Brooding

Throughout the collection, the difficult lives that these characters lead result in episodes of vortex-like mental states, which stylistically perform the brooding they describe. As Refentše sits drinking in his apartment, shortly before his suicide, he experiences a deeply oppressive mental state:

> Throughout the day, at the university, he has suffered visions of sharp gazes focused on him, and of voices reminding him of what his people had always known would be the inevitable outcome of his stubbornness. The gazes and voices had multiplied in his imagination, becoming sharper and louder by the second. There were moments when he would shrug with fright as he fixed faces, familiar village faces, to the gazes and voices [...] the worst torment was the keen knowledge that what he conjured was what he would see and hear in reality, sooner or later. (32)

Refentše's disturbed thoughts, paranoid projections of his interior suffering, are communicated in an almost incantatory prose, with 'faces', 'gazes', 'voices' looping around in his mind and tormenting him. This state of brooding manifests itself differently in Lerato, who, after Refentše's suicide, sits in her room with a single song on repeat and a 'melancholy look' on her face. She speaks less and less as her youth is 'gnawed away by grief', leaving her in a 'mood of severely haunted brooding' (72). Her mother later finds her in bed, dead from an overdose, the song still repeating on the CD player.[44] The compulsive relistening, combined with gnawing grief and haunted brooding, all suggest the constant occupation of present thought by past events recurring as present anxieties. Likewise, Sammy is tortured by his betrayal of Refentše and by his role in accusing Refentše's mother of witchcraft, which leads to her being burned to death. As he tries to sleep he '[remember[s] vividly the crushed corpse face of his late friend' (88) and fantasises about saving Refentše's mother from the flames.

---

44 The song, Stimela's 'See the World Through the Eyes of a Child', is described in *Hillbrow* as 'a song of prolonged pain and suffering; but it was also a song of hope and love. It reminded you strongly of your own loneliness and fear of rejection at certain dark times of your life.' Phaswane Mpe, *Welcome to Our Hillbrow* (Pietermaritzburg: University of Natal Press, 2001), p. 84.

His behaviour becomes ever more erratic, as he would 'shrug and scream unexpectedly' (89) and suffers from auditory and visual hallucinations, which 'flash rapidly and incomprehensibly across his eyes' (90), eventually driving him to 'the sanctuary of his insanity' (93).

Sammy's inability to escape these brooding patterns of thought emphasises the past's iterative repetition in the present, and this sense of the past's perpetuation in the present is doubled when the collection broods on a single event, retold across two stories from different perspectives. The stories, 'Lerato's Ordeal' and 'Refentše's Ordeal', recount a stick-up in a bar, when a group of armed youths break in to steal a set of car keys. We read the story first from Lerato's perspective, then from Refentše's. Including both stories in the collection is interesting in several regards. The first is the proximity of violence that marks the lives of Mpe's characters. Not only do the characters undergo an armed robbery, but Lerato also fears the threat of sexual violence, to which her friend has recently been subjected. The immediate events of the story play out against a wider backdrop of threat, increasing the sense of lives lived under the brooding clouds of structural and spectacular violence. Secondly, the recursive dwelling on a single traumatic scene causes the reader to experience the retelling as if it were a flashback to a past event, but one that also unfolds in the present of the time of reading. This account of the formal workings of recursion is further complicated if we consider that the publication of *Brooding Clouds* in the form in which it currently appears was due to Mpe's tragic and untimely death. As noted above, the collection was published posthumously, and it is unclear whether Mpe would have included both versions of the story had he published the book himself, or if they were rather experiments with perspective as he considered how best to recount the events. Passages recur verbatim or in a nearly identical form across the two stories: almost a half a page appears in the same form (21, 27), raising the question of whether this was an intentional device, designed to show the perspectival aspects of reality while formally bringing the past's immanence to the present into view, or if this was rather the result of Mpe's working process, which was left incomplete. What might, in one reading, be legible as a formal device developed to foreground the text's brooding character is equally legible as the textual trace of a foreshortened life, in which written materials remain necessarily unfinished.

If retelling a single event from multiple perspectives is one technique with which Mpe articulates his aesthetics of brooding, another comes in his use of digressive or recursive narrative development. The stories in this collection are often marked by an unwillingness to move forwards, with individual stories interrupted by background detail or contextual information. Elsewhere, Mpe's frequent foreshadowing and retrospection, sometimes within stories and sometimes across them, gives the reader a formal experience of the ruminatory brooding in which his characters engage. On the one hand, such narrative digression might suggest some influence of oral forms on Mpe's writing practice. It is a common feature of oral storytelling to loop back, elaborate on, or circle around a central line of story. On the other, there is something here of Andrew van der Vlies's observation of the 'state of suspension, and the concomitant sense of disappointment experienced affectively and temporally' that marks many post-apartheid texts, or Leon de Kock's diagnosis of 'plot loss' as post-apartheid texts struggle to find a cohesive narrative amid the disillusionment of transition.[45] The effect of this narrative stalling is amplified by an almost obsessive return to central themes and ideas. This lends the collection a sense of inertia which is in many ways at odds with the often spectacularly violent events that punctuate the book.

The disjunction between these two perspectives is an important component of Mpe's aesthetics of brooding, in which a state of constant activity results in very little forward progress. Take, for example, the fragmentary recounting of Refentše's suicide in 'Occasion for Brooding'. The opening of the story is told in the present tense and depicts Refentše sitting on a balcony wall, drinking, and trapped in a 'maze of brooding' (32). A few paragraphs later we read that '[t]here had been nothing to suggest that the coming funeral would become one of the most talked about events', and we might immediately think that it is Tshepo's funeral that is being discussed, but it is in fact Refentše's own. The strange temporal structure of the sentence – first a past perfect 'there had been' then the future 'would become' – leaves us again in the present, but this is not the same present that opened the story. The effect is one of temporal confusion, in which present, future, and past are one, and all are occupied by the dead and living alike. What follows is a story that works its way through Refentše's recent life via various detours, including the social mores of Tiragalong, Tshepo's funeral,

---

45 Van der Vlies, *Present Imperfect*, p. 3; Leon de Kock, *Losing the Plot: Crime, Reality and Fiction in Postapartheid South African Writing* (Johannesburg: Wits University Press, 2016), p. 3.

the English curriculum at the University of Johannesburg, problems with his previous girlfriends, and reflections on suicide, before finally arriving at the harrowing scene of seeing his girlfriend Lerato in bed with his best friend Sammy. This final event, which is the immediate cause that pushes Refentše to suicide, comes in the last sentence of the story and trails off with an ellipsis: 'He found Lerato still in bed. With her eyes and legs open, and Sammy, moaning...' (46).

The structure of the story is, then, quite strange, with seemingly unnecessary detail impinging on its main events, and one of its central events pushed to the close, but temporally preceding its opening. There is something here of Scheherazade's deferral of death in *1001 Nights*, but Refentše's digressions do not so much stave death off as circle around it in ever-closing concentric spirals. This structure is best understood as a narrative realisation of Refentše's thought processes as he sits on the balcony brooding. The reader is shown his brooding and given a formal experience that approximates the feeling it engenders. It is not that the style is mimetic of what it describes, but rather that it creates in the reader an affective proxy for Refentše's mental state. While in some sense the story's structure frustrates the reader, it gives an experience in miniature of the inescapability of the cumulative factors that contribute to Refentše's state of mind. The effect, as in Gordimer's 'Jump', is one of a paralysing stasis in which past events are compulsively replayed.

The collection's tendency to replay past events, and to obsessively return to its central concerns of poverty, witchcraft, violence, and betrayal, recalls what Sam Durrant terms 'pathological instances of a repetition compulsion' in processes of mourning, but this is not mourning only for past loss.[46] That is certainly one component – Refentše's 'companion' on the balcony is 'the fond memory of Tshepo' (35) – but Refentše's mind is also occupied by 'his thoughts of the pain families have to continue to endure because of the sudden deaths of those who should be in a position to relieve them of their poverty' (35). It is not only the deaths that pain him, but the present endurance of the pain they cause. It is not only the lost lives that he mourns, but the lost chance to escape from poverty that they represent. If Mpe's collection obsessively returns to its central concerns, it is not only due to the great

---

46 Sam Durrant, *Postcolonial Narrative and the Work of Mourning: J.M. Coetzee, Wilson Harris, and Toni Morrison* (Albany: State University of New York Press, 2004), p. 10.

difficulty of living with grief and trauma, but also because it broods on a present state that is itself a source of suffering.

Rather than attributing the source of brooding solely to apartheid's nefarious effects – however powerful these effects might be – the collection refuses this anterior and monocausal explanation. Rather, Mpe's short stories give a sense of at-onceness, in which individual and societal factors, past and present conditions, are intimately connected, and co-shape experience. This effect is created both by the stories he tells and through how they are told, via foreshadowing and retrospection, digression and repetition, and the obsessive dwelling on topics and events that characterise his aesthetics of brooding. At the end of the collection, Mpe foregrounds the reductiveness of the kind of monocausal aetiology that his collection refuses. After Refentše's death,

> Bits and pieces of intelligence as to the cause of the suicide finally found their way onto the N1 to Pietersburg, where Tiragalong was situated. The village refused to gather the pieces together and order them into a coherent story. Ten years after Refentše's death, Tiragalong would still insist that his suicide showed how bad the Jo'burg women were. (95)

While the villagers are keen to attribute Refentše's suicide to a single, immediate cause, the picture we have built up of curtailed lives denies us this convenience. Refentše's betrayal by Lerato is but one piece in a life structured by restricted chances and thwarted opportunity that, together with Refentše's depressive tendencies, leads to him taking his own life. Mpe's short fiction asks us to think of these plural causes as irreducible and mutually reinforcing, and does so through an experience of form.

The End of Brooding

Up to this point my focus has been on brooding in its bleakest and most harrowing forms, appearing as depressive states, threatening atmospheres, and compulsive behaviours. To bring my discussion to an end, however, I want to turn to the other sense that brooding carries, that of thinking through, fostering, or cherishing. At no point does Mpe's collection fully allow this positive sense to efface or outweigh brooding's darker associations, but in the collection's final story, 'Revived Memories', there is a turn towards how brooding might allow readers not only to be more attuned to the determinations of the present, but to forge some path beyond them. The story recounts the experience of Leruo, Refentše's cousin, whose life has many parallels with that of his older relative, as Refentše's life paralleled Tshepo's. Like Refentše, Leruo is academically gifted and succeeds at university. He becomes an accountant and earns good money in Johannesburg, where he falls in love with Beth, who turns out to be Lerato's sister. This uncanny doubling, and Leruo's hubris in the eyes of Tiragalong, are taken as a sign that Leruo will meet the same fate as Refentše and Tshepo before him. However, while Refentše was tied to the mores of the village, and so tortured by its demands on his financial and romantic life, Leruo refuses to 'glorify poverty' (96) and 'choose suffering' (97) when he feels an alternative is available. To the disgust of the villagers – here a form of Greek chorus to Leruo's ascent – the story ends with Leruo and Beth married, and seemingly living a comfortable life. It remains unresolved whether the tragic logic suggested by Leruo's ascent will reach a cathartic crescendo or if the couple will escape the brooding that blighted Refentše's life. The story ends with 'the village's already brooding memory' (103) aggravated by Leruo's decisions to live in a wealthy area and marry an educated woman. Perhaps the suggestion is that Tiragalong, the village that features so prominently as Hillbrow's shadow other, here represents a past mode of life that is being superseded, but the question remains unresolved.[47] The echoes of Refentše's story in Leruo's, and Tiragalong brooding over these parallels, suggests that the threat of the earlier stories is still present. However, Leruo and Beth seem to care for one another deeply. This opens the possibility for brooding in the sense of cherishing or caring for, with their 'two hearts melting and flowing into each other', and foreshadowings of 'later days of reminiscence' (102) of their early love. With this, Mpe's aesthetics of brooding takes on a somewhat different perspective, in which the possibility of another life is offered, albeit with considerable impediments presented to its realisation. The rest of the collection offers very little in terms of hope, but this final story does at least leave some window open on a world beyond the restricted life opportunities that Mpe describes.

---

47 The name Tiragalong literally means 'place of the ancestors', suggesting its association with an older set of mores and expectations. Trengove, 'Lightning and Fiction', p. 45.

There is a productive dialogue here between what Mpe describes as 'brooding' and what van der Vlies has theorised as the 'present imperfect' of post-apartheid fiction, in which texts are marked by 'states of affective dysphoria and temporal disjuncture'.[48] Van der Vlies's analysis is often concerned with how texts offer ways to 'turn missed appointments and bad feelings into new appointments with the unfolding experience of alternative lives and possible futures', or elsewhere 'looking backwards, but also with educated hopefulness'.[49] Van der Vlies's analysis offers a fascinating opportunity to think form, affect, and societal conditions together, and Mpe's work with the short story in *Brooding Clouds* takes advantage of the genre's brevity and tendency towards unfinishedness to articulate a generically informed version of this unsettled socio-affective state. What interests me in *Brooding Clouds* is that whatever 'educated hopefulness' the volume offers happens almost exclusively in the final story, with all the others remaining staunchly pessimistic. The effect, then, is not to turn what has come before into an inevitable progression towards brighter 'possible futures', but rather to juxtapose the wholly valid position of pessimism with an equally valid one of optimism. Many aspects of the present that Mpe describes – poverty, missed opportunities, withered futures, acts of violence, suicides, failures of communication, instances of infidelity and treachery – are left to stand without redemption. And yet it is not a world without hope, even though its realisation remains elusive, fleeting, and inaccessible to many. As the stories relate to one another almost spatially rather than chronologically, the optimistic ending both does and does not resolve the suffering depicted elsewhere, or perhaps, in the manner of Sharpe's thinking, formally instantiates the impossibility of such a resolution.

What opportunities for political thinking might be allowed by texts such as those found in *Brooding Clouds*, which seem to offer so little in terms of future possibility? Michael Green notes that the elegiac quality of *Welcome to Our Hillbrow* risks a 'kind of political retreat', as Mpe's particular use of the 'second person does not, finally, generate a national project adequate to the needs of a post for apartheid'.[50] It may be the case that Mpe's writing either does not or cannot offer the kind of 'specifically directed engagement'

---

48 Van der Vlies, *Present Imperfect*, p. 7.
49 Van der Vlies, *Present Imperfect*, pp. 20, 22.
50 Green, 'Translating the Nation', p. 340.

that Green is looking for, but we do find other kinds of stimulus to socially oriented thought, and importantly ones that insist on recognising both the past's determining influence on the present and the new forms of exclusion produced by the present.[51] The challenge in realising the political affordances of Mpe's collection is that his focus is not on a single clear object so much as a diffuse general state, a social compound of poverty, racism, thwarted ambition, professional disappointment, and personal suffering. The antagonist here is not a single monolithic political structure based on racial segregation, but rather a social climate in which harmful historical structures are perpetuated and developed through economic policy, urban planning, intersubjective acts, and mental states. Neville Hoad, drawing on José Esteban Muñoz and David Eng who have made 'powerful arguments for the further depathologizing of melancholia in the face of so much premature death', argues that Mpe's *Welcome* mobilises melancholia to political ends, and that fiction becomes 'a way of never laying the dead to rest'.[52] This is a useful way to think about *Brooding Clouds*, although the melancholic animation of the unrestful dead should be combined with attention to how Mpe increases our sensitivity to the absolute character of a present, evolving social whole that is premised on racialised societal exclusion.

Previous generations of South African writers thought through the politics and ethics of whether to depict spectacular violence or to promote Njabulo Ndebele's much-discussed 'rediscovery of the ordinary'.[53] Mpe, for his part, fuses the spectacular impulse with a depiction of the ordinary that incorporates the structural violence of daily life, a violence that still striates the experience of many South Africans. The short story plays an important role in Mpe's articulation of this brooding state. What we find in this collection are a series of endings that are not endings, stories that turn in circles around symbolic and thematic centres without resolution, recurring parallelisms that imply but never affirm causality, and a diffuse but undeniable atmosphere of threat. In this, Mpe finds a literary mode in which, in Hartman's words, he can 'give expression to these outrages without exacerbating the indifferent suffering that is the

---

51 Ibid., p. 341.
52 Hoad, 'An Elegy for African Cosmopolitanism', pp. 114–15.
53 Njabulo S. Ndebele, 'The Rediscovery of the Ordinary: Some New Writings in South Africa', *Journal of Southern African Studies*, 12.2 (1986), 143–57.

consequence of the benumbing spectacle'.[54] This everyday structural violence sometimes produces individual acts of spectacular violence, but equally it appears as a slow accretive force that inhibits opportunity, determines life chances, and saturates the mental state of those who live under its influence. By particularising the conditions through the experience of individual characters, but presenting that experience in curtailed, recursive, *brooding* short stories, Mpe finds a form with which to articulate South Africa's particular version of the past's inhabitation of the present. Mpe's brooding requires us to recognise the powerful disturbance caused by the past, to perform acts of mourning for past and present deaths, to insist on the need to sit with the present trouble, and to encourage an awakened state of consciousness. This state impels us to hold the outrage of social violence in thought, but without promising any narrative of utopian possibility.

---

54 Saidiya V. Hartman, *Scenes of Subjection: Terror, Slavery, and Self-Making in Nineteenth-Century America* (New York: Oxford University Press, 1997), p. 4.

CHAPTER FIVE

Spatial Form in Henrietta Rose-Innes

In this final chapter, I turn my attention to the short fiction of Henrietta Rose-Innes. Her stories, like those of Gordimer, Vladislavić, Wicomb, and Mpe, are sites of a productive struggle between formal and extra-formal concerns. In Rose-Innes's case, the most interesting example of this lies in her use of spatial closures, and how they draw into focus the multiple spatial logics of the short story. While the authors discussed in the previous chapters have received considerable critical attention, Rose-Innes's writing has so far only had a handful of articles and chapters devoted to it, and this mostly for her longer prose works.[1] The relative lack of academic criticism on her work is surprising, given her qualities. The blurbs on her books are often provided by J.M. Coetzee – who supervised her master's thesis in creative writing – and Ivan Vladislavić, and her work has been recognised with various prizes: she won the Caine Prize for African Writing in 2008 for her short story 'Poison', and came second in the 2012 BBC (Inter)national Short Story Award for 'Sanctuary'. Two of her novels – *Shark's Egg* (2000) and *Nineveh* (2011) – were shortlisted for the M-Net Literary Award, with the latter also shortlisted for the Sunday Times Prize for Fiction.

Early in her career, Rose-Innes was often portrayed as a member of a new generation of South African writers whose concerns had moved

---

1 To date she has published four novels: *Shark's Egg* (Cape Town: Kwela, 2000), *The Rock Alphabet* (Cape Town: Kwela, 2004), *Nineveh* (Cape Town: Umuzi, 2011), *Green Lion* (Cape Town: Umuzi, 2015), as well as the short story collection *Homing* (Cape Town: Umuzi, 2010). She has also translated Etienne van Heerden's *Die biblioteek aan die einde van die wêreld* as *A Library to Flee* (Cape Town: Queillerie, 2022).

on from those of their apartheid-era predecessors.[2] Cecily van Gend, for example, writes that 'what is refreshing about the work [*Shark's Egg*] is that its subject is removed from the public themes and preoccupations which have dominated South African literature for so long'.[3] However, Rose-Innes has never been comfortable with this characterisation, seeing the politics of her work as operating in less obvious but still important terms.[4] Rose-Innes's works are often concerned with questions of space and place, and these take on a particular quality in her short fiction, in which forms of spatiality internal to the text and those external to it are vividly brought into dialogue. Her stories are often told from highly focused perspectives, in which immediate experience can seem bracketed off from a broader sociopolitical context. However, not only do real places at times emerge in the stories, but in moving between different forms of spatiality, her stories allow for new ways of conceiving how texts intersect with the world outside them.

To fully account for how space in Rose-Innes's short stories mediates between the word and the world, I first bring South African literature's long-standing preoccupation with the politics of space into dialogue with an expanded sense of Joseph Frank's theory of spatial form. Through this conception, I consider the different planes on which space might operate in texts, and how this can generate a composite spatial form which pushes back against Frank's more strictly formalist conception. I then look in detail at how this broader conception of spatial form can be traced in Rose-Innes's short fiction. Analysing three stories – 'Falling', 'Homing', and 'Bad Places' – from her 2010 collection *Homing*, I argue that there is an unresolved tension between the aesthetic demands of the short story's 'spatiality' and the spatially segregated post-apartheid nation. Rose-Innes negotiates spatial anxieties in her short stories through repeated stagings of home-leaving and homecoming, a feature that Susan Lohafer sees as common to much short fiction. Rose-Innes's

---

2 Other names often cited include Diane Awerbuck, Lauren Beukes, K. Sello Duiker, Niq Mhlongo, Phaswane Mpe, and Mary Watson
3 Cecily van Gend, 'Meet Henrietta Rose-Innes', *The Cape Librarian*, 45.2 (2001), 23–24 (p. 23).
4 Michael Barron and Henrietta Rose-Innes, 'One Chip of Colour in a Bigger Mosaic: An Interview with South African Writer Henrietta Rose-Innes', *Culture Trip*, 2017, <https://theculturetrip.com/africa/south-africa/articles/one-chip-of-colour-in-a-bigger-mosaic-an-interview-with-south-african-writer-henrietta-rose-innes/> (accessed 26 October 2022).

stories enact their homecoming through spatial cadences, that is, spatial means of resolving narrative material: a climb up and then down, or a voyage out and back, that provide a spatial closure to essentially psychological subject matter. These cadences come in various forms, but common to them all is what, in musical terms, would be called their 'imperfect' character. These cadences do not resolve fully, and it is this feature that makes them most interesting in offering readers ways of conceiving the social. These imperfect cadences create rich aesthetic experiences, but are also the points at which formal solutions sit in tension with extra-textual spatial inequalities. It is by putting the reader in a position between formal satisfaction and extra-formal dissatisfaction that these stories do their most interesting political work.

Before turning to how Rose-Innes's stories help shape our understanding of these spatial calibrations, it is useful to consider the material and discursive dimensions of space in South Africa. Uneven distribution of land and discriminatory access to space are two of South Africa's most visible markers of societal inequality. As Rita Barnard observes in *Apartheid and Beyond: South African Writers and the Politics of Place*, '[a]partheid [...] clearly represents an extreme [...] instance of the territorialisation of power'.[5] Although the post-apartheid period has brought with it new spatial freedoms, the country's distribution of space is still clearly unequal. By reason of poverty, many continue to live in the areas previously designated to them, and spaces that were once 'landscapes of oppression [...] sites of deprivation' are being transformed into equally exclusionary 'mediascapes of leisure and tourism' – shopping malls, hotels, gated communities, safari parks etc. – as the grip of privatisation tightens.[6] Although since 1994 there have been legal means in place by which land can be regained, actual ownership of the land remains largely unaffected. In 1994 close to 90% of the land was owned by white South Africans, who make up less than 10% of the population. By 2010 under 7% had been redistributed, a rate of change far below even the most conservative estimates.[7] In 2016 parliament passed a bill that would end the 'willing-buyer, willing seller' land reform strategy, giving the government the right to pay an

---

5 Barnard, *Apartheid and Beyond*, p. 5.
6 Ibid., p. 150.
7 Edward Lahiff, 'Q&A: Land Reform in South Africa', *PBS*, 2010, <http://archive.pov.org/promisedland/land-reform-in-south-africa/> (accessed 12 October 2022).

adjudicator value for land, even without the seller's consent. The ANC went even further in 2017 by adopting a resolution to redistribute land without compensation, a movement which was supported by parliament for inclusion in the constitution in 2018. The pace of change remains slow, however, with black South Africans, who make up roughly 80% of the population, owning only 4% of agricultural land.

The built environment also bears the imprint of the country's past: Vladislavić observes that 'the actual physical structures of apartheid South Africa are difficult if not impossible to erase, and [...] we're going to be living within those structures for a very long time'.[8] These structures are physically extended in space, but encode a temporality that spans the gap between past and present. In the previous chapter, I described how the apartheid government's manipulation of public services created a calcified class structure that persisted even after apartheid's end, and the same has been true for city planning and infrastructure. Apartheid's spatial politics are built into these structures, and they continue to strongly shape post-apartheid life.

The apartheid years and the post-apartheid period that has followed have been strongly marked by the distribution of space, and as critics such as Barnard have shown, authors have responded imaginatively to a long history of topographical myths and spatial segregations. Rose-Innes's short fiction presents a particularly interesting recent example of how literature can not only capture something of contemporary spatial experience, but can also to some extent mould our perceptive capacities, and so inflect out experience of the world beyond the text. To better envision the relation of different types of spatiality at work in Rose-Innes's fiction, I now turn to some existing models of how spatiality can be conceived in literature, and how Rose-Innes's works sit in relation to them. I draw on Frank's original concept of 'spatial form', his return to the idea later in his career, and its extension by some of his interlocutors, particularly Roger Shattuck and W.J.T. Mitchell.

For Frank, spatial form is a characteristic of some modernist texts that abandon sequential narrative in favour of a totality formed through an aggregate of parts, and that build meaning through a web of patterned imagery and disjunctive prose.[9] When texts are structured by spatial form, they discourage readers from a diachronic understanding of the text as it

---

8 Vladislavić and Warnes, 'Interview with Ivan Vladislavić', p. 278.
9 Joseph Frank, 'Spatial Form in Modern Literature: An Essay in Three Parts, Part I', *The Sewanee Review*, 53.2 (1945), 221–40.

unfolds in time, and push them towards a synchronic understanding of the work as a simultaneous meaning event, in which self-referentiality, repetition, and other forms of patterning lend coherence and a sense of unity to the work. This can lead to the text seeming decoupled from the temporal world of history, and rather occupying the timeless sphere of myth. Frank's model has consequences for how we think about the act of reading, perhaps most crucially in that it emphasises a retrospective position. While a reader may have various synchronic perceptions while reading a text, it is only when the text has been completed that the spatial form in its entirety can be properly visualised.[10]

Critics have been quick to point out flaws in Frank's model – the spatiality of texts can only be metaphorical; it is not only modernist texts that allow for 'spatial' perceptions, and so on[11] – but these are mostly addressed in Frank's original essays, which neither suggest that our perceptions are literally spatial nor claim a monopoly for modernist texts. More interesting interventions have nuanced Frank's thinking in productive ways. Roger Shattuck, discussing Marcel's Proust's *In Search of Lost Time*, is keen to point out the energising tension between diachronic and synchronic perceptions:

> Far more aptly it [reading the novel] could be represented as a climb to the top of the mountain [...] that allows one's gaze to move at will from feature to feature and to take it in all at once. That view is essentially spatial. But it does not and cannot abolish the climb that took one to the summit, and the temporal order of events in that climb.[12]

If, for Frank, spatial form implies a yearning for an escape from history to myth – not that he thinks texts can ever fully achieve this – Shattuck

---

10 Re-reading is even better: of *Ulysses*, he observes that 'the unified spatial apprehension *cannot* occur on a first reading'. Joseph Frank, 'Spatial Form: An Answer to Critics', *Critical Inquiry*, 4.2 (1977), 231–52 (p. 250).

11 For summaries of these engagements and more, see, for example, Lauriat Lane, 'Spatial Form in Literature: MacLeish's "Einstein"', *ARIEL: A Review of International English Literature*, 15.3 (1984); W.J.T. Mitchell, 'Spatial Form in Literature: Toward a General Theory', *Critical Inquiry*, 6.3 (1980), 539–67; W.J.T. Mitchell, 'Diagrammatology', *Critical Inquiry*, 7.3 (1981), 622–33; Leon Surette, 'Rational Form in Literature', *Critical Inquiry*, 7.3 (1981), 612–21.

12 Roger Shattuck, *Marcel Proust* (Ann Arbor: University of Michigan Press, 1974), p. 116.

emphasises that it is exactly the co-presence of these two perspectives that matters. The two ways of seeing – the climb and the view – are reminders of how texts allow both phenomenological and formalist readings. As will become clear in my analysis of Rose-Innes's work below, her short stories use spatial means to dramatise these twinned perspectives, allowing for a mediation between the diachronic logic of plot development and the synchronic logic of spatial form. To grasp more fully how this works in her stories, Mitchell's extension of Frank's theory offers a useful four-part model that serves as a 'heuristic device for discriminating varieties of spatial form in literature'.[13] Or, perhaps more accurately, he attempts to gain a 'precise understanding of the ways in which spatiality occurs' in literature.[14] The distinction is important, as Mitchell's idea of 'spatiality' is much broader than Frank's idea of spatial form.

The four levels of spatiality that Mitchell outlines are: 1) the physical space of the text on the page; 2) the spatial configuration of the world of the text; 3) the spatial conception we have of a text's temporal movement; and 4) a spatial 'apprehension of the work as a system for generating meanings', or a map of the possible hypotheses for the structures of meaning a text might contain.[15] The first, the physical space of the text, is most pertinent to my discussion of Vladislavić's work in Chapter 2, in which illustrations, photographs, experimental textual effects, and the materiality of the magazine or book turn the physical text into a space to be traversed. It appears also in Nadine Gordimer's and Zoë Wicomb's eschewal of indented dialogue and Phaswane Mpe's juxtaposition of poetry and prose. In my readings of Rose-Innes's stories, however, it is particularly the last three levels that will be important. The second type, the 'spatial configuration of the world of the text', means our mental construction of a spatial world that comes about through our reading, for example, the geography of Milton in Elizabeth Gaskell's *North and South*, or the layout of the court in Franz Kafka's *The Trial*. As my examples suggest, this 'configuration' can be presented as 'stable, solid, and reassuring', but can as easily be 'metamorphic, irrational, heterogeneous, fragmentary', and can even be 'enveloped in temporality'.[16] This last point, that the relationship between space and time is often one of 'complex interaction, interdependence, and interpenetration', has

13 Mitchell, 'Spatial Form in Literature', p. 550.
14 Ibid., p. 547.
15 Ibid., pp. 550–54.
16 Ibid., p. 551.

particular bearing on Rose-Innes's short stories, in which place, time, form, and experience are tightly bound.[17] The third level becomes more abstract yet: for Mitchell, we become aware of the third level '[a]ny time we feel that we have discovered the principle which governs the order or sequence of presentation in a text [...] any time we sense a "map" or outline of our temporal movement through the text'.[18] Here I take him to mean that as we read, we sustain a mental image of both *fabula* and *syuzhet*. The fourth and final level is perhaps closest to Frank's model, but differs from it in one important way. Mitchell explains this level by analogy with the experience of seeing, in the sense of seeing what something or someone means, a flash that allows us suddenly to see an image of what a text could mean. This is distinct from saying a text has a singular 'meaning'; rather than seeing '*the* whole *of* it' we see '*a* whole *in* it'.[19]

In an important departure from Frank's theory, this spatial perception does not depend on having finished the work – it rather develops as we read and is revised as we go. Further, it is not, as form is sometimes conceived, static or permanent: a vision of the whole may be ephemeral, subject to revision over time and with rereading, or be best considered one of many 'falsifiable hypotheses to test against the order of textual particulars'.[20] As is my contention for how form works as an interlocutor to thought, the model we have developed of a work at any point will influence our understanding of what comes next, and so must be conceived of as an iterative process rather than the perception of a pre-existing absolute. If Frankian spatial form, to borrow Shattock's metaphor, favours the view from the summit, Mitchell's model overlays that perspective with the shifting landscape revealed by the climb, with the interaction between the two creating an evolving matrix of meaning events that never settle into a definitive structure.[21]

This debate already provides a rich framing for Rose-Innes's short fiction, in which different forms of spatialisation combine in the production of meaning events, and offers a starting point for understanding how her writing articulates with the social. However,

17 Ibid., p. 544.
18 Ibid., p. 552.
19 Ibid., p. 554.
20 Ibid., p. 554.
21 I use the term 'meaning' here guardedly, but can find no better alternative for the different kinds of sense – propositional, affective, ethical, and so on – that a work might generate.

while Frank and Mitchell focus their enquiries on the formal properties of texts, here understood as bracketed off from extra-textual reality, I am interested in how these formal features articulate with the world outside the text, and how these aspects might illuminate one another. In order to do this, it is helpful to introduce one more kind of space into the models outlined so far, namely the external world to which Rose-Innes's texts, with varying degrees of fidelity, refer. She has spent most of her life in Cape Town, and many of the stories in *Homing* are set in or around some version of the city, bringing a legacy of spatial relations that surfaces at different points. Of course, this setting does not determine the meaning of the stories – the stories happen in Cape Town in a limited sense only and the importance we might attribute to this may vary – but for an analysis concerned with how reading short fiction might articulate with the social, it is an important factor. The perceptual tools offered by the stories I analyse below are most fully realised by understanding Frankian spatial form as operating in counterpoint with Mitchell's expanded idea of spatiality, and with the spaces and places in the world to which Rose-Innes's texts refer.

The interest in bringing the short story into dialogue with spatial form lies in the form's shortness combined with its generic tendency towards creating meaning through patterning, which together cause a strong impulse towards grasping the story as a whole. Short stories are frequently singled out in criticism for their tendency towards such formal 'spatiality': Nadine Gordimer says a short story is like 'an egg; it's all there'; A.L. Kennedy says writing a short story is like 'casting a bell'.[22] Rose-Innes speaks of her own stories in similar terms. She says that in contrast with the 'sprawling material of the life-size novel', she has 'an intuitive sense of the whole shape of a short story, indeed an aerial view; something I can take in at a glance'.[23] She further notes that her way of perceiving the world, and her writing process, are similar to the concept of spatial form. She apprehends the world 'in

---

22 Nancy Topping Bazin and Marilyn Dallman Seymour (eds), *Conversations with Nadine Gordimer* (Jackson, MS: University Press of Mississippi, 1990), p. 287; A.L. Kennedy, '"Small in a Way That a Bullet is Small": Reflections on Writing Short Stories', in *The Short Story*, ed. Ailsa Cox (Newcastle: Cambridge Scholars Publishing, 2008), pp. 1–10 (p. 4).

23 Henrietta Rose-Innes and Graham K. Riach, '"Concrete Fragments": An Interview with Henrietta Rose-Innes', *The Journal of Commonwealth Literature*, 55.1 (2020), 111–20 (p. 115).

concrete fragments, singular images and intuitive flashes, rather than in terms of an overarching narrative',[24] and describes her 'labour' as 'finding a narrative to link and explicate these images, rather than creating images to illustrate a story I consciously needed to tell'.[25] The primary vector of sense making here, like Gordimer's 'flash of fireflies', is the sudden vivid image rather than development in time. However, the stories I analyse here do not abandon narrative altogether, and are not spatial in quite the same mode as the modernist works that Frank discusses. Rose-Innes describes her short fiction as 'writing where plot is not the strong driver', but plot plays a role nevertheless.[26] This dual perspective, of paradigmatic wholeness and syntagmatic development, makes Rose-Innes's short fiction a particularly interesting case study for deepening our understanding of spatial form, and of the role genre might play in that understanding.

One of the key spatial dynamics in Rose-Innes's short fiction, and one that brings it into dialogue with broader generic traits of the short story, is her repeated staging of homecomings and home-leavings. Lohafer proposes that these tropes are part of the mythic substructure of short narratives, and can appear as literal journeys out and back, but can also come about metaphorically, for example through a character moving from a place of psychological safety into danger and back again. For Lohafer, such tropes recur in short narratives because they 'rest on a very fundamental binary human experience of security and insecurity [...] As a metaphor for this primal, binary relationship to the world, homecoming and home-leaving [...] combines both the spatial and linear elements.'[27] When Lohafer describes 'the spatial and linear' elements, she is referring to the tension between fiction's 'spatial', paradigmatic aspect and its syntagmatic, 'linear' narrative progression. To her mind, figures of homecoming and home-leaving fulfil the demands of both linearity and spatiality, in that they provide plot movement by allowing a narrative progression from one space to another, while establishing a structural binary between safety and

---

24 Ibid., p. 113.
25 Henrietta Rose-Innes, 'Sea Creatures of the Southern Deep: A Novel' (unpublished MA thesis, University of Cape Town, 1999), p. xi, OpenUCT <http://hdl.handle.net/11427/19135> (accessed 3 May 2023).
26 Rose-Innes and Riach, '"Concrete Fragments"', p. 116.
27 Michael Trussler, 'The Short Story Today: An Interview with Susan Lohafer and Charles E. May', *Wascana Review*, 33.1 (1998), 14–24 (p. 20).

danger. In Rose-Innes's stories, this trope often appears as a literal movement out and back, up and down, that takes on the character of a recurring Freudian *fort-da*, moving from safety to danger and back, or from a position of comfort to discomfort and then returning.[28] These symbolic endings do not provide some all-encompassing resolution, but rather offer a spatially executed symbol of closure that ambiguously resolves narrative or psychological material.

The deep-rooted dynamics between safety and threat in Lohafer's model take on a particular urgency in the South African literary imaginary, in which a discursive history of writing about the land has been shaped by, although never identical with, conflicts over the land. As Malvern van Wyk Smith observes,

> [j]ust as the history of South Africa essentially becomes the history of the struggle for the land and its resources, so its serious literature would turn out to be a record of the mythology developed by its people to justify or resist that process. Thus every subject treated [...] has turned out to be another act, another aspect, of an endless drama of domicile and challenge.[29]

This 'endless drama' that van Wyk Smith outlines has been described by Michael Chapman as 'key to understanding what it means to live and write as a South African'.[30] On the one hand, South African writers enter into a discursive history of the land as it has been formed in the South African literary imaginary. On the other, representations of space and place in South African fiction come loaded with an unwieldy historical cargo, and so to read them in purely discursive terms would be to ignore an important material dimension. This is an irresolvable but animating tension, and one that Rose-Innes's short works allow readers to think through. In staging narratives of homecoming and

---

28 Sigmund Freud, 'Beyond the Pleasure Principle', in *The Complete Psychological Works of Sigmund Freud*, ed. and trans. James Strachey (London: Hogarth, 1920), XVIII, pp. 7–23.
29 Malvern van Wyk Smith, *Grounds of Contest: A Survey of South African English Literature* (Wynberg: Rustica, 1990). Cited in James Graham, *Land and Nationalism in Fictions from Southern Africa* (Abingdon: Routledge, 2009), p. 6.
30 Michael Titlestad, 'Afterword', in *The Mistress's Dog: Short Stories 1996–2010* (Johannesburg: Picador Africa, 2010), pp. 183–93 (p. 191).

home-leaving – 'domicile and challenge' in van Wyk Smith's words – and making use of multiple forms of spatiality, they offer readers ways of perceiving the social, but are irreducible to that role only. The formal features of Rose-Innes's stories offer experiences of pleasure, displeasure, and a wide range of other affective responses, and these are not simply epiphenomenal or propaedeutic to politically motivated analysis. However, to understand her stories as fully as possible, these formal features and the responses they allow should be understood in how they inflect a socially oriented reading. One form of reading does not trump the other – whatever understanding of the social we bring to our reading experience also affects our experience of formal features – but rather they reciprocally shape one another, without ever settling into a final meaning of the text. Questions of social forms might be raised in the forms of artworks, and the modest scope of the short story can provide a fisheye lens through which to view those social contradictions, or perhaps a macro lens that clarifies our perception, but from an estranging and restricted perspective. These visualisations are experienced in tandem with the affective charge of experiencing literary form, which can intensify, reconfigure, or contradict those speculative acts.

The formal trope that binds together these different strands in Rose-Innes's fiction is her technique of 'expressing human story arcs in terms of architecture and geography', and particularly her use of these features to end her stories.[31] When planning her novel *Green Lion*, she decided it would

> involve somebody going to the top of the mountain and then coming back down, and that would be the entire plot arc: simple. Well, of course it didn't turn out simple at all, but it still has that movement at its heart.[32]

Many of Rose-Innes's short stories are structured around such spatial displacements, and 'Falling', 'Homing', and 'Bad Places' offer three key

31 Henrietta Rose-Innes and Graham K. Riach, unpublished interview, 2013.
32 Henrietta Rose-Innes and Katie Reid, 'Q&A: Henrietta Rose-Innes – "New Voices from South Africa" at the Edinburgh International Book Festival', *Africa in Words*, 2013, <http://africainwords.com/2013/08/23/qa-henrietta-rose-innes-new-voices-from-south-africa-at-the-edinburgh-international-book-festival/> (accessed 30 November 2021).

examples. While they present different sorts of complexity, particularly those that come about through the interaction of multiple forms of spatiality, the movements at their cores remain relatively simple. 'Falling' describes a binary movement of home-leaving and homecoming: a climb up, and a climb down. Protagonist Victor's ascent prompts a series of realisations that allow him a new perspective, and an encounter that he has on his way back down triggers a psychological change that is represented in spatial terms. By setting this story at a shopping mall, Rose-Innes charges the story with a socio-economic voltage that its imperfect spatial cadence does not dissipate. 'Homing' combines vertical and horizontal movement to tease out the spatial politics of economic disparity, when a luxury hotel is built on previously public land. The perimeter wall around the hotel prompts feelings of envy and desire in protagonist Nona, which are shown to be ill-founded when she tries crossing over to the other side. The story's spatially executed closure, as Nona returns to her own side of the wall, provides an aesthetic resolution that sits in oblique relation to the social forces the story describes. 'Bad Places', for its part, is structured horizontally, and concerns a journey out across a beach, an intervening period spent in a liminal space, and then a journey back. This plot of adventure, transformation, and return is a staple of folk tale and myth, but the setting of 'Bad Places' on the beach resists the dehistoricisation typical of these genres. The imperfect spatial cadence that closes the story is neither an example of what Fredric Jameson calls 'formal "solutions" to unresolvable social contradictions', nor does it work by a purely formal logic, but it rather offers the reader a way to think through how the formal and the social might intersect.[33]

Rose-Innes uses these spatial plot arcs to explore how her characters' surroundings overlap with their inner landscapes. As Devi Sarinjeive observes of Rose-Innes's first book, *Shark's Egg*, 'the main character's inner being, inscapes as it were, [are] reflected in a way in the landscapes'.[34] Using space and place to depict human states may not seem particularly innovative at first glance – setting functioning as a projection of inner feelings is a staple of realist fiction – but Rose-Innes is doing something more here. Not only do landscapes and built environments serve as projections of inner states, but these exterior

---

33 Jameson, *The Political Unconscious*, p. 79.
34 Devi Sarinjeive, 'Book Review', *English Academy Review*, 18.1 (2001), 166–72 (p. 166).

features are also reflected in the characters that people them. People and places shape one another, and Rose-Innes is particularly 'interested in the intimate ways in which the changing city alters, and is altered by, its inhabitants'.[35] As Barnard argues is the case in Gordimer's writing, Rose-Innes's places are 'not just metaphorically expressive [...] but are also [...] ideologically productive: the ordinary enclosures in which we live shape, as much as they represent, dominant social relations'.[36] These stories, then, participate in a tradition in the liberal South African short story, in which 'setting [...] [functions] as an agent in the production of character and plot'.[37] The physical spaces in which actions take place both determine and express what happens in them. The three spaces I look at – the mall, the luxury hotel, and the beach – all bring with them norms of behaviour as much as they serve as indices of inner states, and these resonate and clash with the stories' formal and symbolic logics. To take this one step further, as people are shaped by the structures they inhabit, so are we shaped by the structures that come to inhabit us through reading. Our ways of thinking are altered by the texts we read, and Rose-Innes's spatial imagination invites us to deepen our understanding of the social through the aesthetic affordances of short narrative forms.

Before turning to an analysis of the three stories, it is worth registering an important aspect of Rose-Innes's practice as a writer. She is a meticulous reworker of her stories; in her words, she 'won't let go of the text, right up until [her] fingers are being nipped by the actual rollers of the printing press'.[38] Editor Helen Moffett describes Rose-Innes as 'the best rewriter of fiction in this country', noting that her self-editing proceeds in 'cuts and cuts – not in great swathes, but in nibbling increments'.[39] Such piecemeal changes, however, can

---

35 Henrietta Rose-Innes and Diane Awerbuck, 'Interview: Henrietta Rose-Innes', *Times Live*, 29 August 2010, <http://www.timeslive.co.za/lifestyle/books/article626233.ece/Henrietta-Rose-Innes> (accessed 30 November 2013).
36 Barnard, *Apartheid and Beyond*, p. 44.
37 Driver, 'The Fabulous Fifties', p. 391. A typical example of this would be the 'Jim comes to Jo'burg' story, in which the city has a poisonous effect on a character newly arrived from the countryside.
38 Henrietta Rose-Innes and Michelle McGrane, 'Michelle McGrane in Conversation with Henrietta Rose-Innes', *LitNet*, 2006, <http://www.oulitnet.co.za/nosecret/henrietta_rose_innes.asp> (accessed 10 December 2022).
39 Helen Moffett, 'Henrietta Rose-Innes's *Homing*: A Review that's also about Editing', *Books LIVE*, 2010, <http://helenmoffett.bookslive.co.za/

dramatically alter a short story, and reworked passages reveal points of hesitation or fracture in an author's creative process. When these changes are significant or revealing I signal them in the footnotes.

'Falling': The Mall and the Meeting

The central movement of 'Falling', like the up-and-down movement that structures *Green Lion*, is relatively simple.[40] Victor, a young man, climbs to the top of the glass dome of a shopping mall, from where he looks down into the space below. Doing so triggers a traumatic childhood memory of being at the mall during its construction with his architect father, when he accidentally kicked a brick down an exposed shaft and may have hit a black site worker on a lower floor. Back in the present, a security guard in the mall spots Victor and climbs the dome to bring him down, but he begins to feel dizzy, so Victor helps him down. Victor and the guard walk towards the exit, but at some point the guard is left behind and Victor walks out of the mall alone. However, describing the plot in this linear manner misses the more interesting ways in which 'Falling' operates. The story jumps back and forth between past and present, while weaving a tightly patterned web of imagery. This encourages a reading sensitive to the workings of spatial form, in which significance is generated through different means from narrative progression. There is a constant pull in the story between the diachronic unfolding plot and the synchronic forms of meaning generated by spatial form – the climb and the view in Shattuck's terms – and the extra-textual world to which the story refers.

The dynamic between these perspectives is established from the story's opening paragraph. 'Falling' opens with Victor high above the ground:

> Victor selects a square of glass and touches it with his palms. He's very high up: from where he stands, he can see the whole long flank

---

blog/2010/09/17/henrietta-rose-inness-homing-a-review-thats-also-about-editing/> (accessed 12 October 2022).

40 'Falling' was first published in *Willesden Herald: New Short Stories 4*, and there are some important differences between the two printings. Henrietta Rose-Innes, 'Falling', in *Willesden Herald: New Short Stories 4*, ed. Stephen Moran (London: Pretend Genius, 2010), pp. 211–22.

of the mountain and, on the other side, the Cape Town suburbs fanning out to the sea. At his feet is a stained concrete surface never meant to be seen, and before him rises a shining dome, three times his height. It reflects the soft pink sunrise and his own lean figure. His face is severe, deeply lined for a man still in his thirties, and determined. Only Victor himself can see something daunted in the eyes.[41]

The location is quickly established as Cape Town, and its depiction in the nervy suspension of the present tense establishes a troubled relationship with place that runs through the story. The protagonist's name implies a sense of dominance, and his elevation seems to put him in what Mary Louise Pratt calls the 'monarch-of-all-I-survey' position, in which a traveller surveys the land from altitude and so lays claim to it.[42] Pratt pinpoints the 'standard elements' of this trope as being 'mastery of the landscape [...] estheticizing adjectives [and a] broad panorama anchored in the seer'.[43] While Victor's view from on high opens the possibility for such a visual appropriation of the land around him, this is troubled by the story's title. If this is a story about falling, height signals danger, not power.

The precarity of Victor's position is further brought out by the unusual presentation of his surroundings. Rather than describing a scene 'anchored in the seer' that then extends outwards, with Victor as the phenomenological subject intuiting his environs and rendering them intelligible, this description of landscape contracts towards the eye, or 'I', of the seer. It begins in the distance with the mountain, sea, and suburbs, before sharply drawing in to the 'stained concrete' under Victor's feet, and then panning up to a 'shining dome, three times his height', with the unit of measurement emphasising his smallness before it. The 'soft pink sunrise' and 'long flank of the mountain' connote a feminised corporeal generosity in the landscape that risks slipping into colonial tropes of fecundity and virgin land, but Victor's 'lean figure'

---

41 Henrietta Rose-Innes, 'Falling', in *Homing* (Cape Town: Umuzi, 2010), pp. 87–98 (p. 74). All further references to this work are given parenthetically in the text until the end of this section.
42 Mary Louise Pratt, *Imperial Eyes: Travel Writing and Transculturation* (London: Routledge, 1992), p. 201.
43 Ibid., p. 209.

stands ill at ease in it.⁴⁴ The view is then restricted to Victor's 'deeply lined' face, before a further cinematic crop shows only his eyes. Pratt's book might be titled *Imperial Eyes*, but Victor's eyes are 'daunted', with the 'monarch-of-all-I-survey' perspective unavailable to him.⁴⁵

As Victor begins to climb the dome, multiple layers accrete onto the physical space he occupies. The beams, which from 'street level [...] seem[ed] as delicate as lines of latitude and longitude on a model globe', now reveal gaps 'wide enough to admit fingers' (87). The world is, in effect, reduced to a scale on which the 'daunted' Victor can once more gain purchase, and so his climb represents both a physical displacement and a testing of psychological limits.⁴⁶ In Lohafer's terms, this act of 'home-leaving' provides both narrative movement and psychological significance, and sets the stage for a transformative experience and final return. The 'gradient eases out to almost horizontal' (87) and Victor lies face down against the glass. Victor's climb is not, however, reducible to either a convenience of plot or a psychological projection of his 'inscape'.⁴⁷ As the clock turns nine, the 'interior lights snap on' (87) in a harsh parody of the sun's soft rise, and the building is revealed as a mall.

---

44 In the *Willesden Herald* printing of this story, the links between the eye and the landscape are more explicit – in this opening paragraph, 'The only light is pink sunrise, reflecting into his eyes'. Rose-Innes, 'Falling', p. 211.

45 The line 'His face is severe, deeply lined for a man still in his thirties, and determined' reads in the earlier printing: 'He's in his mid-thirties, a strong man.' Replacing 'strong' with 'determined' changes his characterisation by emphasising purpose over ability, and de-emphasising a gendered relationship to space. Although this is not my focus here, Rose-Innes's disruptions of gender norms are consistently intriguing.

46 In the earlier printing, this sentence read 'From street level, these lines of latitude and longitude seem delicate as ruled pencil marks, but up close each is as wide as a strong man's wrist' (211). The insertion of 'on a model globe' in *Homing* adds to the patterning of geographical imagery in the story, and draws attention to a recurring trope of miniaturisation in Rose-Innes's fiction. This perspectival telescoping recurs across the whole collection, in stories such as 'Bad Places', 'Homing', 'The Boulder', and 'Burning Buildings', but also in Rose-Innes's other books *Shark's Egg*, *The Rock Alphabet*, and *Nineveh*. Rose-Innes describes her 'fascination of miniaturization and miniature landscapes' as stemming from 'a fear of the real full-sized world', and from a 'desire for control [...] A desire to make [the world] small and close'. Rose-Innes and Riach, unpublished interview, p. 115.

47 Sarinjeive, 'Book Review', p. 166.

The mall in South Africa is a contradictory space: in a city such as Cape Town, which is short on public space, the mall perhaps comes closest to serving this function, in that it is one of the few spaces in which strangers mingle. However, it differs greatly from actual public space, most obviously in that it is private, and is policed by security guards who restrict access to it. Both its securitisation and its role in facilitating consumerism determine the kind of behaviour the mall allows, and control who is welcome to access it. The mall's exclusionary politics are effectively conducted on the grounds of class, and as I argue in relation to Wicomb's work, in South Africa this distinction is unavoidably racialised. The use of space in the story is then physical, psychological, and socio-economic, and these three strata interpenetrate one another. While the theorisations of spatiality offered by Frank, Mitchell, and Lohafer go a certain way in thinking through Rose-Innes's short stories, it is when these are read alongside the material world outside the text that the full import of their spatiality can be understood.

When Victor reaches the top, his elevated position offers less stability than he might have hoped for. Looking down into the mall, the trajectory of his perception moves in the reverse direction to the story's opening, his gaze shifting 'in increments from near to far' (88) as the mall's interior is revealed to him. Although this movement might suggest a recentring of the subject, this is quickly undermined as Victor looks down, imagining the dome below him giving way:

> a soft, percussive popping as glass and metal shifted, trying to adjust to a balance of forces fatally skewed [...] each failure in the structure triggering the next until tiny cracks infested the dome.
> And then the collapse; and a million fragments debouching into the waiting vault, losing their brilliance all at once, like a swarm of bees dropping from sunlight into shadow. (88)

Given the layered meaning of the space he occupies, his anxiety might then be thought to stem at once from his physical position, high above the ground, his apprehensive psychological state, and as the economic vocabulary – 'vault', 'forces fatally skewed', 'failure in the structure'[48] – suggests, from an economic position. Shane Graham identifies such 'distrust of the solidity of built environments' as a recurring trope

---

48 This economic lexis is more emphasised in the earlier printing, in which 'gems' (213) stands in place of 'fragments'.

of South African 'post-millennial anxiety'.⁴⁹ His diagnosis of this phenomenon is socio-economic, citing narratives that 'strip away the surface layers' to 'deconstruct the urban spaces that are [late capitalism's] primary vector for propagation'.⁵⁰ This is certainly true for 'Falling', but it must be supplemented by a psychological stripping back, when it transpires that Victor's fear is a 'specific and unique' one from his childhood, a 'heavier dread' that is attached to a fear of falling 'like an anchor at the end of a weed-slimed chain' (89), and that demands the plumbing of his past to bring it back to the surface.⁵¹ As Victor's gaze penetrates further into the mall, it is accompanied by a backwards movement in time, as we see Victor at ten years old, visiting the mall's construction site with his father, the building's architect.

This analepsis disturbs the linear progression of the story, with a temporal telescoping into the past that tracks the spatial extension of Victor's gaze down into the mall. The non-linearity of the plot draws attention to the story's 'spatial form', in that, as John Gerlach argues, '[w]hen there is a significant [...] disjunction between the chronological sequence of events and the actual telling [...] emplotment generates a more paradigmatic perception'.⁵² The story's chronology begins to make different demands on the reader from those of linear narratives, asking them to perceive meaning in patterning and in the juxtaposition of temporally distinct events. Spatial form attempts, in William Holtz's words, to 'negate the temporal principle inherent in language and to force the apprehension of [the] work as a total "thing" in a moment of time rather than as a sequence of things', but in Rose-Innes's short stories, this movement towards spatial form is resisted by the press of narrative development and worldly causality.⁵³ The depiction of physical space, which in this story bears psychological and socio-economic weight, is overlaid with the demands of spatial form, meaning that the text is

---

49 Shane Graham, 'The Entropy of Built Things: Postapartheid Anxiety and the Production of Space in Henrietta Rose-Innes' *Nineveh* and Lauren Beukes' *Zoo City*', *Safundi*, 16.1 (2015), 64–77 (p. 64).
50 Ibid., p. 67.
51 This section was added in the *Homing* version, suggesting that Rose-Innes felt the link between memory and place was insufficiently developed in the earlier version.
52 Gerlach, 'Narrative, Lyric and Plot', p. 50.
53 William Holtz, 'Spatial Form in Modern Literature: A Reconsideration', *Critical Inquiry*, 4.2 (1977), 271–83 (p. 273).

experienced as pulling towards both a temporally experienced chain of narrative development and as a single synchronous structure.

This tension becomes more intense as Victor wanders away from his father, and in a structural echo of the story's opening, moves to a spot where he can look down into the site's central shaft, the area that will eventually become the space under the dome. The doubling of present and past scenes of downward viewing brings these distinct moments symbolically together – we move from 'climb' to 'view' – and the patterning across the story of looking below the surface creates a seam of imagery suggesting the excavatory retrieval of the repressed.[54] Victor watches two labourers at work, 'engaged in a vertical dance' (91), as one throws bricks upwards into another's waiting hands. They are at first described in entirely bodily terms, as 'sinews pull in the man's arm, the pads of muscle in his dark chest shifting', and their movements are mechanical: 'Tireless: bend, hoist, release... [...] They were pushing, parts of a machine worked past its limits, strained to breaking' (91). It is only when Victor thinks his eyes have met those of the worker that he 'looked away, strangely shamed' (91).[55] It is only in this moment of human contact that the depersonalising effect of the place, and the societal structure that produces it, is stripped away.

The tension between the different forms of spatialisation reaches its climax as the action shifts back to the young Victor, 'caught in the rhythm of the brick dance' (92). He does not notice his foot catch a loose half-brick sitting on the edge of the shaft above which he sits. The passage that describes this scene is remarkable first for the shocking event it describes, and secondly for the way in which that event is represented, a lyric intensification that seems to halt narrative time:

> He only saw it hanging mid-air – a cartoon brick – before it was plucked down straight, as if pulled on a string. A line in a drawing, connecting the tip of his running shoe to the forehead of the man at the bottom. That face far below, turned up to meet the blow.

---

[54] This is another trope that Graham identifies as recurrent across post-apartheid literature. See Shane Graham, *South African Literature after the Truth Commission: Mapping Loss* (Basingstoke: Palgrave Macmillan, 2009), pp. 135–78.

[55] In the earlier printing, Victor is here described as 'shamefully small and pale' (215), emphasising racial over socio-economic difference.

One quick step backwards, and the scene was concealed, the men erased, as if they'd never been. If there was a cry, it was lost in the noise of construction. (92)

This passage is highly worked: the odd syntax of 'plucked down straight' creates three consecutive stressed syllables that whisk the brick down; 'That face far below, turned up to meet the blow' sets up a disturbing contrast between the jingling rhythm, alliteration and rhyme, and the violence of the scene.[56] This leads into the chiasmic verse-like patterning of '[o]ne quick step backwards, and the scene was concealed, the men erased, as if they'd never been'. The assonant 'e' sounds of 'concealed' and 'been' rhyme with 'scene', emphasising the theatrical closure of the sentence as the men are made to disappear from view. These effects add to the emotional intensity of the scene, but also raise the question of whether the man's cry, lost in the bustle of the building site, might also be 'lost in the noise of [literary] construction', with the representation of actual physical harm sublated into well-crafted lyric intensity. While on the one hand the temporal suspension that comes about through this intensification focuses the scene, and provokes a strong affective response, it also prompts a shift in attention from the content of what is described to the means of its description. The balance of the text swings at this point from space *in* the story, the mall's building site, to the space *of* the story, its network of formal relations. And yet it is at the very moment of the brick's drop that the story's depiction of societal inequality is at its most urgent and vivid. Rose-Innes puts the reader in an impossible position, torn between the pleasure of the text and the shock of the world.

It is clear that Victor's childhood experience affected him deeply. He runs to his father, saying nothing of what happened. As the two descend the spiral parking ramp together, Victor wets himself, and 'all the way down, [he] did not turn to look back, nor did he release his father's hand' (93).[57] Victor's childhood encounter with the worker finds

---

56 The *Willesden Herald* version has: 'The last thing Victor saw before he ducked back was that face far below, turned up to meet the blow' (216). This reworking suggests that the rhythm was important here. Similarly, in the earlier version, 'they'd never been' read 'they had never been'. By removing the extra syllable, the rhythm becomes almost iambic, suggesting that Rose-Innes reworked this passage with its metre in mind.

57 In the *Willesden Herald* edition this reads 'All the way down, Victor did not release his father's hand' (217). The addition of Victor not looking back in

a structural parallel in the story's present, when a security guard spots Victor from inside the mall, and makes his way up to where he lies. The guard looks down through the glass dome, and his 'body stiffen[s]' (96). Victor 'sees something enter him, some kind of crushing weight [...] as if his personal gravity has just increased fourfold' (96). Victor helps the guard down, placing his trembling feet one by one in the gaps between the glass panes, and supporting him as they walk. This tender act in some sense offers a symbolic repentance for the wrongs he may have committed in the past. Victor holds the guard's hand as they make their way down the spiral ramp to the parking garage below, and the further down they go, the less tightly the guard holds Victor's hand, until finally he lets go. In contrast with the previous descent, however, this time Victor looks back to check the guard is still there, resisting the urge to turn away.

As the story ends, Victor has climbed down from the glass dome and is making his way out of the mall's parking lot. This presents the reader with a spatial cadence that offers some formal satisfaction – what went up has come down – but this is troubled by the story's closing lines. At the bottom of the ramp Victor and the guard have one last exchange, and then

> [Victor] turns and goes on through the dark of the parking garage, heading for its mouth. His walk is steady. As he exits past the ticket machines and into the sunlight and the air, he feels something shatter, some shell as light and transparent as blown glass. And then he is through. (98)

This spatially enacted epiphanic closure has Victor walking out of the mall a changed man. It creates an aesthetically satisfying final cadence to the story, as verticality shifts to horizontality, and constriction dilates. If Victor's ascent of the mall is to be understood as a psychological exploration of unfamiliar territory, a testing of the self, then his antithetical descent suggests homecoming and the recentring of the subject. However, this moment is troubled, first by the multivalent image of a shattering shell of glass, and secondly by the exclusionary nature of the spatial closure. Glass becomes increasingly overdetermined as the story progresses, becoming associated with reflection, vision, separation,

---

Homing thickens the story's patterning of visual imagery, and constitutes a foreshadowing of the story's final scene.

6. Statue of a miner at the Clocktower Mall, Cape Town, author's photograph.

danger, and, here, the sloughing of a past self. Taken together, these factors generate some ungraspable meaning that exceeds the sum of its parts, providing what Mitchell calls a 'system for generating meanings', in which the physical properties of glass and the psychological dynamics of the story refract one another.

This formal spatiality is usefully read, however, in counterpoint with the spatial divisions that the story describes. While Victor may walk into the light in a moment of self-liberating and ephemeral epiphany, the black security guard is left inside. While it is well and good for Victor to come away from his encounter changed, as Benita Parry has argued in discussing the Truth and Reconciliation Commission, it is difficult to see how the 'demands of reconciliation can be met without a radical restructuring of those economic, social, political and cultural circumstances which would render the wrongs of the past as properly transcended, thus enabling new modes of consciousness, new psychic dispositions to grow'.[58] Victor leaves the guard behind, and the structural inequality that first caused his unease remains in place. Victor's gesture of turning away is performed structurally by the story, as the narrative turns away from the security guard, making him effectively disappear from view.

These exclusionary spatial politics take on an added resonance in that the fictional mall that Rose-Innes describes in 'Falling' shares many characteristics with an actual mall: the Clocktower Shopping Centre at the V&A Waterfront in Cape Town. Both have a glass dome with a concrete lip, both have a compass rose on the floor, and the Clocktower Centre boasts a statue that could have inspired the 'vertical dance' of the labourers that Rose-Innes describes, in which 'sinews pull in the man's arm, the pads of muscle in his dark chest shifting' (91) (fig. 6). The statue in the mall is of a miner, while Rose-Innes's character is a construction site labourer, but the similarity is nevertheless striking. If Rose-Innes's mall is, in some sense, the Clocktower Centre – of course it is never identical with it – it also sits on the site of the Chavonnes Battery, one of the oldest European structures in the country, dating from the early 1700s, and cemented with a mixture made by burning sea-shells on Robben Island. As Victor leaves the car park at the story's close, he would arrive on Fish Quay, where tourists wait to be ferried to see Nelson Mandela's former cell. It is, then, a fitting site to show the stubbornness of spatial politics, and the tenacity of their historical roots.

The links between the battery, site of early settlement, the prison island, epitome of spatialised exclusion, and the shopping centre, the post-apartheid manifestation of spatial segregation, are already striking, but there is more. Jewellery designer Charmaine Taylor has transformed the wire fence that once surrounded the prison on Robben Island into pieces of bespoke jewellery that are sold in the mall. Pieces such as the 'Justice Cuff' and 'Liberty Bangle' are made from chopped-up sections of the fence, which are coated in gold or silver and turned into necklaces and bracelets that sell for up to R9,300 (£475).[59] The physical fence that demarcated apartheid spatiality has been removed, but its transformation

---

[58] Benita Parry, *Postcolonial Studies: A Materialist Critique* (London: Routledge, 2004), p. 183.

[59] Charmaine Taylor, 'Robben Island Jewellery – Legacy Collection by Charmaine Taylor', *Legacy Collection*, 2022, <https://legacycollection.org/?c=a3368f18ef71> (accessed 17 September 2022).

into luxury jewellery on sale in a securitised mall is a telling symbol of how apartheid-era spatial politics continue to be reproduced in the decades that have followed. Depending on one's attitude towards Taylor's project, it could be understood as an opportunistic seizure of part of South Africa's history, which aestheticises and commodifies past suffering for a wealthy audience. A more sympathetic reading would see it as an initiative that salvaged the fence – an important part of South Africa's history that was bound for landfill – and converted it into pieces of art. In the process, 10% of all sales are donated to sustainable development projects such as Abalimi Bezekhaya (The Planters) and Harvest of Hope.

How, then, might we read the spatial resolution of the story and the unresolved spatial fractures of Cape Town together? One solution, following Jameson, would be to read this spatial closure as an ideological act which offers 'imaginary or formal "solutions" to unresolvable social contradictions'.[60] In this model, it is the critic's role to reveal the social reality that form has displaced through its spatialising, mythicising tendency. To the extent that the analysis of formal features can focalise one's perspective on a societal complex, this is a useful exercise; while a symptomatic reading of this kind may not explain away the text, by thinking through an experience of form, a reader can clarify their existing thoughts, much as a lens might focus a ray of light. What this approach accounts for less well is how the reader might be transformed by reading, through the 'climb' as the text unfolds, the 'view' as we reach the end, and what these together might allow them to know. On the one hand, this knowledge might be of art: in the compact form of the short story, 'Falling' offers us a vivid experience of being pulled between narrative flow and its precipitation into meaning. The spatialising tendency of the short story sensitises us to this phenomenon and offers it up in a way that differs from both the intense moment of lyric poetry and the extended, though often interrupted, duration of novel reading. We might also consider how 'Falling' offers a way of understanding with purchase outside the sphere of art, in that it combines the synthetic perspective of structure with the processual perspective of change, and moreover, shows these forces as being mutually influencing and each subject to revision. It would be reductive to describe 'Falling' as an allegory of the social, or to say that its forms are strongly determined by social forces. However, by presenting us

60 Jameson, *The Political Unconscious*, p. 79.

with an arrangement of details which take on significance through their patterning – certainly of Frankian spatial form, but also here between different kinds of spatiality, both in and outside the text – it asks us to maintain a finer awareness of the spaces in which we live, their striations of access, inequality, memory, and intersubjective encounter, and the role art plays in their mediation.

'Homing': An Aerial Perspective

While in 'Falling', Victor experiences an ambiguous epiphany by scaling a mall and coming back down, in 'Homing', protagonist Nona comes to a realisation by leaving her modest home, spending the night high up in a neighbouring luxury hotel, and then returning. As the title suggests, the narrative arc of the story partakes of Lohafer's mythic tropes of home-leaving and homecoming, and as in 'Falling', the story's formal spatiality intersects with more worldly spatial concerns, as the narrative movement in the story is prompted by the reorganisation of the built environment through the construction of a luxury hotel. Hotels, along with malls, are two quintessential spaces of urban postmodernism, and this hotel shares a number of attributes with the Westin Bonaventure Hotel, the disorienting building that Jameson famously uses to decrypt the architectural logic of late capitalism.[61] This similarity invites a reading of the building's spatial distortions as outward projections of the excesses of capital, of the psychological disturbances its inequalities provoke, and of what role the short story might play in our understanding of them. However, this reading is not entirely allowed by the story's internal logics, which resist any mapping of the experience it describes onto the social, while leaving no remainder.

The plot of 'Homing', like that of 'Falling', is quite straightforward. Nona and her husband Ray are a retired couple whose lives are changed when a hotel built on a neighbouring plot casts their home into darkness. The hotel is, in the first instance, a physical structure that alters Ray and Nona's way of being, disrupting their daily routine by disorienting the birds they feed each morning, and degrading the relationship they have with their surroundings. Physical environments influence one's sense of self, and the hotel serves as a stark reminder to Ray and Nona

---

61 Fredric Jameson, *Postmodernism: Or, the Cultural Logic of Late Capitalism* (Durham, NC: Duke University Press, 1991), pp. 1–54.

of their relative insignificance in a societal hierarchy of wealth. While they do not seem particularly poor, their lives are modest. Their names, Rose-Innes says, are 'old fashioned, unfashionable names that were perhaps to indicate a particular class'.[62] Nona feels at once resentful and envious of the hotel's patrons, until a chance happening makes her decide, without her husband's knowledge, to book a room in the hotel, where she undergoes a transformative experience.

In 'Falling', the built environment serves as a vehicle of memory and both reflects and projects psychological unease. In 'Homing', by contrast, it is more the operations of desire that are given spatial expression, and particularly how desire interacts with late capitalist space. The hotel that is built next to Ray and Nona's house transforms the 'place' of their home into a depersonalised, commodified 'space'.[63] Once there was a sports field opposite their house that provided a democratic public space for local 'dog walkers, soccer players, domestic workers taking the short cut down to the taxi rank', and further down the road was an old folks' home they imagined themselves one day moving into.[64] With alarming suddenness, however, the home is closed, and its residents are shipped out to the 'bleak northern suburbs' (10) as the construction of the hotel begins. The hotel is swift and resolute in its reorganisation of space. Within a week, where the home and sports field were,

> [a] high wall rose at amazing speed and was painted a peachy pink, and behind it there reared the pink backside of a new hotel [...] the greatest affront was the size and fleshy colour of the thing. Set down like a giant monopoly piece, fatly overflowing its monopoly square, the hotel filled up the space where the old-age home had been [...] Brash, three storeys tall, and featureless except for a row of mirrored windows that faced them over the top of the new wall. (10)

---

62 When I put it to Rose-Innes that Nona was also one of the Roman Fates, responsible for spinning the thread of life, she replied: 'Was she now? [...] You can't call anybody anything without finding out they were one of the fates.' Rose-Innes and Riach, unpublished interview.

63 Place is space as it is lived, a space textured and fleshed out through human interaction.

64 Henrietta Rose-Innes, 'Homing', in *Homing* (Cape Town: Umuzi, 2010), pp. 9–23 (p. 9). All further references to this work are given parenthetically in the text until the end of this section.

While Nona and Ray's long habitation in the street has led to a strong sense of place, by their very nature hotels are spaces of transitory habitation, the antithesis of rooted living; their residents are temporary, with little investment in the people and places around them. The hotel is ringed by a high wall, is compared to a 'monopoly piece', and is corporeally grotesque, with greedy, 'overflowing' proportions. As with the mall in 'Homing', this hotel seems likely to have been based on a real building in Cape Town, the Belmond Mount Nelson Hotel, a bright pink luxury hotel that sits on land that was owned by the governor of the Cape in 1743. The building as reimagined in Rose-Innes's story is 'brash' and 'featureless', with 'mirrored' windows that would allow observation only from the inside out. The new building blocks the morning light, and in the evenings the hotel's reflective windows transform the cul-de-sac into a defamiliarised and artificial space: 'The alleyway was strangely illuminated, as if with several weak spotlights. Indeed, it was the mirror-glass windows of the hotel [...] flashing sunset light directly down at them' (11). This inversion of the natural order gives them a 'counterfeit sunset' in exchange for a 'stolen [...] sunrise', with the spotlight effect adding a 'distressing' (11) simulacral veneer. As is the case for Jameson's analysis of the Bonaventure Hotel, this mirroring repels those outside, while reflecting 'distorted images of everything that surrounds it'.[65] The sports field was a piece of public ground, and the street their home, but the privatisation of the terrain in front of their house transforms the place they live into a reified, synthetic space.

Ray is quick to 'mak[e] his peace with the new lie of the land' (12); he sets up deckchairs in the artificial light and feeds the pigeons that have been disoriented by the false sunset. For Nona, however, the hotel's construction engenders feelings of envy, antipathy, and desire: 'Every glance at the bland pink wall was a small humiliation' (12), as she imagines 'wealthy guests' (12) occupying the rooms. She reads in the *Cape Argus* that the hotel is patronised by 'politicians and celebrities, both local and international' (14), but all she sees and hears of what goes on in it are reflections of 'the coloured glaze of party lights' and the 'vibrations of popular songs' (14). These exclusions breed both resentment and aspiration, repulsion and compulsion in equal measure. She complains about the noise to Ray, but 'what she did not confess [...] was how the pulse of the music excited her' (14). The hotel represents for Nona a life she never had the chance to live – she has only stayed

---

65 Jameson, *Postmodernism*, p. 42.

in 'rundown country hotels, or campsites' (16) – and its wall serves as a physical manifestation of her exclusion from the glamorous lifestyle she covets.

Until this point, the story has been in a largely realist mode, albeit one slightly skewed by the simulacral effects of the hotel. There is a shift towards a more symbolic or spatial register, however, as a rogue champagne cork flies over the wall to land in Nona's lap. This detritus of luxury from the other side is the first sign of permeability between Nona's life and that in the hotel, and she 'grip[s] the cork with her fingernails, digging them deep' (14). This gesture is ambivalent, showing both anger and frustrated desire at the privilege the hotel represents. There is resentment towards the inequality the cork represents, but also a guilty wish to be included in that privileged group, as well as a distinctly erotic overtone in the popping cork and digging fingernails. As such, it serves as a form of objective correlative or image, which holds a complex inner state in a single spatialised moment, asking the reader to become alert to the story as a 'system for generating meanings' as well as a plotted narrative.[66]

It will be clear from the examples offered so far that Rose-Innes's tropes of spatial patterning in the stories that make up *Homing* begin to create a larger-order spatial logic across the collection, in which the boundaries of setting and inscape are permeable, and boundary crossings and liminal zones become important vectors of sense. What might be less apparent is that there is a further form of spatialisation introduced here, in that the cork alludes to Raymond Carver's 'Errand', in which the central symbol is a champagne cork picked up by a hotel bellboy from the bottle Anton Chekhov drinks from before he dies.[67] This gesture to the Carverian and Chekhovian short story creates a form of meta-spatiality, in which symbolic patterning might accrete across a genre rather than in a single story or collection only.

Carver's story has been described as 'uncanny realism' that 'combines familiarity and strangeness, *déja vu* and *jamais vu*', and it is the champagne cork in 'Homing' that marks a shift towards a more spatial register.[68] In an elliptic jump, the action shifts to Nona making her

---

66 Mitchell, 'Spatial Form in Literature', pp. 550–54.
67 Raymond Carver, 'Errand', *The New Yorker*, 1 June 1987, pp. 30–31.
68 Claudine Verley, '"Errand," or Raymond Carver's Realism in a Champagne Cork', *Journal of the Short Story in English. Les Cahiers de La Nouvelle*, 46 (2006), 147–63 (p. 157).

way around the hotel's perimeter and approaching its 'grand, curlicued, wrought-iron' (15) gate. In the symbolic logic of the story, the cork crossing the perimeter wall both causes this temporal jump and marks entry into a world that operates in irrealist terms. Passing through the threshold of the gate, Nona enters a dream space. The building before her is 'indistinct: a shimmer of pink, the suggestion of steps ascending' (15), the ethereal vocabulary here combining with paratactic syntax to conjure up an imagistic, oneiric state. The dream space of the hotel is anamorphic, its scale shifting queasily: 'Luxury, ease, light; it was disorienting [...] the avenue was longer than it seemed' (15). This unreal quality is emphasised when she reaches the reception to see the 'brass tags [of the keys] that gleamed like a dragon's flank in a cave', the elevator that conducts her to 'a higher realm', a corridor that 'seemed to her unaccustomed eyes to be carpeted in gold', and a 'wondrous carpet' that seems to 'fl[y] her' (16) to her room. While this description is, on the one hand, the stuff of fantasy, its luxurious excesses and seemingly magical convenience are markers of the hyper-real space into which Nona's world has been temporarily transformed.

As for Victor in 'Falling', Nona's climb to a 'higher realm' gives her a bird's-eye view which is at once a literal vantage point and a site from which patterns can be perceived in the mess of daily experience. Nona looks from the third-floor window, and sees her home from an 'unfamiliar angle' (17). She sees all the flaws of the house she loves: it appears to her as 'shameful: repulsive, even. She felt a hotel guest's resentment of this disappointing view' (17), and also sees her husband, whose head appears as a 'blunt, grey knob, pushed into the frame' (17). While 'down on the ground, at home, she never noticed [the shabbiness of her house and her husband's advancing age]', from the hotel window, 'with height and distance the blemishes pulled into focus' (17). The physical space of the hotel, towering over her house, shapes her behaviour, and the view from above grants knowledge that destabilises as much as it empowers. It allows Nona a more comprehensive understanding of her lot, in that she gains perspective on her position within a societal hierarchy of wealth, but this knowledge brings with it scorn for what once made her happy. At the thought of this, and of the white lie she told her husband – that she was going to visit her sister, rather than to stay in the hotel – she 'drop[s] her eyes' (18).

The story's invitation to a spatial reading becomes more explicit when, after an evening spent in the hotel bar, Nona returns somewhat drunk to her room and falls asleep, before waking to find it filled with homing pigeons. These birds are famed for their ability to return home, and so bear a symbolic freight of centripetal movement, of homecoming after the journey out. Their reappearance gives the story a structural cohesion, as they appear at various pivotal moments. They are there in the opening paragraph, 'specks against the blue of Table Mountain' (9), then reappear as the newly built hotel's false sunset 'depolarise[s]' (13) them, at which point Ray and Nona take to feeding them. Nona sees them again when she looks down at Ray from the hotel window, and they are associated with him through one landing on his wrist. When the pigeons reappear in Nona's room, she sees them as 'small but troubling shapes in the dimness [...] Hunched figures [...] A fidgeting crowd of small, dour spectators' (20). These shady apparitions are as much projections of Nona's anxieties as real-world objects – she sees in the birds' eyes 'a husband's chastisement' (20) for straying from home – and further require a mode of reading that creates sense out of the story seen as a single functioning unit as much as a temporally extended act of reading.

The multivalent meaning of the birds – markers of routine, boundary crossers, ciphers of homecoming, silent judges – is multiplied as Nona drifts in and out of sleep and begins to dream:

> She dreamt she was walking in the hotel, down a long gold corridor, looking for a way through the building. A flight path. But there were no exits here, no clear routes. The birds were with her and they were trapped, battering up against glazed windows, winging down corridors into dead ends, tangling in elevator cables. She pushed at the walls with her hands, searching for secret doorways; but the hotel could not be unbuilt. (22)

While the hotel was previously both the site of Nona's projected desire for a more glamorous life and a materialisation of commodified space, the dream transforms it into a nightmarish site of entrapment and panic. The luxurious 'gold corridor' has no exit, its space depicted as restrictive and insular. The corridors that transported Nona as if by magic have morphed into suffocating 'dead ends', and the elevator that took her to a 'higher realm' is now a perilous mechanism. Nona and the pigeons' efforts to escape are repeatedly checked by the hotel's architecture. Like the perplexing space of the Bonaventure Hotel, once inside this hotel, and by extension the cultural logic for which it stands, it is a daunting task to try to leave. The architecture of both hotels, in Jameson's words, 'transcend[s] the capacities of the individual human body to locate itself, to organise its immediate surroundings perceptually, and cognitively to map its position in a mappable external world'.[69] In so doing, it constitutes an 'analogon' of our incapacity to understand our subjective position in 'the great global multinational and decentred communicational network' in which we live.[70]

If an analogon is taken to mean an allegorical substitution in a blunt sense – the hotel *stands for* or *symbolises* late capitalism – this would be to miss the more interesting sense Jameson attributes to the term, and how it functions in Rose-Innes's story. In Jameson's usage, informed by Jean-Paul Sartre's thought in *L'Imaginaire: Psychologie phénoménologique de l'imagination*, the analogon is something that allows the mental equivalent of a perceptual act, which for Sartre means that it is formed from a combination of past knowledge and our intention towards it.[71] For example, a lock of hair can stand in for an absent person, and we might even transfer the feelings we have for the person onto the object. In other words, the analogon can take on new qualities depending on one's orientation towards it. Much like spatial form, the analogon is an amalgam of existing properties and their apprehension by an imagining consciousness, and so might better be conceived of as a possible way of understanding that is shaped by an artwork rather than as a one-to-one equivalent for an extra-textual reality. This hotel leaves Nona disoriented, both in a literal, physical sense, and in that her subjective and affective coordinates have been misaligned. Not only is she trapped in a fiction of her own making, the world of her desires transforming before her eyes into a maze of obsession, but she is also ensnared in the trap of spatial privatisation.

Nona wakes late the next day, and the surfaces of the room now strike her as 'cool, promiscuous', as she senses it 'shrugging off its brief habitation' (22). The room is ready to return to its 'pristine blankness, thoughtless, faithless, without memory' (22). She decides to leave a day early, and returns to her husband, who is fretting that the pigeons did not come for their morning feed. Nona takes her husband's arm, saying: '"Oh Ray. They'll be back [...] Those birds they know which side their bread is buttered"' (23). The couple sit, 'their backs to the

---

69 Jameson, *Postmodernism*, p. 44.
70 Ibid., p. 44.
71 Jean-Paul Sartre, *L'imaginaire: psychologie phénoménologique de l'imagination* (Paris: Gallimard, 1940).

new hotel', on the 'old road: altered but familiar, stolen from them and yet theirs. Waiting, in that changing and mysterious light, for the birds to find their way' (23). This conciliatory return to home and husband signals, in one possible reading, that the life on offer in the hotel is less attractive than she had imagined. Rose-Innes has discussed her interest in deflating false wishes; she sees in many of her protagonists an 'aspir[ation] to comfort, or power, I suppose, and when they attain it, it is uneasy, or [...] precarious. I think I am interested in undermining not necessarily power, but undermining false dreams, false aspirations.'[72] Nona's homecoming comes to signify a foregoing of the false aspirations caused by the hotel's distorting reflections and disorienting spaces, and a return to the safety of familiarity.

However, something in Nona's return home rankles. On the one hand, she is once more content with her life; her adventure has satisfied her desire for change, allowing a happy return to her life at home. Further, the sense of closure that her homecoming provides is aesthetically satisfying; it balances the journey out, and in returning to the point of origin creates a pleasing parabolic structure to the narrative. This sense of contentment jars, however, in that her acquiescence to the changes imposed on her is a frustratingly passive acceptance of the hotel's invasive spatial encroachment. Privilege, it would seem, is to be accommodated rather than contested, with adaptation the best possible response. The feeling of dissatisfaction this causes is both disempowering and enabling. Rose-Innes creates a disjunction between the story's spatial cadence and that cadence's inability to resolve the very real spatial problems voiced in the story. The political space the story opens up sits in the gap between formal satisfaction and referential dissatisfaction, between the exigencies of form and the unfinished project of post-apartheid spatial distribution. It is not that this formal solution is a manifestation of some prior extra-textual social condition. Rather, in staging a story that operates on multiple spatial levels simultaneously, it allows a way of thinking that draws a complex of formal and extra-formal features together, and does so in a small-scale model that allows these different dimensions to be conceived as if at once.

---

72 Rose-Innes and Riach, unpublished interview.

'Bad Places': The Voyage Out, and Back

The interaction between different modes of spatiality takes on a different aspect in 'Bad Places', in which the spatial structure underlying the story is out and back rather than up and down.[73] Rather than attaining an elevated vantage point from which sense can be gleaned, this suggests a transformative process structured by other logics. The story is focalised through Elly, a young woman who wakes up on the beach beside her two friends Nadia and Mac the morning after a wild party, still in fancy dress as a mermaid. While her friends continue to sleep, Elly realises that her car keys are missing, and retraces her steps from the night before to look for them. She finds another set of tracks mixed with her own, and follows them along the beach and over the dunes, where she unexpectedly finds a cave dwelling. She goes inside, and after dozing briefly, wakes to realise that the cave is occupied, and that the sleeping occupant, a 'bergie', has her keys on a shelf above him.[74] Her attempts to retrieve them wake him up, and he grabs her by the arm and slaps her before robbing her and chasing her out, flinging her keys after her. She makes her way back across the dunes and returns to her worried friends.

The significance of this story's spatial politics are best understood through the material and discursive histories of the beach in South Africa. During the 1980s, as the struggle against apartheid became increasingly acute, beaches became sites of peaceful political protest as the Mass Democratic Movement mounted a defiance campaign on 'whites-only' beaches. The beaches were occupied, a movement that contributed to the relaxation and eventual repeal of petty-apartheid legislation around public space. Arguments in the 1980s and early 1990s over who should have access to beaches were often conducted in terms of civility and propriety, with defenders of segregation complaining that the black beachgoers were acting inappropriately. A newspaper article from January 1990, just months after desegregation, reported

---

73 This story was first published in *New Contrast* in 2003, seven years before its appearance in *Homing*. Henrietta Rose-Innes, 'Bad Places', *New Contrast*, 31 (2003), 26–34.

74 The word 'bergie' is a mildly pejorative term used to describe an Afrikaans-speaking section of Cape Town's homeless population, and is also used to refer to homeless people more generally. Henrietta Rose-Innes, 'Bad Places', in *Homing* (Cape Town: Umuzi, 2010), pp. 129–38 (p. 135). All further references to this work are given parenthetically in the text until the end of this section.

that city officials had been inundated with 'more than 400 phone calls from irate whites complaining that blacks were littering, stripping naked, playing loud music, and sleeping and relieving themselves on the beach'.[75] As petty apartheid crumbled, the beach became a site where differing expectations of public space came into conflict. The behaviour that provoked the most vituperative response, however, was that of conducting political protest on the beach, a space conceived of by segregationists as a site of 'refuge from public politics'.[76] By bringing politics to the beach, black beachgoers were thought to have broken some unspoken agreement of political propriety.

Although all beaches were formally desegregated in 1989, many have remained, in Kevin Durrheim and John Dixon's words, 'informally segregated', with 'beaches previously defined as black, white, Indian and coloured [...] still occupied predominantly by people who were so categorised by apartheid'.[77] As noted in Chapter 3, Patrick Bond describes post-apartheid South Africa as structured by 'class apartheid', and the still-divided use of the beaches shows the spatial effects that these economic disparities produce.[78] The ongoing racialised partition of space serves as a good example of how difficult the spatial politics of previous eras are to undo, and furthermore demonstrates how infrastructure can determine the use of a place. Many of the beaches around Cape Town that are used primarily by whites are inaccessible by public transport, and so are unreachable for those without the means to own a car. It is no accident that in 'Bad Places' it is Elly's car keys that go missing, as not only is the car a particularly concentrated example of the privatisation of space, it is also the means by which many of the country's restricted spaces become accessible.

If the physical beach has been the site of fractious social struggle, South African literature's discursive engagement with that space has often seen it as a site of tentative possibility beyond apartheid's

---

75 David Zucchino, 'In South Africa, Mingling Peacefully Despite Fears of Race Riots, the Beaches were Quiet', *Philly*, 9 January 1990, <http://articles.philly.com/1990-01-09/news/25910265_1_whites-only-beaches-allan-hendrickse-race-riots> (accessed 10 December 2013).
76 Kevin Durrheim and John Dixon, 'Racism on South Africa's Beaches: Then and Now', *Perspectives on Kwa-Zulu Natal*, 1.6 (2001), <http://www.cherylgoodenough.com/docs/racismonsabeaches.pdf> (accessed 12 October 2013).
77 Ibid.
78 Bond, 'The Mandela Years in Power'.

segregations and their post-apartheid consequences. In Meg Samuelson's account of the beach in South African writing, which stretches from the 1572 *Lusiads* to the early 2010s, she notes that the South African beach has been '[s]potted crimson during the colonial encounter while infused with thwarted desire for communicative exchange, inscribed with the regulatory zeal of apartheid and haunted by bloody apparitions of its aftermath'; but the beach as imagined in literature is more often 'a contact zone and threshold' that provides 'a setting in which to imagine the emergent state' and to explore 'alternative positions to those produced out of a politics of difference'.[79] This is certainly the case for Rose-Innes's story, in which her spatial imaginary and the transformative potential of the beach are brought into dialogue. In the reading I offer below, her story can be thought of as engaged in two overlapping but non-identical contexts: that of the history of the beach in South Africa and that of how the country's literature has imagined and rewritten that space.

The plot arc of 'Bad Places', like those of 'Falling' and 'Homing', is spatial at its core. The physical movement this time is that of a journey out and back across a beach, with time spent midway in no-man's land. The structure is akin to what David Trotter calls the 'anthropological' or 'rite of passage' short story, in which a character moves from society to a liminal space, and spends time there before returning in some way transformed.[80] In such stories, the transformation often comes about through an encounter with a liminal figure. The beach is a shifting and uncertain threshold where land and sea mingle, and as such provides a suitable location for narratives of transformation. In the words of poet and marine biologist Douglas Livingstone, the 'littoral zone' is a 'mysterious border that [...] has [...] always reflected that blurred and uneasy divide between humanity's physical and psychic elements'.[81]

---

79 Meg Samuelson, 'Literary Inscriptions on the South African Beach: Ambiguous Settings, Ambivalent Textualities', in *The Beach in Anglophone Literatures and Cultures: Reading Littoral Space*, ed. Virginia Richter and Ursula Kluwick (Farnham: Ashgate, 2015), pp. 121–38 (pp. 121, 135–36).

80 David Trotter, 'Modernist Anthropology', paper presented at the 20th Century Seminar, University of Cambridge, 2014. These three phases are described by Arnold van Gennep as 'separation', 'transition', and 'aggregation'. See Arnold van Gennep, *The Rites of Passage*, trans. Monika B. Vizedom and Gabrielle L. Caffee (London: Routledge, 1960), p. 11.

81 Douglas Livingstone, *A Littoral Zone* (Cape Town: Carrefour, 1991), p. 62.

The beach, a site of both leisure and political struggle, is in 'Bad Places' equally a psychological projection of Elly's inscape, with the dunes she crosses marking off a taboo area at the conceptual limits of her world. This structure allows a shuttling between Elly's physical exploration, the testing of her psychological boundaries of safety and threat, and a spatial formulation of Lohafer's mythic tropes of homecoming and home-leaving.

Rose-Innes creates uneasiness around home-leaving by defamiliarising vision, perspective, and scale on Elly's journey out. Elly walks 'without thought – five minutes, ten, until colour and detail bleached from her vision', with the heat 'like a dense liquid sinking into her scalp' (131). This passage marks a process of transition from the everyday world into an altered space, governed by different logics. There is an interpermeability between body and landscape, as the heat sinks into her, and her surroundings become an extension of her 'inscape', here depicted as colourless, blank, and hence open to reinscription. She reaches the crest of the dunes, and from the top the footprints behind her become 'insect-tracks' (131). In the other direction, the 'secret side of the dune' (213) is revealed, a 'narrow and intimate' dip, 'like the cleft between a sleeper's arm and body' (213). Place and body become further commingled, as place takes on the dream state of a sleeper, and perspective and scale are skewed. This point at the dune's crest marks the boundary between two worlds, a distinction emphasised by the relative silence of the shady side. She feels quietness 'infiltrate her, like some cool fluid, saturating, insulating. She could hear the tiniest sounds now: a faint insect rasping [...]' (131). Rose-Innes's characteristic visual telescoping is here matched by an auditory one, in which the background sound is brought sharply to the foreground, causing a switch in perspective that reorients the relationship between subject and surroundings. The perspective oscillates between Elly's and that of the insects she hears, as a 'flame-red mite, the size of a grain of salt, crawl[s] over her toe, carefully negotiate[s] one hair, two, and trek[s] out across the blue-varnished toenail' (131). While the dunes are shrunk to the size of the body, the body becomes extended to that of a world. This perspectival inversion suggests the destabilisation that Elly experiences on her journey from safety to threat, and further draws attention to how size and scale can shape understanding. The smallness of frame offered by the short story does not just give a curtailed version of what a novel offers; rather, in giving less, it leads us to attribute greater significance to detail. The short story's shortness, in other words, makes detail take on meaning in ways that the novel usually does not. It is not that the detail necessarily differs, but it is rather that its prominence becomes magnified or distorted when read in a short form. Elly's voyage out, and the recalibration of her perspective this entails, is doubled by the reader's need to attune their attention more precisely.

At first glance, the space over the dunes appears uninhabited, made up of 'textures of sand, stone, leaves, the gaps and cracks of shade between them, random and harmonious' (132). As such, it adheres to the principles Coetzee describes as necessary to representations of the land in white writing: the landscape must be aestheticised and depicted as empty of human habitation.[82] Elly, thinking herself out of sight, 'squat[s] to pee' (131), but suddenly becomes aware of something she had not noticed. In a hallucinatory shift, the 'landscape's camouflage fell away. The stones slid into a different focus, revealing their arrangement and their function: not ten metres away stood a house, with walls, a roof, a door' (132). This dwelling, which appears out of the landscape as if by a conjurer's trick, is uncannily homely. Or better, it is quite literally *unheimlich*, in that its uncanniness arises through becoming suddenly 'unhidden'. Leading up to the structure are 'two neat lines of stones [that] marked a pathway to this rough entrance, and the sand was trampled flat' (132).[83] While Elly uses the public beach as her toilet, recalling the arguments over appropriate conduct on the beach in the 1990s, this house is the very model of private ownership and civility. The doorstep is a threshold space, here marking the division between public and private. If, as Mikhail Bakhtin suggests, thresholds in fiction draw attention to 'the breaking point of a life, the moment of crisis, the decision that changes a life', then Elly's approach signifies not only the entry into a new physical space, but also a possible psychological turning point.[84]

She enters the cave on her hands and knees, a movement that signals the entrance into what Anne McClintock calls 'anachronistic space', that

---

82 J.M. Coetzee, *White Writing: On the Culture of Letters in South Africa* (New Haven, CT: Yale University Press, 1988).

83 This odd homeliness is emphasised in an earlier printing in the Caine Prize anthology, in which the house is even more ornate, sporting a 'kind of portico' and a 'silvery curtain' marking the entrance. Henrietta Rose-Innes, 'Bad Places', in *Jambula Tree & Other Stories: The Caine Prize for African Writing 8th Annual Collection* (Auckland Park: Jacana Media, 2008), pp. 49–56 (p. 51).

84 Mikhail Bakhtin, *The Dialogic Imagination: Four Essays*, trans. Michael Holquist and Caryl Emerson (Austin: University of Texas Press, 1981), p. 248.

is, a space that also encodes a prior time, and with it a 'regression to an earlier moment of racial development'.[85] The weird spatio-temporality of the cave is further emphasised by its later description as a 'wormhole' (137) through which she passes out into the light of day. McClintock describes how in colonial discourse, '[g]eographical difference across space is figured as a historical difference across time', but what Elly sees inside the cave is not so simply compartmentalised into either modernity or an atavistic space.[86] The cave is first described in primordial, organic terms: the floor is 'damp, spongy', shapes are 'soft [...] smooth, round', with the '[w]alls and floor flowing into each other' (133), yet the floor is carpeted with cardboard. The table and tools are of stone, the wall of boulder, the decorations made from shells, and the shelf formed of driftwood, pre-modern fittings that hold modern objects: a chipped china cow, a peacock tea tray, and decorative fish tins that create a parody of domesticity, a jerry-rigged 'bourgeois interior' of the kind I discussed in relation to Wicomb's stories in Chapter 3.[87] These may be modern objects, but they are of a kind salvaged from the detritus of modernity, and when framed in this cave dwelling, they point to the synchronicity of different times occupying a shared space.

Elly drifts off in a 'shallow pit in the floor, lined with dimpled mauve cardboard' that constitutes a 'giant's easy chair' (133), but jolts awake as she realises that someone else is sleeping in the cave, hidden behind the fishing net. She smells the 'sour stench of an unwashed body' as she makes out a figure with 'huge, charcoaled soles [...] feet [...] shod with calluses as tough as hooves', a 'sinewy neck', and a throat emitting a 'ferocious snore' (134). It is unclear whether this ogre-like depiction is a fairy tale externalisation of Elly's inner anxieties, or if, rather, it realistically illustrates the kind of societal grotesque produced by the juxtaposition of extremes of wealth, in which prolonged poverty *can* and *does* make people appear as if monsters. Elly's noonday nightmares are at once projections of her inscape and reflections of the spatial inequalities of where she lives. In 'Falling', Victor's deepest terror lies in the conjunction of his own childhood trauma with the

---

85 McClintock, *Imperial Leather*, p. 112. The cave in South African literature has a long discursive history. See Lucy Valerie Graham, 'Re-Imagining the Cave: Gender, Land and Imperialism in Olive Schreiner's *Trooper Peter Halket of Mashonaland* (1897)', *English Studies in Africa*, 50.1 (2007), 25–40.
86 McClintock, *Imperial Leather*, p. 40.
87 Brown, *The Bourgeois Interior*.

moral instability of his current position. In 'Homing', Nona's hallucinatory half-dreams are rooted equally in her guilty desire for a more glamorous life and in the emotional and spatial exclusions this entails. Elly's fears in 'Bad Places' are aggregations of psychological, even mythic threats and the consequence of society choosing to ignore one part of its population.

As the story progresses, the 'bergie' becomes overdetermined by a host of competing meanings. Elly notices her keys, adorned with an alien figurine keyring, gleaming on a shelf above the sleeping man. These keys are the reason for Elly's trek out across the beach, but they also hold symbolic value, both as the key for Elly to unlock some knowledge about herself (from which she is 'alienated'), and as a synecdoche for private ownership itself. When she tries to retrieve her keys from above the 'giant' (135), she suddenly finds her arm clamped in his grip, a 'stone cuff' of a hand, 'unlike any human's she had yet experienced' (135). This geological comparison leads to a further association between the man and the land through his 'muddy' skin with 'mineral grey' 'ridges and prominences' (136) his 'charcoal' (134) soles, his palm 'like a piece of wood' (136) and his fingers that click 'like branches snapping' (137).[88] At first there is a hint of sexual threat, as his 'mouth comes close to her cheek' (135), and he becomes fascinated by her painted face and sequined skirt.[89] However, he makes no advance, rather slapping her in the face, saying in a 'husky', 'unused' voice: '"This is my place [...] Mine"' (136). His anger is directed in the first instance at Elly's trespassing into what he feels to be his property. As he asserts his right to ownership, he appears to her 'like a great sand lion' (137), an embodiment of the land itself. The 'bergie', literally a 'mountain man' in Afrikaans, comes to occupy multiple sites of meaning in the story's spatial economy: he is a monstrous embodiment of otherness and threat; a taboo figure who provides a foil for Elly's psychological transformation; a grotesque product of the unequal distribution of property and wealth; and, on the most concrete level, he is the cave's occupant, making of Elly an intruder. He takes her cigarettes and wallet, and threatens her with another slap.

---

88 In *New Contrast*, his skin is 'muddy tea brown' (32), drawing greater attention to racial difference.

89 For more on the persistent trope of interracial rape in South African fiction, see Lucy Valerie Graham, *State of Peril: Race and Rape in South African Literature* (Oxford: Oxford University Press, 2012).

Elly stumbles backwards out of the cave, reversing the story's spatial trajectory. He throws her keys out after her, and she once again crosses the 'waste-land' liminal space towards the dunes, although it is now transformed into an abject space, filled with 'broken glass and bottlenecks and human shit, flies gathering around bloody things in the bushes' (137). This macabre landscape, filled with gruesome objects, represents, on a metaphorical level, whatever pollutants Ellie is leaving behind. However, these wholly unromantic objects also show a stripping away of her fantasies, and serve as a reminder that the beach is as much a real physical space as it is a vehicle for the tenor of Elly's psychological state. The very title of the story, 'Bad Places', suggests a fairy-tale world of clear polarities and paradigmatic exempla, but this stability is constantly troubled by the ragged and unpredictable nature of the reality it describes. The 'Bad Places' to which the title refers are both the dark spots of the subconscious and those of the material world, and these two are shown to be mutually determining.

As Elly crests the dune, the narration switches from the past tense to the present, giving a sense of a rush back into reality. She 'knows she is changed, quite changed' (138) by her experience. Her friends now appear to her as 'children' (138) and they see her differently, '[t]aller, maybe, more substantial; and walking with the long, deliberate stride of some much larger being' (138). This harks back to earlier in the story, when Elly tried with great difficulty to walk in the wide-spaced steps she found. She can now presumably do so, implying that she has overcome some insufficiency. However, this spatial closure, like those of 'Homing' and 'Falling', is troublesome. On a literal level, by experiencing at first hand how those much poorer than her live, she comes back wiser. The implication is also that she has gone through some inner process of change, with the taboo figure of the 'bergie' allowing her to progress to some new and perhaps less insular phase of her life. On a more abstract level, the progression from safety to danger and back satisfies Lohafer's model of homecoming and so provides an aesthetic sense of closure. However, as with Victor's relation to the security guard in 'Falling', the narrative of progress that Elly enjoys is not shared by the story's homeless man. She returns to her former life changed, but, as far as we can tell, the man in the cave continues to live in his makeshift home, living on the flotsam and jetsam gleaned from a culture that has no place for him.

In each of the stories I analyse here, Rose-Innes's depiction of space is multilayered, with contesting and interwoven understandings. Each story is structured around a simple spatial movement, and in each case that movement tracks and produces a psychological change in the protagonist. In the case of 'Falling', Victor's individual emancipation from the shameful burden of his past is realised spatially in walking out of the mall that caused his trauma. However, this catharsis fails to extend to the security guard who helps him, and so does little to change the structural relations that lie behind his unease. In 'Homing', Nona's conflicting desires lead to a disorientation of her system of values. She eventually discovers contentment in what she already had, but the spatial cadence of her return home implies a quietist position when faced with inequality, even though the formal closure is a source of pleasure. 'Bad Places' uses a journey to a taboo space and back to explore Elly's anxieties of alterity. She returns from her ordeal changed, but again this development is a luxury afforded her only, and not the homeless man, whose continuing societal exclusion is the prerequisite for his narrative function.

Across these three stories there is an unresolved tension between the dehistoricising tendencies of spatial form and the material histories of where the stories take place – the mall, the hotel, and the beach – sites where public and private conceptions of space come into conflict. In Rose-Innes's stories, space shifts between personal, social, metaphorical, and political registers, and the imperfect spatial cadences that close these stories cannot be explained away as primarily reflections of, or indices to, a prior social reality. Such a reading would see literary form as the (false) resolution of historical contradiction, and it would be the critic's job to find the fissures and cracks that reveal the ideological struggle of the world in which the text was produced. While these stories certainly allow such a reading, a fuller understanding of them requires seeing this affordance of form – to allow a reading of the social – as only one component of a more complex meaning event, in which our experience of different levels of narrative spatiality work with and against one another. The tension in these short stories between spatial organisation, in which symbolic patterning takes precedence, and a continuing commitment to narrative unfolding offers readers a scale model for seeing seemingly unchanging spatial realities as working in dialogue with historical change. The experience of these short stories, in which mythic abstraction, narrative development, and extra-textual historical reality are experienced together, offers a way to help think through how change might emerge in seemingly unchanging structures, and does so through a sensuous experience of form.

These stories can, of course, be seen as reflecting reality or masking its ideological premises, but by thinking of them as actively shaping knowledge of the world, there is conceptual gain to be accrued. These works offer us in the first instance a reading experience in which attunement to detail and finding pattern and sense in seemingly disconnected material is rewarded. By drawing our attention to their microcosms, these stories reveal a fractal richness that further reveals itself the longer we look. This is its own reward, but these same characteristics also offer us unique structures through which to conceive of the social, in which we understand our partial experience as bound up with that of others, albeit by logics that may for now elude us. It is our role to think how these seemingly disparate lives are conjoined, and for this to be an ongoing process of reinvention.

Conclusion
Small Medium at Large

This book has made the case for the short story's importance to post-apartheid literature, and has done so by analysing how its formal capabilities might inform our conception of the social world. The kind of political work these stories do is not that of direct response to rolling events, nor is it that of indexing societal conditions; rather, it is achieved by allowing readers to reframe and filter their understanding of the social through literary forms. These stories are at no point reducible to such a function, and consistently exceed their determination by social forces. In the post-apartheid short story, the 'rhetoric of urgency' that Louise Bethlehem identified in apartheid-era writing and criticism is no longer as pressing.[1] Writing that was once understood, in Es'kia Mphahlele's words, as 'a response to the immediate, to the instant, and [as] a direct, urgent confrontation with the dominant political morality', now offers a set of conceptual resources for readers, mediations of the social world that allow readers to participate in its remaking.[2] By focusing on the form and style of these stories, while insisting that these features are enmeshed with the subject matter of the stories and their material 'worldliness', I have offered examples of how postcolonial criticism might respond more fully to how literature articulates with the social.[3]

---

1 Louise Bethlehem, '"A Primary Need as Strong as Hunger": The Rhetoric of Urgency in South African Literary Culture under Apartheid', *Poetics Today*, 22.2 (2001), 365–89.
2 Es'kia Mphahlele, 'South African Literature vs the Political Morality', *English Academy Review*, 1.1 (1983), 8–28 (p. 14).
3 Edward Said, *The World, the Text, and the Critic* (Cambridge, MA: Harvard University Press, 1983), p. 35.

In making the case for an approach to postcolonial literary analysis that is sensitive to questions of form and genre, I have tried to clarify a broader point about putting formalism to political use. Namely, we should recognise that the transfer between work and world rests in part on what Jonathan Loesberg calls 'a mental construct that recognizes its separateness from the real bases of the objects it perceives'.[4] This is to say that what I am calling form is not solely a property of texts, nor is it determined by extra-textual events, but rather it is a provisional and mutable entanglement between readers and texts. This 'mental construct', formed through an aesthetic encounter, allows a certain hermeneutic vantage point on the world should a reader wish it to do so. The kind of knowledge this produces – perhaps 'route towards knowledge' would be closer – is inevitably partial, fissile, and subject to revision. In this regard, the experience of artworks serves social thought as a temporary scaffolding, or what I.A. Richards calls, to very different ends, a 'machine for thinking'.[5] How would the world look, these texts allow us to ask, if we thought about it like *this*?

The kind of answers we might arrive at are informed by a text's formal and generic characteristics. Genres are not a neutral means of presenting information, but rather play an important role in how we understand what is before us. Genre is, in John Frow's words, a 'framework for processing information', and it is one that 'actively shapes the way we understand the world'.[6] My examples are drawn from the short story, but through this I hope to encourage others to explore other critically neglected genres. It is heartening in this regard to see Ed Charlton's *Improvising Reconciliation: Confession After the Truth Commission*, which offers a deft analysis of contemporary South African theatre and film in the wake of the TRC. It would be of great interest to see similar attention paid to contemporary South African poetry, which is inexplicably under-represented in criticism, and indeed to the novel read more explicitly in terms of form and genre.

The stories I have discussed offer experiences of form that help readers to analyse the texture and detail of their lives and to be aware that its organising logics are not simply given. We might even say that the kinds of reading that short stories call out for can turn us into different kinds of reader. If there is a world-changing dimension to these works, perhaps

---

4 Loesberg, *A Return to Aesthetics*, p. 6.
5 Richards, *Principles*, p. 1.
6 John Frow, *Genre* (Abingdon: Routledge, 2006), pp. 80, 2.

this is where it lies: these texts help make the kinds of readers they need by facilitating thought without strongly determining it, showing us that other ways of thinking, of being, are possible. This has entailed revisiting some of the central concerns of post-apartheid literature to see how the short story offers different ways of understanding them. To be clear, I am not suggesting that the short story alone can do this, but rather that it is something that short stories are able to do. In her short fiction, Gordimer disturbs narrative temporality, depicting scenes of retrospection that reflect on South Africa's troubled past while asking what style of writing could meet the demands of contemporary engaged authorship. In Ivan Vladislavić's hands, the short story's accommodation of absence can help readers think through the politics of memorialising troubled pasts, and highlights the political affordances of different art forms. Zoë Wicomb's texts foreground how elliptical aesthetics both allow and disallow thinking about the 'problem of class'. In Phaswane Mpe's only collection he creates an aesthetics of brooding that bears witness to state necropolitics while remaining irreducible to its logics. In the final chapter, I claimed that Rose-Innes's fictions overlay different modalities of space and in so doing put pressure on the spatial logics of the period after apartheid. Together, these five authors offer readers new ways of understanding the social, but in no way could we say that these affordances have exhausted the text. Rather, they provide forms through which such thought can move. In each case, the short story offers a form in which the aesthetic demands of short fiction are held in productive tension with the political overdetermination of South African writing.

Perhaps inevitably, alongside the things I hope this book does do, there are many things that it does not. *The Short Story after Apartheid* is not, and in fact is not intended to be, a survey of the post-apartheid short story. My focus has rather been on a selection of formally and stylistically experimental texts, and as a result there are many excellent short stories – both experimental and less so – that I do not include. Moreover, my selection of authors has privileged those who write 'after' apartheid, here implying in relation to it, and hence authors whose concerns lie fully elsewhere are under-represented. Finally, my selection is further restricted in that I deal with English-language texts only. This is indeed a shortcoming, but my abilities in South Africa's other languages are simply not yet up to the standard that this kind of analysis would require. I sincerely hope that other researchers – or perhaps a future version of myself – will be able to take up this task.

Across *The Short Story after Apartheid*'s five chapters, several threads have emerged that stitch the work of these authors together. A first gathering of such threads would show these authors' engagement with temporality in the short story, both within the text and in relation to the world outside it. All of the stories I analyse are concerned with how the short story, a form known for its temporal immediacy, might offer resources with which to mediate on the past's long hold on the present. Gordimer's recursive poetics, Vladislavić's apophatic forms, Wicomb's ellipses, Mpe's brooding, and Rose-Innes's spatio-temporal forms are all examples of this. This engagement with the past has been one of the defining characteristics of post-apartheid literature, and the short story has been shown to offer experiences of form that orient the reader towards this trope in new and interesting ways. The short story is most immediately associated with presentness and the current moment – Gordimer's 'flash of fireflies' – but these texts have used this to show the past's continuance in, and immediacy to, that present.

If revisiting the past is one common line through these authors, another can be found in how they make use of the short story's bifurcation between its narrative and lyrical aspects. What I mean by this is that the short story often holds within it two kinds of happening: a diachronic plot that advances in time and a synchronic stilling that allows us to think about what those happenings might mean. This stilling character appears, for example, in Gordimer's allegorisation, Vladislavić's lyrical intensifications, and Mpe's stylistic vortices. The implications of the duality between a text's syntagmatic and paradigmatic dimensions – one that pertains in most literary forms, but that takes on a different weighting in the short story – were further explored in Wicomb's use of heightened affective states to slow the reader, increasing our attention while inhibiting our understanding. Likewise, Rose-Innes's historically mediated spatial forms juxtapose the stilling quality of formal resolution and the unfolding historical present. The curtailed temporal experience imposed by brevity illuminates, in the stories I analyse, our mortal finitude and how we might negotiate our end-stopped lives. Gordimer and Vladislavić explore these questions through their stories' juxtaposition of human lives with the enduring myths of the national imaginary, and through a revisiting of their previous stylistic innovations that brings into view the temporality of authorial change. Mpe brings the short story's end-consciousness and preference for radically isolated experience into dialogue with an African cosmology in which people are who they are through others, and death is not a final endpoint.

These temporal concerns provide one important through line for understanding the short story after apartheid, and operate mostly on the level of literary form, albeit as it opens out onto broader societal concerns. Another way of looking at this body of texts, and one that is woven through the previous chapters, is the importance to the short story of more obviously material concerns. These include opportunities for publishing, the effect of paratexts on a story's reception, and the variant versions that proliferate when stories are published and republished in different venues. Gordimer's stories were often published in magazines worldwide before being collected in book form, Vladislavić's often appear in multimedia formats alongside photographs, illustrations, and other artworks. In Wicomb's case, the story 'In the Botanic Gardens' appeared in the early 1990s in contexts that proclaimed their political commitment, and then again in a revised form and with a more playful framing in the 2010s, illuminating the central tension in her work between political and aesthetic commitment. Mpe's *Brooding Clouds* did not find a publisher during his lifetime, and so went through a posthumous editing process that brings into relief the concerns of mortality he addresses in his writing. Rose-Innes's republished stories are transformed at a granular level, with the 'nibbling increments' of her editing often adding up to substantial reworkings.[7] Being able to track these changes is not only fascinating in terms of what it tells us about an author's process, but also shows just how sensitive the short story is to even minor reworkings, and hence the intensity of attention it requires of us as readers.

These material aspects of short story publication, and the available infrastructure for the form in South Africa, continue to shape how the form will likely develop. I began this book with a claim made by Craig MacKenzie, that the short story was 'destined to play a major role in bodying forth South Africa's future in imaginative terms', and the innovative, formally daring stories I have discussed certainly suggest that he may be correct.[8] My main focus throughout *The Short Story after Apartheid* has been these formal dimensions, but I want to conclude by drawing attention to some material factors that will likely shape the form in the coming years. The first concerns South African

---

7 Moffett, 'Henrietta Rose-Innes's *Homing*'.
8 Gareth Cornwell, Dirk Klopper, and Craig MacKenzie (eds), *The Columbia Guide to South African Literature in English since 1945* (New York: Columbia University Press, 2010), p. 181.

publishers' assessment of the form's commercial viability, and so their willingness to publish short story collections. As Tom Eaton reported in 2005, the head of one unnamed South African publisher put it to him succinctly: 'When I hear "short stories", I break out in cold sweats.'[9] Since then, things have perhaps improved somewhat. At the time of writing, Penguin Random House South and Jonathan Ball do not accept submissions for short story collections. Nb Publishers, which includes Kwela and Human and Rousseau, and Jacana Media sometimes publish them. One Kwela collection, Niq Mhlongo's *Soweto, Under the Apricot Tree*, sold well for a South African book, with nearly 2,000 copies selling in two months. For context, publishers often print 'less than a thousand copies of a South African novel in English, hoping to sell between six hundred and eight hundred'.[10] This scale of these sales is in no small measure due to Mhlongo's dynamic engagement with book clubs, where many copies of his collection were sold. These groups and the great success of Mhlongo's writings may well open future opportunities for short story publication.

Several magazines and online platforms also provide venues for new work. Discussing the South African short story in the 1960s, Walter Ehmeir noted that '[t]he great importance of short fiction in South African imaginative writing can be explained to a large extent by th[e] particular infrastructure of publication possibilities actually available to writers. Short texts were perfectly suited to publication in such a medium as the magazine.'[11] During the period Ehmeir describes, *Drum* and *Staffrider* regularly published short stories, but this stopped after their transformation or demise. There are, however, still a few magazine outlets: *New Contrast* continues to publish short stories, as do online venues such as *The Chimurenga Chronic*, the *Kalahari Review*, and the *Johannesburg Review of Books*. Until 2019, *Prufrock* put out six print issues a year, and often featured short fiction. Publications such as these provide essential forums for authors at the beginning of their careers as well as more established names.

---

9 Tom Eaton, 'Editorial', *New Contrast*, 33.1 (2005), v–vi (p. v).
10 Niq Mhlongo, 'South Africa's Cultural Game-Changers: Niq Mhlongo Believes Book Clubs are Changing the Literary Landscape', *The Johannesburg Review of Books*, 2018, <https://johannesburgreviewofbooks.com/2018/07/02/city-editor-south-africas-cultural-game-changers-niq-mhlongo-believes-book-clubs-are-changing-the-literary-landscape/> (accessed 22 October 2022).
11 Ehmeir, 'Publishing South African Literature', p. 114.

Publishing opportunities for short fiction offer a somewhat mixed picture, but another development looks likely to promote the short story in South Africa: the growth of the creative writing programme. Another version of *The Short Story after Apartheid*, one weighted more towards the sociology of literature than literary form, might easily have spent more time on this major shift. In America and the UK there has been something of a revival in short fiction, a phenomenon that author and journalist William Boyd attributes to 'the massive increase in creative-writing degree courses'.[12] Although perhaps not to the same degree as in America and the UK, there has also been a sharp increase in the number of creative writing programmes in South Africa.[13] Creative writing master's degrees are now offered at most of the major South African universities, including Cape Town (founded 1992), UKZN (2000), Stellenbosch (2000), the Witwatersrand (2008/9), the University of the Free State (2009), Pretoria (2009), Rhodes (2011), and Nelson Mandela Metropolitan University (2015). This boom in such programmes provides a welcome space for literary endeavour, while indicating the increasing professionalisation of writing, not to mention the lucrative financial potential such programmes hold for universities.

Among the authors I discuss, three out of five have either studied or taught creative writing in a university context. While Gordimer and Mpe did not, to the best of my knowledge, study or teach creative writing in an institutional context, Rose-Innes completed an MA at the University of Cape Town's Centre for Creative Writing under J.M. Coetzee in 1999, and later taught on the course before completing a PhD in creative writing at the University of East Anglia in 2018. Zoë Wicomb, until her retirement in 2012, was a professor of creative writing at the University of Strathclyde in Glasgow, Scotland, and has also taught in South Africa. Ivan Vladislavić is currently Distinguished Professor of Creative Writing at the University of the Witwatersrand. Many other prominent South African authors, such as Lauren Beukes, Breyten Breytenbach, André Brink, Imraan Coovadia, Damon Galgut, Etienne van Heerden, Christopher Hope, Leon de Kock, Siphiwo Mahala, Rian Malan, Deon

---

12 William Boyd, 'Brief Encounters', *The Guardian*, 2 October 2004, <http://www.theguardian.com/books/2004/oct/02/featuresreviews.guardianreview38> (accessed 20 October 2022).
13 Kasia Boddy provides data showing that the number of MFA programmes in the USA increased from 32 in 1975 to 153 in 2009, with an increase of 44 programmes since 2004 alone. Boddy, *The American Short Story*, p. 104.

Meyer, Niq Mhlongo, and Masande Ntshanga have either studied or taught on creative writing programmes, suggesting that these spaces play an important role in shaping contemporary literary culture. Rose-Innes, for example, describes these programmes as 'instrumental in generating a large number of proficient manuscripts and many new writers in a way that I think is having a growing effect on publishing in South Africa'.[14]

The expansion of creative writing degrees is likely to have at least three important consequences for the short story in South Africa. First, more short stories will be written. While the goal for most creative writing students is publication, which in the current publishing climate often means a novel, shorter texts are more manageable for teaching purposes, and so students regularly write short stories. This increase in the number of stories being written will surely lead to more being published. Secondly, more short stories will be read, as teaching how to write inevitably entails teaching how to read. As Mary Rohrberger observes of American MFAs, 'the university was not only hiring writers and producing writers skilled in the form but also training readers. In this way, the academy created a reading public knowledgeable in how to read a short story.'[15] Training readers is also central to South African creative writing programmes. Henning J. Pieterse, who has written an overview of creative writing programmes in South Africa, notes that across all of the programmes he has analysed, '[e]en kernkomponent is duidelik: studente word deur die bank gedwing om wyd te lees' [One key component stands out: without exception, students are forced to read widely].[16] This is backed up by Wicomb's comments on her teaching, which includes directed writing exercises, but also 'exercises in close reading of exemplary set texts […] A writer has after all to be a competent reader.'[17] Training readers in this way will further create a market for the short story, as emerging writers seek examples through which to master the form.

---

14 Henrietta Rose-Innes, 'Unlike Lightning "Poison" Has Struck Twice', *The M&G Online*, <https://mg.co.za/article/2008-07-23-unlike-lightning-poison-has-struck-twice/> (accessed 5 October 2019).

15 Erin Fallon and others (eds), *A Reader's Companion to the Short Story in English* (Westport, CT: Greenwood, 2001), p. 1. Cited in March-Russell, *The Short Story*, p. 77.

16 Henning J. Pieterse, 'Die Dosering van Skryfkuns Aan Suid-Afrikaanse Universiteite: 'n Oorsig', *Literator*, 34.2 (2013), 1–12 (p. 11). My translation.

17 Wicomb and Attridge, 'Zoë Wicomb in Conversation'.

A third consequence, perhaps more speculative, is that such programmes could shape the kinds of writing produced, perhaps even leading to a distillation of certain aesthetic and thematic precepts. As greater numbers of published authors pass through such programmes, and some eventually then teach on them, this could have a focalising influence on the kinds of stories written and published. For example, Rose-Innes observes that while she was 'always aware of rhythm and word choice', it was the experience of having 'pages marked up by J.M. Coetzee' that fully made her aware of 'the degree of word-by-word attention that was necessary'.[18] It is precisely this close attention to sentence-level detail that makes her work so vivid and appealing. Wicomb notes that in her teaching she has students 'practise various modes of narration, for example, free indirect speech, focalizing through a character, representation of thought', three aspects in which her own fiction excels.[19] This kind of attention to sentence-level detail and the nuts and bolts of fiction writing suggests that greater technical proficiency may emerge from these programmes. Further, Mark McGurl, in his study of American MFA programmes, notes that these courses are often generative of particular kinds of writing. He sees this as stemming from three tenets of creative writing teaching – experience, creativity, and craft – that are epitomised in the mantras: 'Write what you know', 'Find your voice', and 'Show don't tell'.[20] If the first of these promotes a focus on exploring one's identity, and the second on extending a capacity for expression beyond individual selfhood, the last suggests a preference for texts written in a sparse, elliptical, implicatory style. Creative writing programmes in South Africa have certainly been influenced by the American model in terms of their format, most often that of the workshop seminar, but it is probably too early to tell if the same tenets will be followed or if different kinds of aesthetic change might come about. In any case, they are likely to grapple with similar issues of identity, voice, and style.

Creative writing programmes in South Africa attract not only local students, but also students from other African countries and beyond. This global dimension promises a greater opening out of South African

---

18 Henrietta Rose-Innes and Ashraf Jamal, 'Ashraf Jamal in Conversation with Henrietta Rose-Innes', 2006, <http://www.oulitnet.co.za/chain/ashraf_jamal_vs_henrietta_rose_innes.asp> (accessed 17 October 2022).
19 Wicomb and Attridge, 'Zoë Wicomb in Conversation', p. 218.
20 Mark McGurl, *The Program Era: Postwar Fiction and the Rise of Creative Writing* (Cambridge, MA: Harvard University Press, 2009), p. 23.

fiction onto other geographies, and perhaps points towards a closer alignment with the 'global literary marketplace' of an international reading public.[21] Depending on one's point of view, this is either to be celebrated or mourned. Jack Cope, writing in 1970, was already critical of the effects of internationalisation. While acknowledging that '[o]n some counts, the sifting and refining process of "grooming" work for a sophisticated foreign market will result in improvements in style and technique', he held that 'in most ways the effect is harmful; it produces a kind of polyglot writing, dulled insights, and a loss of verbal clarity and colour'.[22] This statement perhaps underplays the global dimension of earlier South African fiction, but in any case the increasing internationalisation of post-apartheid writing – visible for example in Wicomb's translocal texts, Vladislavić's melancholy wanderings amid German monuments, and the cosmopolitan settings of S.J. Naudé's *The Alphabet of Birds* – suggests an extension of the geographical boundaries of the South African literary imaginary.[23] This has not, however, caused the dulling and desaturation that Cope feared. Rather, it has initiated a new and exciting phase of South African writing, in which fresh vistas are opening on what it means to be a South African writer.

Given the breadth of talent in contemporary South African short story writing, it is time the form received the attention it is due from publishers, readers, and critics, both at home and abroad. I have begun this work by arguing that South African authors have made use of the short story to produce works that offer, should readers wish, structures for thinking through the unfinished project of apartheid's end. These structures do not offer the consolatory pleasure of resolution, but rather the aesthetically coherent suspension of such resolution, and so an invitation for readers to think with the text. The short story's accommodation of ellipses and aporias, fragmentary narratives, non-linear plots, and above all its very *shortness*, have allowed these authors to create striking and original works of fiction that both frustrate and satisfy, offering, in Amy Hempel's words, 'a tiny way into a huge subject'.[24]

---

21 Sarah Brouillette, *Postcolonial Writers in the Global Literary Marketplace* (Basingstoke: Palgrave Macmillan, 2007).
22 Jack Cope, 'South Africa', *The Kenyon Review*, 32.1 (1970), 78–84 (p. 82).
23 'Zoe Wicomb and the Translocal: Scotland and South Africa', <http://wicombandthetranslocal.wordpress.com/about/> (accessed 6 May 2013]; Naudé and Vladislavić, 'In Conversation'.
24 Schumacher and Hempel, 'Amy Hempel', p. 31.

Bibliography

Abrahamsson, Hans, and Anders Nilsson, *Mozambique, the Troubled Transition: From Socialist Construction to Free Market Capitalism* (London: Zed Books, 1995)
Achebe, Chinua, 'The Novelist as Teacher', in *Morning Yet on Creation Day: Essays* (Garden City, NY: Anchor, 1975), pp. 67–74
Adesokan, Akinwumi, *Postcolonial Artists and Global Aesthetics* (Bloomington: Indiana University Press, 2011)
Adhikari, Mohamed, *Burdened by Race: Coloured Identities in Southern Africa* (Cape Town: Double Storey, 2009)
———, *Not White Enough, Not Black Enough: Racial Identity in the South African Coloured Community* (Cape Town: Double Storey, 2005)
Anker, Elizabeth S., and Rita Felski (eds), *Critique and Postcritique* (Durham, NC: Duke University Press, 2017)
Attridge, Derek, *J.M. Coetzee & the Ethics of Reading: Literature in the Event* (Chicago: University of Chicago Press, 2004)
———, '"No Escape from Home": History, Affect and Art in Zoë Wicomb's Translocal Coincidences', in *Zoë Wicomb & the Translocal: Writing Scotland & South Africa*, ed. Kai Easton and Derek Attridge (Abingdon: Routledge, 2017), pp. 49–63
———, *The Singularity of Literature* (London: Routledge, 2004)
Attwell, David, *Rewriting Modernity: Studies in Black South African Literary History* (Pietermaritzburg: University of Kwa-Zulu Natal Press, 2005)
Attwell, David, and Derek Attridge, 'Introduction', in *The Cambridge History of South African Literature*, ed. David Attwell and Derek Attridge (Cambridge: Cambridge University Press, 2012), pp. 1–13
Awadalla, Maggie, and Paul March-Russell (eds), *The Postcolonial Short Story: Contemporary Essays* (Basingstoke: Palgrave Macmillan, 2013)
Bahri, Deepika, *Native Intelligence: Aesthetics, Politics, and Postcolonial Literature* (Minneapolis: University of Minnesota Press, 2003)

Bailey, Julius, and Scott Rosenberg, 'Reading Twentieth Century Urban Black Cultural Movements through Popular Periodicals: A Case Study of the Harlem Renaissance and South Africa's Sophiatown', *Safundi*, 17.1 (2016), 63–86

Bakhtin, Mikhail, *The Dialogic Imagination: Four Essays*, trans. Michael Holquist and Caryl Emerson (Austin: University of Texas Press, 1981)

Balibar, Étienne, and Immanuel Maurice Wallerstein, *Race, Nation, Class: Ambiguous Identities* (London: Verso, 1991)

Balogun, F. Odun, *Tradition and Modernity in the African Short Story: An Introduction to a Literature in Search of Critics* (New York: Greenwood, 1991)

Barkham, John, 'Nadine Gordimer', *Saturday Review*, 12 January 1963, 63

Barnard, Ian, 'The "Tagtigers"? The (Un) Politics of Language in the "New" Afrikaans Fiction', *Research in African Literatures*, 23.4 (1992), 77–95

Barnard, Rita, *Apartheid and Beyond: South African Writers and the Politics of Place* (Oxford: Oxford University Press, 2007)

———, 'Locating Gordimer: Modernism, Postcolonialism, Realism', in *Modernism, Postcolonialism, and Globalism: Anglophone Literature, 1950 to the Present*, ed. Richard Begam and Michael Valdez Moses (Oxford: Oxford University Press, 2018), pp. 99–122

———, 'Nadine Gordimer's Transitions: Modernism, Realism, Rupture', *Cycnos*, 34.3 (2018), 19–33

———, 'Relocating Gordimer: Modernism, Postcolonialism, Realism' (talk given at Queen Mary University of London, 2014)

Barnett, Clive, 'Constructions of Apartheid in the International Reception of the Novels of J. M. Coetzee', *Journal of Southern African Studies*, 25.2 (1999), 287–301

Barris, Ken, 'Fiction of Ideas', *Southern African Review of Books*, 3.6 (1990), 6–7

Barron, Michael, and Henrietta Rose-Innes, 'One Chip of Colour in a Bigger Mosaic: An Interview with South African Writer Henrietta Rose-Innes', *Culture Trip*, 2017, <https://theculturetrip.com/africa/south-africa/articles/one-chip-of-colour-in-a-bigger-mosaic-an-interview-with-south-african-writer-henrietta-rose-innes/> (accessed 26 October 2022)

Bartels-Swindells, Aaron, 'The Metapragmatics of the "Minor Writer": Zoë Wicomb, Literary Value, and the Windham-Campbell Prize Festival', *Representations*, 137 (2017), 88–111

Basseler, Michael, *An Organon of Life Knowledge: Genres and Functions of the Short Story in North America* (Bielefeld: Transcript, 2019)

Bazin, Nancy Topping, and Marilyn Dallman Seymour (eds), *Conversations with Nadine Gordimer* (Jackson, MS: University Press of Mississippi, 1990)

Beal, Joan, 'Syntax and Morphology', in *The Edinburgh History of the Scots Language*, ed. Charles Jones (Edinburgh: Edinburgh University Press, 1997), pp. 335–77
Beckett, Samuel, *Proust and Three Dialogues with Georges Duthuit* (London: Jonathan Calder, 1965)
Bendixen, Alfred, and James Nagel (eds), *A Companion to the American Short Story* (Oxford: Blackwell, 2010)
Benjamin, Walter, 'Theses on the Philosophy of History', in *Illuminations: Essays and Reflections*, ed. Hannah Arendt, trans. Harry Zohn (New York: Schocken Books, 2007), pp. 253–64
–––, 'The Storyteller: Reflections on the Works of Nikolai Leskov', in *Illuminations: Essays and Reflections*, ed. Hannah Arendt, trans. Harry Zohn (New York: Schocken Books, 2007), pp. 83–109
Bennett, Bruce, *Australian Short Fiction: A History* (St Lucia, Australia: University of Queensland Press, 2002)
Berlant, Lauren, 'Slow Death (Sovereignty, Obesity, Lateral Agency)', *Critical Inquiry*, 33.4 (2007), 754–80
Best, Stephen, and Sharon Marcus, 'Surface Reading: An Introduction', *Representations*, 108.1 (2009), 1–21
Bethlehem, Louise, '"A Primary Need as Strong as Hunger": The Rhetoric of Urgency in South African Literary Culture under Apartheid', *Poetics Today*, 22.2 (2001), 365–89
Bezuidenhout, Andries, Christine Bischoff, and Ntsehiseng Nthejane, 'Is Cosatu Still a Working-Class Movement?', in *Labour Beyond Cosatu*, ed. Andries Bezuidenhout and Malehoko Tshoaedi (Johannesburg: Wits University Press, 2017), pp. 48–61
Bhattacharya, Sourit, *Postcolonial Modernity and the Indian Novel: On Catastrophic Realism* (Basingstoke: Palgrave Macmillan, 2020)
Blair, Peter, 'The Liberal Tradition in Fiction', in *The Cambridge History of South African Literature*, ed. David Attwell and Derek Attridge (Cambridge: Cambridge University Press, 2012), pp. 474–99
Blanchot, Maurice, *The Gaze of Orpheus*, ed. P. Adams Sitney, trans. Lydia Davis (Barrytown, NY: Station Hill, 1981)
Boddy, Kasia, *The American Short Story Since 1950* (Edinburgh: Edinburgh University Press, 2010)
Boehmer, Elleke, 'Endings and New Beginnings: South African Fiction in Transition', in *Altered State? Writing and South Africa*, ed. Elleke Boehmer, Laura Chrisman, and Kenneth Parker (Hebden Bridge: Dangaroo, 1994), pp. 43–56
–––, *Postcolonial Poetics: 21st-Century Critical Readings* (Basingstoke: Palgrave Macmillan, 2018)

de Bolla, Peter, *Art Matters* (Cambridge, MA: Harvard University Press, 2001)
Bond, Patrick, 'The Mandela Years in Power: Did He Jump or Was He Pushed?', *Counterpunch*, 6 December 2013, <http://www.counterpunch.org/2013/12/06/the-mandela-years-in-power/> (accessed 12 October 2022)
Bongie, Chris, *Friends and Enemies: The Scribal Politics of Post/Colonial Literature* (Liverpool: Liverpool University Press, 2008)
'Book Review: *Loot* by Nadine Gordimer', *PublishersWeekly.Com*, <https://www.publishersweekly.com/978-0-374-19090-3> (accessed 10 October 2022)
Bornstein, George, *Material Modernism: The Politics of the Page* (Cambridge: Cambridge University Press, 2001)
Bourdieu, Pierre, *The Logic of Practice*, trans. Richard Nice (Palo Alto, CA: Stanford University Press, 1990)
Bowen, Elizabeth, 'The Faber Book of Modern Short Stories', in *The New Short Story Theories*, ed. Charles E. May (Athens, OH: Ohio University Press, 1994), pp. 256–62
Boyd, William, 'Brief Encounters', *The Guardian*, 2 October 2004, <http://www.theguardian.com/books/2004/oct/02/featuresreviews.guardianreview38> (accessed 20 October 2022)
Bradbury, Ray, *Farenheit 451* (New York: Ballantine, 1953)
Bregin, Elana, 'Editor's Preface', in *Brooding Clouds* (Scottsville: University of KwaZulu-Natal Press, 2008)
Brennan, Timothy, *At Home in the World: Cosmopolitanism Now* (Cambridge, MA: Harvard University Press, 1997)
Brink, André, *Kennis van die Aand* (Cape Town: Buren, 1973)
Brosch, Renate, 'English Summary of Short Story: Textsorte und Leseerfahrung', *WVT Trier*, 2007, <http://www.wvttrier.de/top/summary%20(Short%20Story)%20_%20Brosch.pdf> (accessed 23 August 2022)
Brouillette, Sarah, 'Literature is Liberalism', *Jacobin Magazine*, 2014, <https://www.jacobinmag.com/2014/10/literature-is-liberalism/> (accessed 22 October 2014)
———, *Postcolonial Writers in the Global Literary Marketplace* (Basingstoke: Palgrave Macmillan, 2007)
Brown, Julia Prewitt, *The Bourgeois Interior: How the Middle Class Imagines Itself in Literature and Film* (Charlottesville: University of Virginia Press, 2008)
Brown, Nicholas, *Utopian Generations: The Political Horizon of Twentieth-Century Literature* (Princeton, NJ: Princeton University Press, 2005)
Byrnes, Rita M., *South Africa: A Country Study*, 3rd edn (Washington, DC: Library of Congress Federal Research Division, 1997)
Cameron, Sharon, *Lyric Time: Dickinson and the Limits of Genre* (Baltimore, MD: Johns Hopkins University Press, 1981)

Carver, Raymond, 'Errand', *The New Yorker*, 1 June 1987, pp. 30–31
Cave, Terence, *Thinking with Literature: Towards a Cognitive Criticism* (Oxford: Oxford University Press, 2016)
Chapman, Michael, 'A Case of Story: Coetzee, Gordimer, Bosman...!', *Current Writing*, 16.1 (2004), 1–14
———, (ed.), *The Drum Decade: Stories From the 1950s* (Pietermaritzburg: University of Natal Press, 2001)
———, (ed.) *Omnibus of a Century of South African Short Stories* (Johannesburg and Cape Town: Ad Donker, 2007)
———, *SA Lit: Beyond 2000* (Scottsville: University of KwaZulu-Natal Press, 2011)
———, 'Storyteller and Journalist: Can Themba in Sophiatown', in *Art Talk, Politics Talk: A Consideration of Categories* (Scottsville: University of KwaZulu-Natal Press, 2006), pp. 47–57
Charlton, Ed, *Improvising Reconciliation: Confession After the Truth Commission* (Liverpool: Liverpool University Press, 2021)
Clarkson, Carrol, 'Locating Identity in Phaswane Mpe's *Welcome to Our Hillbrow*', *Third World Quarterly*, 26.3 (2005), 451–59
Clingman, Stephen, *The Novels of Nadine Gordimer: History from the Inside*, 2nd edn (Amherst: University of Massachusetts Press, 1992)
———, 'Surviving Murder: Oscillation and Triangulation in Nadine Gordimer's *The House Gun*', *MFS: Modern Fiction Studies*, 46.1 (2000), 139–58
Cloninger, Curt, *Some Ways of Making Nothing: Apophatic Apparatuses in Contemporary Art* (Santa Barbara, CA: Punctum Books, 2021)
Coetzee, J.M., *White Writing: On the Culture of Letters in South Africa* (New Haven, CT: Yale University Press, 1988)
Cohn, Alison S., 'Nobel Winner's "Beethoven" an Uneven Performance', *The Crimson*, 2007, <http://www.thecrimson.com/article/2007/12/14/nobel-winners-beethoven-an-uneven-performance/> (accessed 20 February 2020)
Colie, Rosalie L., *The Resources of Kind: Genre-Theory in the Renaissance* (Berkeley: University of California Press, 1973)
Colleran, Jeanne, 'Archive of Apartheid: Nadine Gordimer's Short Fiction at the End of the Interregnum', in *The Later Fiction of Nadine Gordimer*, ed. Bruce King (Basingstoke: Palgrave Macmillan, 1993), pp. 237–45
Collett, Anne, 'Writing Freedom: Nadine Gordimer and *The New Yorker*', in *Experiences of Freedom in Postcolonial Literatures and Cultures*, ed. Annalisa Oboe and Shaul Bassi (Abingdon: Routledge, 2011), pp. 341–52
Combe, Dominique, 'Preface', in *Postcolonial Poetics: Genre and Form*, ed. Patrick Crowley and Jane Hiddleston (Liverpool: Liverpool University Press, 2011), pp. vii–xii

Coovadia, Imraan, and Eve Gerber, 'The Best South African Fiction', *Five Books*, 2011, <https://fivebooks.com/best-books/south-african-fiction-imraan-coovadia/> (accessed 6 September 2022)

Cope, Jack, 'South Africa', *The Kenyon Review*, 32.1 (1970), 78–84

Cornwell, Gareth, Dirk Klopper, and Craig MacKenzie (eds), *The Columbia Guide to South African Literature in English since 1945* (New York: Columbia University Press, 2010)

Cox, Ailsa (ed.), *The Short Story* (Newcastle: Cambridge Scholars Publishing, 2008)

Crowley, Patrick, and Jane Hiddleston (eds), *Postcolonial Poetics: Genre and Form* (Liverpool: Liverpool University Press, 2011)

Currey, James, 'Representing South Africa in the African Writers Series', *English in Africa*, 34.1 (2007), 5–20

Currie, Mark, *About Time: Narrative, Fiction and the Philosophy of Time* (Edinburgh: Edinburgh University Press, 2007)

Davids, Yul Derek, Benjamin Roberts, Gregory Houston, and Nazeem Mustapha, 'Race and Class Perceptions of Poverty in South Africa', in *Paradise Lost: Race and Racism in Post-Apartheid South Africa*, ed. Gregory Houston, Modimowabarwa Kanyane, and Yul Derek Davids (Leiden: Brill, 2022), pp. 200–29

Davidson, Jeremy H.C.S., and Helen Cordell, *The Short Story in South East Asia: Aspects of a Genre* (London: School of Oriental and African Studies, University of London, 1982)

Davis, Emily S., 'Contagion, Cosmopolitanism, and Human Rights in Phaswane Mpe's *Welcome to Our Hillbrow*', *College Literature*, 40.3 (2013), 99–112

Delaney, Paul, and Adrian Hunter (eds), *The Edinburgh Companion to the Short Story in English* (Edinburgh: Edinburgh University Press, 2019)

D'hoker, Elke, 'The Short Story Anthology', in *The Edinburgh Companion to the Short Story in English*, ed. Paul Delaney and Adrian Hunter (Edinburgh: Edinburgh University Press, 2019), pp. 108–24

Dickinson, Philip, *Romanticism and Aesthetic Life in Postcolonial Writing* (Basingstoke: Palgrave Macmillan, 2018)

Dimitriu, Ileana, 'Shifts in Gordimer's Recent Short Fiction: Story-telling after Apartheid', *Current Writing: Text and Reception in Southern Africa*, 17.1 (2005), 90–107

Driver, Dorothy, 'The Fabulous Fifties: Short Fiction in English', in *The Cambridge History of South African Literature*, ed. David Attwell and Derek Attridge (Cambridge: Cambridge University Press, 2012), pp. 387–409

———, 'Modern South African Literature in English: A Reader's Guide to Some Recent Critical and Bibliographic Resources', *World Literature Today*, 70.1 (1996), 99–106

———, 'The Struggle over the Sign: Writing and History in Zoë Wicomb's Art', *Journal of Southern African Studies*, 36.3 (2010), 523–42

Driver, Dorothy, Ann Dry, Craig MacKenzie, and John Read (eds), *Nadine Gordimer: A Bibliography of Primary and Secondary Sources, 1937–1992* (London: Hans Zell, 1994)

Dube, Kgauhelo, Corinne Sandwith, Khulukazi Soldati-Kahimbaara, and Rebecca Fasselt, 'LongStorySHORT: Decolonising the Reading Landscape – A Conversation with Kgauhelo Dube', in *The Short Story in South Africa: Contemporary Trends and Perspectives*, ed. Rebecca Fasselt and Corinne Sandwith (Abingdon: Routledge, 2022), pp. 226–41

Dubow, Saul, *Scientific Racism in Modern South Africa* (Cambridge: Cambridge University Press, 1995)

Dunton, Chris, 'Between Rural Roots and Urban Possibility', *The Sunday Independent*, 11 May 2008, p. 17

Durrant, Sam, 'The Invention of Mourning in Post-Apartheid Literature', *Third World Quarterly*, 26.3 (2005), 441–50

———, *Postcolonial Narrative and the Work of Mourning: J.M. Coetzee, Wilson Harris, and Toni Morrison* (Albany: State University of New York Press, 2004)

Durrheim, Kevin, and John Dixon, 'Racism on South Africa's Beaches: Then and Now', *Perspectives on Kwa-Zulu Natal*, 1.6 (2001), <http://www.cheryl-goodenough.com/docs/racismonsabeaches.pdf> (accessed 12 October 2013)

Eagleton, Terry, *Marxism and Literary Criticism* (Berkeley: University of California Press, 1976)

Eaton, Tom, 'Editorial', *New Contrast*, 33.1 (2005), v–vi

Ehmeir, Walter, 'Publishing South African Literature in English in the 1960s', *Research in African Literatures*, 26.1 (1995), 111–31

Emenyonu, Ernest N. (ed.), *Writing Africa in the Short Story: African Literature Today* (Woodbridge, Suffolk: James Currey, 2013)

Etherington, Ben, and Sean Pryor, 'Historical Poetics and the Problem of Exemplarity', *Critical Quarterly*, 61.1 (2019), 3–17

Evans, Lucy, *Communities in Contemporary Anglophone Caribbean Short Stories* (Liverpool: Liverpool University Press, 2014)

Evans, Lucy, Mark McWatt, and Emma Smith (eds), *The Caribbean Short Story: Critical Perspectives* (Leeds: Peepal Tree, 2011)

Eyers, Tom, *Speculative Formalism: Literature, Theory, and the Critical Present* (Evanston, IL: Northwestern University Press, 2017)

Eyre, Ronald, Frederic Raphael, John Wells, Nadine Gordimer, Richard Rodriguez, Nigel Hamilton, and others, *Frontiers* (London: BBC Books, 1990)

Fallon, Erin, R.C. Feddersen, James Kurtzleben, Maurice E. Lee, and Susan Rochette-Crawley (eds), *A Reader's Companion to the Short Story in English* (Westport, CT: Greenwood, 2001)

Farred, Grant, *Midfielder's Moment: Coloured Literature and Culture in Contemporary South Africa* (Boulder, CO: Westview Press, 2001)

Fasselt, Rebecca, Corinne Sandwith, and Khulukazi Soldati-Kahimbaara, 'Introduction: The Short Story in South Africa – New Trends and Perspectives', in *The Short Story in South Africa: Contemporary Trends and Perspectives*, ed. Rebecca Fasselt and Corinne Sandwith (Abingdon: Routledge, 2022), pp. 1–27

February, V.A., *Mind Your Colour: The 'Coloured' Stereotype in South African Literature* (London: Kegan Paul International, 1981)

Felski, Rita, *Hooked: Art and Attachment* (Chicago: University of Chicago Press, 2020)

–––, *The Limits of Critique* (Chicago: University of Chicago Press, 2015)

Feuser, Willfried, *Jazz and Palm Wine, and Other Stories* (Harlow: Longman, 1981)

Filling, Brian, and Susan Stuart (eds), *The End of a Regime? An Anthology: Scottish–South African Writing Against Apartheid* (Aberdeen: Aberdeen University Press, 1991)

Finnegan, William, *A Complicated War: The Harrowing of Mozambique* (Oakland: University of California Press, 1993)

Flatley, Jonathan, 'How A Revolutionary Counter-Mood is Made', *New Literary History*, 43.3 (2012), 503–25

Fourie, Abrie, 'Oblique', *Abriefourie.Com*, <http://www.abriefourie.com/oblique_01.html> (accessed 10 April 2021)

Frank, Joseph, 'Spatial Form: An Answer to Critics', *Critical Inquiry*, 4.2 (1977), 231–52

–––, 'Spatial Form in Modern Literature: An Essay in Three Parts, Part I', *The Sewanee Review*, 53.2 (1945), 221–40

Freud, Sigmund, 'Beyond the Pleasure Principle', in *The Complete Psychological Works of Sigmund Freud*, ed. and trans. James Strachey (London: Hogarth, 1920), XVIII, pp. 7–23

Frow, John, *Genre* (Abingdon: Routledge, 2006)

Gallagher, Catherine, 'Formalism and Time', *MLQ: Modern Language Quarterly*, 61.1 (2000), 229–51

Gandhi, Leela, *Postcolonial Theory: A Critical Introduction* (New York: Columbia University Press, 1998)

Garuba, Harry, 'The Unbearable Lightness of Being: Re-Figuring Trends in Recent Nigerian Poetry', *English in Africa*, 32.1 (2005), 51–72

Gaylard, Rob, 'R.R.R. Dhlomo and the Early Black South African Short Story in English', *Current Writing*, 17.1 (2005), 52–69

———, 'Writing Black: The South African Short Story by Black Writers' (unpublished DLitt thesis, University of Stellenbosch, 2008), <http://hdl.handle.net/10019.1/1202> (accessed 12 October 2022)
Gend, Cecily van, 'Meet Henrietta Rose-Innes', *The Cape Librarian*, 45.2 (2001), 23–24
Gennep, Arnold van, *The Rites of Passage*, trans. Monika B. Vizedom and Gabrielle L. Caffee (London: Routledge, 1960)
Gerlach, John, 'Narrative, Lyric and Plot in Chris Offutt's *Out of the Woods*', in *The Art of Brevity: Excursions in Short Fiction Theory and Analysis*, ed. Per Winther, Jakob Lothe, and Hans Hanssen Skei (Columbia: University of South Carolina Press, 2004), pp. 44–56
Ghosh, William, 'The Formalist Genesis of "Postcolonial" Reading: Brathwaite, Bhabha, and *A House for Mr Biswas*', *ELH*, 84.3 (2017), 765–89
Goldin, Ian, *Making Race: The Politics and Economics of Coloured Identity in South Africa* (Cape Town: Maskew Miller Longman, 1987)
'Gordimer Looks Towards End', *BBC*, 6 June 2003, <http://news.bbc.co.uk/1/hi/entertainment/arts/2966732.stm> (accessed 20 January 2015)
Gordimer, Nadine, 'Adam's Rib: Fictions and Realities', in *Writing and Being* (Cambridge, MA: Harvard University Press, 1995), pp. 1–19
———, 'Beethoven Was One-Sixteenth Black', in *Beethoven Was One-Sixteenth Black and Other Stories* (London: Bloomsbury, 2007), pp. 1–16
———, *Beethoven Was One-Sixteenth Black and Other Stories* (London: Bloomsbury, 2007)
———, 'A Beneficiary', in *Beethoven Was One-Sixteenth Black and Other Stories* (London: Bloomsbury, 2007), pp. 115–35
———, 'A Bolter and the Invincible Summer', in *Telling Times: Writing and Living, 1950–2008* (London: Bloomsbury, 2010), pp. 112–21
———, 'English-Language Literature and Politics in South Africa', *Journal of Southern African Studies*, 2.2 (1976), 131–50
———, 'The Essential Gesture', in *Telling Times: Writing and Living, 1950–2008* (London: Bloomsbury, 2010), pp. 409–23
———, *Face to Face: Short Stories* (Johannesburg: Silver Leaf, 1949)
———, 'The Flash of Fireflies', in *The New Short Story Theories*, ed. Charles E. May (Athens, OH: Ohio University Press, 1994), pp. 263–67
———, 'The Idea of Gardening', *The New York Review of Books*, 2 February 1984, pp. 3–6
———, *July's People* (New York: Penguin, 1981)
———, 'Jump', *Harper's Magazine*, October 1989, pp. 55–61
———, *Jump and Other Stories* (London: Bloomsbury, 1991)
———, *Livingstone's Companions* (London: Jonathan Cape, 1971)
———, 'Loot', in *Loot and Other Stories* (London: Penguin, 2004), pp. 1–6
———, *Loot and Other Stories* (London: Penguin, 2004)

— — —, *Writing and Being* (Cambridge, MA: Harvard University Press, 1995)

Gordimer, Nadine, and Ángel Gurría-Quintana, 'Taking Tea with Nadine Gordimer', *Prospect*, 21 July 2014, <http://www.prospectmagazine.co.uk/world/taking-tea-with-nadine-gordimer> (accessed 6 September 2022)

Gordimer, Nadine, and Jannika Hurwitt, 'Nadine Gordimer, The Art of Fiction No. 77', *Paris Review*, summer 1983, <https://www.theparisreview.org/interviews/3060/the-art-of-fiction-no-77-nadine-gordimer> (accessed 12 January 2021)

Gordimer, Nadine, and Hermione Lee, 'Nadine Gordimer with Hermione Lee', in *Writing Across Worlds: Contemporary Writers Talk*, ed. Susheila Nasta (London: Routledge, 2004), pp. 315–26

Gordimer, Nadine, and Henk Rossouw, 'An Interview with Nadine Gordimer', *VQR: A National Journal of Literature & Discussion*, 2007, <http://www.vqronline.org/web-exclusive/interview-nadine-gordimer> (accessed 7 October 2022)

Graham, James, *Land and Nationalism in Fictions from Southern Africa* (Abingdon: Routledge, 2009)

Graham, Lucy Valerie, 'Re-Imagining the Cave: Gender, Land and Imperialism in Olive Schreiner's *Trooper Peter Halket of Mashonaland* (1897)', *English Studies in Africa*, 50.1 (2007), 25–40

— — —, *State of Peril: Race and Rape in South African Literature* (Oxford: Oxford University Press, 2012)

Graham, Shane, 'Cultural Exchange in a Black Atlantic Web: South African Literature, Langston Hughes, and Negritude', *Twentieth-Century Literature*, 60.4 (2014), 481–512

— — —, 'The Entropy of Built Things: Postapartheid Anxiety and the Production of Space in Henrietta Rose-Innes' *Nineveh* and Lauren Beukes' *Zoo City*', *Safundi*, 16.1 (2015), 64–77

— — —, *South African Literature after the Truth Commission: Mapping Loss* (Basingstoke: Palgrave Macmillan, 2009)

Gray, Stephen (ed.), *The Penguin Book of Contemporary South African Short Stories* (Johannesburg: Penguin, 1993)

Green, Michael, 'Translating the Nation: From Plaatje to Mpe', *Journal of Southern African Studies*, 34.2 (2008), 325–42

Griem, Julika, '"The Trick Lies in Repetitions": The Politics of Genre in Zoë Wicomb's *The One That Got Away*', *Safundi*, 12.3–4 (2011), 389–406

Hallward, Peter, *Absolutely Postcolonial: Writing Between the Singular and the Specific* (Manchester: Manchester University Press, 2001)

Hanson, Clare, 'Introduction', in *Re-Reading the Short Story*, ed. by Clare Hanson (London: Macmillan, 1989), 1–9

Harrison, Nicholas, *Postcolonial Criticism: History, Theory and the Work of Fiction* (Cambridge: Polity, 2003)

Hartman, Saidiya V., *Lose Your Mother: A Journey Along the Atlantic Slave Route* (New York: Farrar, Straus, and Giroux, 2007)
―――, *Scenes of Subjection: Terror, Slavery, and Self-Making in Nineteenth-Century America* (New York: Oxford University Press, 1997)
Haugh, Robert F., *Nadine Gordimer* (New York: Twayne, 1974)
Head, Dominic, *The Modernist Short Story: A Study in Theory and Practice* (Cambridge: Cambridge University Press, 2009)
―――, *Nadine Gordimer* (Cambridge: Cambridge University Press, 1994)
Heerden, Etienne van, *A Library to Flee*, trans. Henrietta Rose-Innes (Cape Town: Queillerie, 2022)
Hemingway, Ernest, *Death in the Afternoon* (New York: Charles Scribner's Sons, 1932)
Heyns, Michiel, '"Separate Families, Separate Worlds, the Same Native Space": Aspects of the South African Short Story', *Current Writing*, 17.1 (2005), 167–84
Hiddleston, Jane, 'Introduction', in *Postcolonial Poetics: Genre and Form*, ed. Patrick Crowley and Jane Hiddleston (Liverpool: Liverpool University Press, 2011), pp. 1–12
Hoad, Neville, 'An Elegy for African Cosmopolitanism: Phaswane Mpe's *Welcome to Our Hillbrow*', in *African Intimacies: Race, Homosexuality, and Globalization* (Minneapolis: University of Minnesota Press, 2007), pp. 113–26
Holtz, William, 'Spatial Form in Modern Literature: A Reconsideration', *Critical Inquiry*, 4.2 (1977), 271–83
Huggan, Graham, 'Echoes from Elsewhere: Gordimer's Short Fiction as Social Critique', *Research in African Literatures*, 25.1 (1994), 61–73
Hunter, Adrian, *The Cambridge Introduction to the Short Story in English* (Cambridge: Cambridge University Press, 2007)
Hunter, Eva, and Craig MacKenzie (eds), *Between the Lines II: Interviews with Nadine Gordimer, Menán Du Plessis, Zoë Wicomb, Lauretta Ngcobo* (Grahamstown: National English Literary Museum, 1993)
Hunter Brown, Suzanne, 'Discourse Analysis and the Short Story', in *Short Story Theory at a Crossroads*, ed. Susan Lohafer and Jo Ellyn Clarey (Baton Rouge: Louisiana State University Press, 1989), pp. 217–48
Ibanez, Jose R., Jose Francisco Fernandez, and Carmen M. Bretones (eds), *Contemporary Debates on the Short Story* (Bern: Peter Lang, 2007)
Ingarden, Roman, *The Literary Work of Art: An Investigation on the Borderlines of Ontology, Logic, and Theory of Literature*, trans. George G. Grabowicz (Evanston, IL: Northwestern University Press, 1973)
Irlam, Shaun, 'Unravelling the Rainbow: The Remission of Nation in Post-Apartheid Literature', *South Atlantic Quarterly*, 103.4 (2004), 695–718

Jacobs, Johan U., 'Finding a Safe House of Fiction in Nadine Gordimer's *Jump and Other Stories*', in *Telling Stories: Postcolonial Short Fiction in English*, ed. Jacqueline Bardolph (Amsterdam: Rodopi, 2001), pp. 197–204

Jameson, Fredric, *The Political Unconscious: Narrative as a Socially Symbolic Act* (Ithaca, NY: Cornell University Press, 1981)

–––, *Postmodernism: Or, the Cultural Logic of Late Capitalism* (Durham, NC: Duke, 1991)

–––, 'Third-World Literature in the Era of Multinational Capitalism', *Social Text*, 15 (1986), 65–88

Jauss, Hans Robert, *Towards an Aesthetic of Reception*, trans. Timothy Bahti (Minneapolis: University of Minnesota Press, 1982)

Kaufman, Robert, 'Everybody Hates Kant: Blakean Formalism and the Symmetries of Laura Moriarty', *MLQ: Modern Language Quarterly*, 61.1 (2000), 131–55

Kennedy, A.L., '"Small in a Way That a Bullet is Small": Reflections on Writing Short Stories', in *The Short Story*, ed. Ailsa Cox (Newcastle: Cambridge Scholars Publishing, 2008), pp. 1–10

King, Bruce, 'Introduction: A Changing Face', in *The Later Fiction of Nadine Gordimer*, ed. Bruce King (Basingstoke: Palgrave Macmillan, 1993), pp. 1–17

Kirschenblatt-Gimblett, Barbara, 'Objects of Ethnography', in *Exhibiting Culture: The Poetics and Politics of Museum Display*, ed. Steven D. Lavine and Ivan Karp (Washington, DC: Smithsonian Institution, 1991), pp. 386–433

Kock, Leon de, *Losing the Plot: Crime, Reality and Fiction in Postapartheid South African Writing* (Johannesburg: Wits University Press, 2016)

Kolski Horwitz, Alan, *Meditations of a Non-White White* (Johannesburg: Dye Hard, 2012)

Kornbluh, Anna, *The Order of Forms: Realism, Formalism, and Social Space* (Chicago: University of Chicago Press, 2019)

Kossew, Sue, 'Re-Reading the Past: Monuments, History and Representation in Short Stories by Ivan Vladislavić and Zoë Wicomb', *Journal of Southern African Studies*, 36.3 (2010), 571–82

Kramnick, Jonathan, and Anahid Nersessian, 'Form and Explanation', *Critical Inquiry*, 43.3 (2017), 650–69

Kunin, Aaron, *Character as Form* (London: Bloomsbury, 2019)

Lacan, Jacques, *Livre V: Les Formations de l'inconscient, 1957–1958*, ed. Jacques-Alain Miller (Paris: Seuil, 1998)

Lahiff, Edward, 'Q&A: Land Reform in South Africa', *PBS*, 2010, <http://archive.pov.org/promisedland/land-reform-in-south-africa/> (accessed 12 October 2022)

Lane, Lauriat, 'Spatial Form in Literature: MacLeish's "Einstein"', *ARIEL: A Review of International English Literature*, 15.3 (1984), 35–47

Lauder, Hugh, 'Introduction', *Landfall*, 44.4 (1990), 395–96

Lazarus, Neil, 'Modernism and Modernity: T.W. Adorno and Contemporary White South African Literature', *Cultural Critique*, 5 (1986), 131–55
———, *The Postcolonial Unconscious* (Cambridge: Cambridge University Press, 2011)
Lec, Stanisław, *Unkempt Thoughts*, trans. Jacek Gałązka (London: Minerva, 1962)
Lefebvre, Henri, *The Production of Space*, trans. Donald Nicholson-Smith (Oxford: Blackwell, 1991)
Lefevere, André, *Translation, Rewriting, and the Manipulation of Literary Fame* (London: Routledge, 1992)
Leibbrandt, Murray, Ingrid Woolard, Arden Finn, and Jonathan Argent, *Trends in South African Income Distribution and Poverty since the Fall of Apartheid* (Paris: Organisation for Economic Co-operation and Development, 28 May 2010), <http://www.oecd-ilibrary.org/content/workingpaper/5kmmsot7p1ms-en> (accessed 13 May 2013)
Leibowitz, Vicki, 'Making Memory Space: Recollection and Reconciliation in Post Apartheid South African Architecture' (unpublished master's thesis, RMIT University, 2008), <https://researchrepository.rmit.edu.au/esploro/outputs/9921861490601341> (accessed 10 August 2022)
Leighton, Angela, *On Form: Poetry, Aestheticism, and the Legacy of a Word* (Oxford: Oxford University Press, 2007)
Lenta, Margaret, 'Introduction', *Current Writing*, 17.1 (2005), i–iv
Levine, Caroline, *Forms: Whole, Rhythm, Hierarchy, Network* (Princeton, NJ: Princeton University Press, 2015)
Levinson, Marjorie, 'What is New Formalism?', *PMLA*, 122.2 (2007), 558–69
Lindfors, Bernth, 'Post-War Literature in English by African Writers from South Africa: A Study of the Effects of Environment upon Literature', *Phylon*, 27 (1966), 50–62
Livingstone, Douglas, *A Littoral Zone* (Cape Town: Carrefour, 1991)
Loesberg, Jonathan, *A Return to Aesthetics: Autonomy, Indifference, and Postmodernism* (Stanford, CA: Stanford University Press, 2005)
Lohafer, Susan, *Coming to Terms with the Short Story* (Baton Rouge: Louisiana State University Press, 1983)
López, María J., 'Communities of Mourning and Vulnerability: Zakes Mda's "Ways of Dying" and Phaswane Mpe's "Welcome to Our Hillbrow"', *English in Africa*, 40.1 (2013), 99–117
MacKenzie, Craig, *The Oral-Style South African Short Story in English: A.W. Drayson to H.C. Bosman* (Amsterdam: Rodopi, 1999)
Macmillan, Hugh William, and Lucy Valerie Graham, 'The "Great Coloured Question" and the Cosmopolitan: Fiction, History and Politics in David's Story', *Safundi*, 12.3-4 (2011), 331–47
MacPherson, Sandra, 'A Little Formalism', *ELH*, 82.2 (2015), 385–405

Marais, Susan, '(Re-)Inventing Our Selves/Ourselves: Identity and Community in Contemporary South African Short Fiction Cycles' (PhD thesis, Rhodes University, 2014), <http://hdl.handle.net/10962/d1016357> (accessed 16 September 2022)

March-Russell, Paul, *The Short Story: An Introduction* (Edinburgh: Edinburgh University Press, 2009)

Maseko, Bheki, *Mamlambo and Other Stories* (Johannesburg: COSAW, 1991)

Matlou, Joël, *Life at Home, and Other Stories* (Johannesburg: COSAW, 1991)

Mbembé, Achille, 'Necropolitics', trans. Libby Meintjes, *Public Culture*, 15.1 (2003), 11–40

McClintock, Anne, *Imperial Leather: Race, Gender, and Sexuality in the Colonial Contest* (New York: Routledge, 1995)

McDonald, Peter D., *The Literature Police: Apartheid Censorship and Its Cultural Consequences* (Oxford: Oxford University Press, 2009)

McGurl, Mark, *The Program Era: Postwar Fiction and the Rise of Creative Writing* (Cambridge, MA: Harvard University Press, 2009)

McKenzie, Ray, and Gary Nisbet, *Public Sculpture of Glasgow* (Liverpool: Liverpool University Press, 2001)

McPherson, Annika, 'Tracing the Rural in the Urban: Re-Reading Phaswane Mpe's *Welcome to Our Hillbrow* through *Brooding Clouds*', in *Re-Inventing the Postcolonial (in the) Metropolis*, ed. Cecile Sandten and Annika Bauer (Leiden: Brill, 2016), pp. 55–69

Melas, Natalie, *All the Difference in the World: Postcoloniality and the Ends of Comparison* (Stanford, CA: Stanford University Press, 2006)

Messud, Claire, 'Lost Things Revealed', *The New York Times*, 4 May 2003, <http://www.nytimes.com/2003/05/04/books/lost-things-revealed.html> (accessed 16 January 2020)

Meyer, Stephan, and Thomas Olver, 'Zoë Wicomb Interviewed on Writing and Nation', *Journal of Literary Studies*, 18.1–2 (2002), 182–98

Mhlongo, Niq, 'South Africa's Cultural Game-Changers: Niq Mhlongo Believes Book Clubs are Changing the Literary Landscape', *The Johannesburg Review of Books*, 2018, <https://johannesburgreviewofbooks.com/2018/07/02/city-editor-south-africas-cultural-game-changers-niq-mhlongo-believes-book-clubs-are-changing-the-literary-landscape/> (accessed 22 October 2022)

Mhlongo, Niq, Rebecca Fasselt, and Corinne Sandwith, '"My Stories Will Remain Written the Way I Talk": A Conversation with Niq Mhlongo', in *The Short Story in South Africa: Contemporary Trends and Perspectives*, ed. Rebecca Fasselt and Corinne Sandwith (Abingdon: Routledge, 2022), pp. 242–55

Miles, Jack, 'A Crime of Passion: Review of *The House Gun*', *New York Times*, 1 February 1998 <http://www.nytimes.com/books/98/02/01/reviews/980201.01milest.html> (accessed 10 October 2022)

Miller, John, and Mariangela Palladino, 'Glasgow's Empire Exhibition and the Interspatial Imagination in "There's the Bird That Never Flew"', in *Zoë Wicomb & the Translocal: Writing Scotland and South Africa*, ed. Kai Easton and Derek Attridge (Abingdon: Routledge, 2017), pp. 148–65

Mitchell, W.J.T., 'Diagrammatology', *Critical Inquiry*, 7.3 (1981), 622–33

———, 'Spatial Form in Literature: Toward a General Theory', *Critical Inquiry*, 6.3 (1980), 539–67

Modisane, Bloke, *Blame Me on History* (London: Thames and Hudson, 1963)

Moffett, Helen, 'Henrietta Rose-Innes's *Homing*: A Review that's also about Editing', *Books LIVE*, 2010, <http://helenmoffett.bookslive.co.za/blog/2010/09/17/henrietta-rose-inness-homing-a-review-thats-also-about-editing/> (accessed 12 October 2022)

Morphet, Tony, 'Stranger Fictions: Trajectories in the Liberal Novel', *World Literature Today*, 70.1 (1996), 53–58

Mpe, Phaswane, *Brooding Clouds* (Scottsville: University of KwaZulu-Natal Press, 2008)

———, *Welcome to Our Hillbrow* (Pietermaritzburg: University of Natal Press, 2001)

Mpe, Phaswane, and Lizzy Attree, 'Healing with Words: Phaswane Mpe Interviewed by Lizzy Attree', *The Journal of Commonwealth Literature*, 40.3 (2005), 139–48

Mphahlele, Es'kia, 'South African Literature vs the Political Morality', *English Academy Review*, 1.1 (1983), 8–28

Munro, Alice, and Cara Feinberg, 'Bringing Life to Life', *The Atlantic*, December 2001, <http://www.theatlantic.com/magazine/archive/2001/12/bringing-life-to-life/303056/> (accessed 3 December 2015)

Mzamane, Mbulelo, 'Introduction', in *Hungry Flames and Other Black South African Short Stories*, ed. Mbulelo Mzamane (London: Longman, 1986), pp. ix–xxvi

Mzamane, Mbulelo Visikhungo (ed.), *Words Gone Two Soon: A Tribute to Phaswane Mpe & K. Sello Duiker* (Pretoria: Umgangatho Media & Communications, 2005)

Naudé, S.J., and Ivan Vladislavić, 'In Conversation: S.J. Naudé and Ivan Vladislavić', *Granta*, 12 December 2014, <https://granta.com/in-conversation-s-j-naude-and-ivan-vladislavic/> (accessed 29 July 2021)

Ndebele, Njabulo S., *Fools and Other Stories* (Johannesburg: Ravan, 1983)

———, 'The Rediscovery of the Ordinary: Some New Writings in South Africa', *Journal of Southern African Studies*, 12.2 (1986), 143–57

Newman, Judie, 'Jump Starts: Nadine Gordimer after Apartheid', in *Apartheid Narratives*, ed. Nahem Yousaf (Amsterdam: Rodopi, 2001), pp. 101–14

———, *Nadine Gordimer* (London: Routledge, 1988)

Niehaus, Isak, 'Witches and Zombies of the South African Lowveld: Discourse, Accusations and Subjective Reality', *The Journal of the Royal Anthropological Institute*, 11.2 (2005), 191–210

Nischik, Reingard M., *The Canadian Short Story: Interpretations* (Rochester, NY: Camden House, 2007)

Nixon, Rob, *Homelands, Harlem, and Hollywood: South African Culture and the World Beyond* (New York: Routledge, 1994)

———, 'Nadine Gordimer', in *British Writers, Supplement II*, ed. George Stade (New York: Scribner, 1992), pp. 1–28

Nkosi, Lewis, *Home and Exile, and Other Selections* (London: Longman, 1983 [1965])

———, 'Postmodernism and Black Writing in South Africa', in *Writing South Africa: Literature, Apartheid, and Democracy 1970–1995*, ed. Derek Attridge and Rosemary Jane Jolly (Cambridge: Cambridge University Press, 1998), pp. 75–90

Nuttall, Sarah, 'Literary City', in *Johannesburg: The Elusive Metropolis*, ed. Sarah Nuttall and Achille Mbembe (Durham, NC: Duke University Press, 2008), pp. 195–218

O'Connor, Frank, *The Lonely Voice: A Study of the Short Story* (Cleveland, OH: World Publishing, 1963)

———, *The Lonely Voice: A Study of the Short Story* (New York: Melville House, 2011)

Ogden, Benjamin H., 'The Palimpsest of Process and the Search for Truth in South Africa: How Phaswane Mpe Wrote *Welcome to Our Hillbrow*', *Safundi*, 14.2 (2013), 191–208

Oliphant, Andries Walter, *At the Rendezvous of Victory and Other Stories* (Cape Town: Kwela, 1999)

———, 'Nonidentity and Reciprocity in Conceptualising South African Literary Studies', *Journal of Literary Studies*, 19.3–4 (2003), 237–54

Park Sorensen, Eli, *Postcolonial Studies and the Literary: Theory, Interpretation and the Novel* (Basingstoke: Palgrave Macmillan, 2010)

Parry, Benita, *Postcolonial Studies: A Materialist Critique* (London: Routledge, 2004)

Peck, Richard, *A Morbid Fascination: White Prose and Politics in Apartheid South Africa* (Westport, CT: Praeger, 1997)

Peterson, Bhekizizwe, 'Spectrality and Inter-Generational Black Narratives in South Africa', *Social Dynamics*, 45.3 (2019), 345–64

Phiri, Aretha, and Zoë Wicomb, 'Black, White and Everything In-between: Unravelling the Times with Zoë Wicomb', *English in Africa*, 45.2 (2018), 117–28

Pieterse, Henning J., 'Die Dosering van Skryfkuns Aan Suid-Afrikaanse Universiteite: 'n Oorsig', *Literator*, 34.2 (2013), 1–12

Poe, Edgar Allan, 'The Philosophy of Composition', in *The New Short Story Theories*, ed. Charles E. May (Athens, OH: Ohio University Press, 1994), pp. 67–69

Pratt, Mary Louise, *Imperial Eyes: Travel Writing and Transculturation* (London: Routledge, 1992)

Pravinchandra, Shital, 'Not Just Prose', *Interventions*, 16.3 (2014), 424–44

Propp, Vladimir Yakovlevich, *Morphology of the Folktale*, trans. Laurence Scott, 2nd edn (Austin: University of Texas Press, 1968)

Quayson, Ato, Debjani Ganguly, and Neil ten Kortenaar, 'Editorial: New Topographies', *Cambridge Journal of Postcolonial Literary Inquiry*, 1.1 (2014), 1–10

Raiskin, Judith L., *Snow on the Cane Fields: Women's Writing and Creole Subjectivity* (Minneapolis: University of Minnesota Press, 1996)

Ramazani, Jahan, *The Hybrid Muse: Postcolonial Poetry in English* (Chicago: University of Chicago Press, 2001)

Rankin, Elizabeth, and Rolf Michael Schneider, *From Memory to Marble: The Historical Frieze of the Voortrekker Monument. Part I: The Frieze* (Berlin: De Gruyter, 2019)

Rehbein, Boike, 'Social Classes, Habitus andAriocultures in South Africa', *Transience*, 9.1 (2018), 19

Reid, Robin Anne, *Ray Bradbury: A Critical Companion* (Westport, CT: Greenwood, 2000)

Riach, Graham K., 'The Late Nadine Gordimer', *Journal of Southern African Studies*, 42.6 (2016), 1077–94

———, 'Sticking Together: Ivan Vladislavić's Collage Practice', *Safundi*, 16.1 (2015), 78–95

Rich, Paul, 'Liberal Realism in South African Fiction, 1948–1966', *English in Africa*, 12.1 (1985), 47–81

Richards, I.A., *Principles of Literary Criticism* (London: Kegan Paul, Trench, Tubner, 1924)

Rive, Richard, *Emergency: A Novel* (Cape Town: David Philip, 1988)

———, *Writing Black* (Cape Town: David Philip, 1981)

Rose-Innes, Henrietta, 'Bad Places', *New Contrast*, 31.4 (2003), 26–34

———, 'Bad Places', in *Jambula Tree & Other Stories: The Caine Prize for African Writing 8th Annual Collection* (Auckland Park: Jacana Media, 2008), pp. 49–56

———, 'Bad Places', in *Homing* (Cape Town: Umuzi, 2010), pp. 129–38

———, 'Falling', in *Homing* (Cape Town: Umuzi, 2010), pp. 87–98
———, 'Falling', in *Willesden Herald: New Short Stories 4*, ed. Stephen Moran (London: Pretend Genius, 2010), pp. 211–22
———, *Green Lion* (Cape Town: Umuzi, 2015)
———, *Homing* (Cape Town: Umuzi, 2010)
———, 'Homing', in *Homing* (Cape Town: Umuzi, 2010), pp. 9–23
———, *Nineveh* (Cape Town: Umuzi, 2011)
———, *The Rock Alphabet* (Cape Town: Kwela, 2004)
———, 'Sea Creatures of the Southern Deep: A Novel' (unpublished MA thesis, University of Cape Town, 1999), OpenUCT, <http://hdl.handle.net/11427/19135> (accessed 3 May 2023)
———, *Shark's Egg* (Cape Town: Kwela, 2000)
———, 'Unlike Lightning "Poison" Has Struck Twice', *The M&G Online*, <https://mg.co.za/article/2008-07-23-unlike-lightning-poison-has-struck-twice/> (accessed 5 October 2019)
Rose-Innes, Henrietta, and Diane Awerbuck, 'Interview: Henrietta Rose-Innes', *Times Live*, 29 August 2010, <http://www.timeslive.co.za/lifestyle/books/article626233.ece/Henrietta-Rose-Innes>(accessed 30 November 2013)
Rose-Innes, Henrietta, and Ashraf Jamal, 'Ashraf Jamal in Conversation with Henrietta Rose-Innes', 2006, <http://www.oulitnet.co.za/chain/ashraf_jamal_vs_henrietta_rose_innes.asp> (accessed 17 October 2022)
Rose-Innes, Henrietta, and Michelle McGrane, 'Michelle McGrane in Conversation with Henrietta Rose-Innes', *LitNet*, 2006, <http://www.oulitnet.co.za/nosecret/henrietta_rose_innes.asp> (accessed 10 December 2022)
Rose-Innes, Henrietta, and Katie Reid, 'Q&A: Henrietta Rose-Innes – "New Voices from South Africa" at the Edinburgh International Book Festival', *Africa in Words*, 2013, <http://africainwords.com/2013/08/23/qa-henrietta-rose-innes-new-voices-from-south-africa-at-the-edinburgh-international-book-festival/> (accessed 30 November 2021)
Rose-Innes, Henrietta, and Graham K. Riach, '"Concrete Fragments": An Interview with Henrietta Rose-Innes', *The Journal of Commonwealth Literature*, 55.1 (2020), 111–20
———, unpublished interview with Henrietta Rose-Innes, 2013
Rossetti, Dante Gabriel, *Ballads and Sonnets* (London: Ellis and White, 1881)
Sachs, Albie, 'Preparing Ourselves for Freedom', in *Spring Is Rebellious: Arguments about Cultural Freedom*, ed. Ingrid de Kok and Karen Press (Cape Town: Buchu, 1990), pp. 19–29
Said, Edward, *The World, the Text, and the Critic* (Cambridge, MA: Harvard University Press, 1983)

Samuelson, Meg, 'Literary Inscriptions on the South African Beach: Ambiguous Settings, Ambivalent Textualities', in *The Beach in Anglophone Literatures and Cultures: Reading Littoral Space*, ed. Virginia Richter and Ursula Kluwick (Farnham: Ashgate, 2015), pp. 121–38

Sarinjeive, Devi, 'Book Review', *English Academy Review*, 18.1 (2001), 166–72

Sartre, Jean-Paul, *L'imaginaire: psychologie phénoménologique de l'imagination* (Paris: Gallimard, 1940)

Schumacher, Michael, and Amy Hempel, 'Amy Hempel', in *Reasons to Believe: New Voices in American Fiction*, ed. Michael Schumacher (New York: St Martins, 1988), pp. 28–45

Scofield, Martin, *The Cambridge Introduction to the American Short Story* (Cambridge: Cambridge University Press, 2006)

Scully, Pamela, 'Zoë Wicomb, Cosmopolitanism, and the Making and Unmaking of History', *Safundi*, 12.3–4 (2011), 299–311

Sedgwick, Eve Kosofsky, *Touching Feeling: Affect, Pedagogy, Performativity* (Durham, NC: Duke University Press, 2003)

Seekings, Jeremy, and Nicoli Nattrass, *Class, Race, and Inequality in South Africa* (New Haven, CT: Yale University Press, 2006)

Shadbolt, Maurice, 'The Hallucinatory Point', in *The New Short Story Theories*, ed. Charles E. May (Athens, OH: Ohio University Press, 1994), pp. 268–72

Sharpe, Christina, *In the Wake: On Blackness and Being* (Durham, NC: Duke University Press, 2016)

Shattuck, Roger, *Marcel Proust* (Ann Arbor: University of Michigan Press, 1974)

Shaw, Valerie, *The Short Story: A Critical Introduction* (Abingdon: Routledge, 2014)

'South African Writers and the Problem of Languages...', *Commonwealth Essays and Studies*, 16.1 (1993), 96–103

Spivak, Gayatri Chakravorty, *Death of a Discipline* (New York: Columbia University Press, 2003)

Steenkamp, Alta, 'Apartheid to Democracy: Representation and Politics in the Voortrekker Monument and Red Location Museum', *Arq: Architectural Research Quarterly*, 10.3–4 (2006), 249–54

Stevens, Quentin, Karen A. Franck, and Ruth Fazakerley, 'Counter-Monuments: The Anti-Monumental and the Dialogic', *The Journal of Architecture*, 17.6 (2012), 951–72

Surette, Leon, 'Rational Form in Literature', *Critical Inquiry*, 7.3 (1981), 612–21

Szczurek, Karina Magdalena (ed.), *Touch: Stories of Contact* (Cape Town: Struik, 2010)

Taylor, Charmaine, 'Robben Island Jewellery – Legacy Collection by Charmaine Taylor', *Legacy Collection*, 2022, <https://legacycollection.org/?c=a3368f18ef71> (accessed 17 September 2022)

Thurman, Christopher, 'Beyond Butlerism: Revisiting Aspects of South African Literary History', *English Studies in Africa*, 51.1 (2008), 47–64

———, '"I Take up My Spade and I Dig": Verwoerd, Tsafendas and the Position of the Writer', in *Marginal Spaces: Reading Ivan Vladislavić*, ed. Gerald Gaylard (Johannesburg: Wits University Press, 2011), pp. 46–69

———, 'Places Elsewhere, Then and Now: Allegory "Before" and "After" South Africa's Transition?', *English Studies in Africa*, 53.1 (2010), 91–103

Titlestad, Michael, 'Afterword', in *The Mistress's Dog: Short Stories 1996–2010* (Johannesburg: Picador Africa, 2010), pp. 183–93

Toner, Anne, *Ellipsis in English Literature: Signs of Omission* (Cambridge: Cambridge University Press, 2015)

Trengove, Estelle, 'Lightning and Fiction: An Engineer Reads Phaswane Mpe's Brooding Clouds', *Current Writing: Text and Reception in Southern Africa*, 27.1 (2015), 38–49

Trotter, David, 'Modernist Anthropology', paper presented at the 20th Century Seminar, University of Cambridge, 2014

Trump, Martin, 'South African Short Fiction in English and Afrikaans since 1948' (unpublished PhD thesis, School of Oriental and African Studies, University of London, 1985), <https://eprints.soas.ac.uk/28643/1/10672803.pdf> (accessed 17 May 2022)

Trussler, Michael, 'Michael Trussler on Hayden White, Paul Ricoeur, and Others', *Narrative*, 20.2 (2012), 163–64

———, 'The Short Story Today: An Interview with Susan Lohafer and Charles E. May', *Wascana Review*, 33.1 (1998), 14–24

Turner-Hospital, Janette, 'What They Did to Tashi', *New York Times Book Review*, 28 June 1992, p. 12

Twidle, Hedley, '|Xam Narratives of the Bleek and Lloyd Collection', in *The Cambridge History of South African Literature*, ed. David Attwell and Derek Attridge (Cambridge: Cambridge University Press, 2012), pp. 19–41

———, 'To Spite His Face: What Happened to Cecil Rhodes's Nose?', *Harper's Magazine*, 11 November 2021, <https://harpers.org/archive/2021/12/to-spite-his-face-what-happened-to-cecil-rhodes-statue-nose/> (accessed 21 September 2022)

van der Vlies, Andrew, *Present Imperfect: Contemporary South African Writing* (Oxford: Oxford University Press, 2017)

———, *South African Textual Cultures: White, Black, Read All Over* (Manchester: Manchester University Press, 2011)

———, 'Zoë Wicomb's Queer Cosmopolitanisms', *Safundi*, 12.3-4 (2011), 425–44, <https://doi.org/10.1080/17533171.2011.586838>

———, 'Zoë Wicomb's South African Essays: Intertextual Ethics, Translative Possibilities, and the Claims of Discursive Variety', in *Race, Nation, Translation: South African Essays, 1990–2013*, ed. Andrew van der Vlies (New Haven, CT: Yale University Press, 2018), pp. 3–33

Vaughan, Michael, '*Staffrider* and Directions within Contemporary South African Literature', in *Literature and Society in South Africa*, ed. Landeg White and Tim Couzens (London: Longman, 1984), pp. 196–212

———, 'Storytelling and Politics in Fiction', in *Rendering Things Visible: Essays on South African Literary Culture*, ed. Martin Trump (Johannesburg: Ravan, 1990), pp. 186–204

Verley, Claudine, '"Errand," or Raymond Carver's Realism in a Champagne Cork', *Journal of the Short Story in English. Les Cahiers de La Nouvelle*, 46 (2006), 147–63

Visser, Nicholas, 'The Politics of Future Projection in South African Fiction', in *Black/White Writing: Essays on South African Literature*, ed. Pauline Fletcher (Cranbury, NJ: Associated University Presses, 1993), pp. 62–82

Vladislavić, Ivan, 'Frieze', in *The Loss Library and Other Unfinished Stories* (Calcutta: Seagull, 2012), pp. 47–54

———, *The Loss Library and Other Unfinished Stories* (Calcutta: Seagull, 2012)

———, 'The Prime Minister is Dead', *Tri Quarterly*, 69 (1987), 447–53

———, 'Save the Pedestals', in *The Yale Review* (Hoboken, NJ: Wiley Blackwell, 2019), pp. 165–86

———, 'Staffrider', *The Chimurenga Chronic*, <https://chimurengachronic.co.za/staffrider/> (accessed 12 October 2022)

———, 'We Came to the Monument', in *Missing Persons* (Cape Town: David Philip, 1989), pp. 69–81

Vladislavić, Ivan, Peter Beilharz, and Sian Supski, 'Ivan Vladislavić – A Tale in Two Cities', *Thesis Eleven*, 136.1 (2016), 20–30

Vladislavić, Ivan, and David Goldblatt, *TJ & Double Negative* (Cape Town: Umuzi, 2010)

Vladislavić, Ivan, and Jennifer Malec, '"The Fallible Memory is Surely at the Heart of Writing Fiction"—Jennifer Malec Interviews Ivan Vladislavić about His Latest Novel, *The Distance*', *The Johannesburg Review of Books*, 2019, <https://johannesburgreviewofbooks.com/2019/05/06/the-fallible-memory-is-surely-at-the-heart-of-writing-fiction-jennifer-malec-interviews-ivan-vladislavic-about-his-latest-novel-the-distance/> (accessed 20 September 2022)

Vladislavić, Ivan, and Corina van der Spoel, 'Ivan Vladislavić Believes Society's Monuments Should be Complex, with a Sense of Irony', *Penguin SA @ Sunday Times Books LIVE*, <http://penguin.bookslive.co.za/blog/2015/12/01/ivan-vladislavic-believes-societys-monuments-should-be-complex-with-a-sense-of-irony-podcast/> (accessed 21 September 2022)

Vladislavić, Ivan, and Jan Steyn, 'Interview with Ivan Vladislavić', *The White Review*, 2012, <http://www.thewhitereview.org/interviews/interview-with-ivan-vladislavic/> (accessed 10 June 2019)

Vladislavić, Ivan, and Christopher Warnes, 'Interview with Ivan Vladislavić', *MFS: Modern Fiction Studies*, 46.1 (2000), 273–81

'The Voortrekker Monument', *VTM*, <https://vtm.org.za/en/the-voortrekker-monument/> (accessed 8 October 2022)

Warnes, Christopher, 'The Making and Unmaking of History in Ivan Vladislavić's *Propaganda by Monuments and Other Stories*', *MFS: Modern Fiction Studies*, 46.1 (2000), 67–89

Watson, Stephen, '*Cry, the Beloved Country* and the Failure of Liberal Vision', *English in Africa*, 9.1 (1982), 29–44

Wicomb, Zoë, 'Boy in a Jute-Sack Hood', in *The One That Got Away* (Nottingham: Five Leaves, 2011), pp. 7–18

———, *David's Story* (Cape Town: Kwela, 2000)

———, '"Good Reliable Fictions": Nostalgia, Narration, and the Literary Narrative', in *Race, Nation, Translation: South African Essays, 1990–2013*, ed. Andrew van der Vlies (New Haven, CT: Yale University Press, 2018), pp. 203–16

———, 'In the Botanic Gardens', *Landfall*, 44.4 (1990), 484–92

———, 'In the Botanic Gardens', in *The One That Got Away* (Nottingham: Five Leaves, 2011), pp. 161–72

———, *The One That Got Away* (Cape Town: Umuzi, 2008)

———, 'South African Short Fiction and Orality', in *Telling Stories: Postcolonial Short Fiction in English*, ed. Jacqueline Bardolph (Amsterdam: Rodopi, 2001), pp. 157–70

———, 'There's the Bird That Never Flew', in *The One That Got Away* (Nottingham: Five Leaves, 2011), pp. 61–74

———, *You Can't Get Lost in Cape Town* (London: Virago, 1987)

Wicomb, Zoë, and Derek Attridge, 'Zoë Wicomb in Conversation with Derek Attridge', in *Zoë Wicomb & the Translocal: Writing Scotland & South Africa*, ed. Kai Easton and Derek Attridge (Abingdon: Routledge, 2017), pp. 209–19

Wicomb, Zoë, and Devi Sankaree Govender, 'A Girl in Short', *Sunday Times*, 8 April 2001, p. 12

Wicomb, Zoë, and Hein Willemse, 'Zoe Wicomb in Conversation with Hein Willemse', *Research in African Literatures*, 33.1 (2002), 144–52

Williams, Raymond, 'Realism and the Contemporary Novel', *Universities & Left Review*, 4 (1958), 23–25

Winters, David, 'Literature is What We Are Lost In', *3:AM Magazine*, 18 March 2012, <http://www.3ammagazine.com/3am/literature-is-what-we-are-lost-in/> (accessed 25 March 2021)

Wright, Austin M., 'Recalcitrance in the Short Story', in *Short Story Theory at a Crossroads*, ed. Susan Lohafer and Jo Ellyn Clarey (Baton Rouge: Louisiana State University Press, 1989), pp. 115–29

Wyk Smith, Malvern van, *Grounds of Contest: A Survey of South African English Literature* (Wynberg: Rustica, 1990)

Young, James E., 'The Counter-Monument: Memory against Itself in Germany Today', *Critical Inquiry*, 18.2 (1992), 267–96

Zimbler, Jarad, Ben Etherington, and Rachel Bower, 'Crafts of World Literature: Field, Material and Translation', *The Journal of Commonwealth Literature*, 49.3 (2014), 273–78

'Zoe Wicomb and the Translocal: Scotland and South Africa', <http://wicombandthetranslocal.wordpress.com/about/> (accessed 6 May 2013)

Zucchino, David, 'In South Africa, Mingling Peacefully Despite Fears of Race Riots, the Beaches were Quiet', *Philly*, 9 January 1990, <http://articles.philly.com/1990-01-09/news/25910265_1_whites-only-beaches-allan-hendrickse-race-riots> (accessed 10 December 2013)

Zumthor, Paul, 'Brevity as Form', trans. Laurence Thiollier Moscato and William Nelles, *Narrative*, 24.1 (2016), 73–81

Zvomuya, Percy, 'Sharp Read: Phaswane Mpe's One Great Novel', *New Frame*, 2021, <https://www.newframe.com/sharp-read-phaswane-mpes-one-great-novel/> (accessed 15 April 2022)

Index

African National Congress (ANC) 2, 3n5, 115, 139, 149, 164
Afrikaans 12, 13, 30, 26n104, 39n115, 40, 81, 118, 119, 133, 199
  literature 77–78
Afrikaner 75n1, 82, 83, 131
allegory 9, 26
  in Gordimer, Nadine 62–65, 67, 74, 206
  in Rose-Innes, Henrietta 184, 191
  in Vladislavić, Ivan 82, 84–85
analogon 191
apartheid 2–4, 14, 30–39, 41, 44, 203, 205
  in Gordimer, Nadine 48, 52–54, 66–68, 70
  in Mpe, Phaswane 138–39, 146–47, 151, 156, 162–64, 183–84, 193–95
  in Vladislavić, Ivan 76–78, 86, 88, 95
  in Wicomb, Zoë 103–04, 108, 109–12, 116, 121, 125–26, 132
Argentina 65

Banerjee, Sunandini 79, 92
Barnard, Rita 14, 50, 51, 54, 62, 72, 163, 164, 173
beaches 193–96

Belmond Mount Nelson Hotel 187
Benjamin, Walter 69–71, 87
  'The Storyteller' 56–57
Bleek and Lloyd Collection 31
Bonaventure Hotel 185, 187, 190
Bosman, Herman Charles 32, 67, 138
Bourdieu, Pierre 126, 134
Bowen, Elizabeth 143
Bregin, Elana 139–42, 145, 147
brevity *see* shortness
British Council 118–20

Caine Prize for African Writing 12, 161, 197n83
Cape Town 36, 75, 109, 115, 168, 175, 177, 183–84, 187, 193–94, 209
Carver, Raymond 188
Chavonnes Battery 183
Chekhov, Anton 52, 188
Chile 63, 65
class 37, 43, 44, 69–70, 103–36, 164, 177, 186, 194
Clingman, Stephen 49, 51
Clocktower Shopping Centre 183–85
Coetzee, J.M. 1, 107, 139, 161, 197
  as a teacher of creative writing 209, 211

coloured 32, 34, 66, 108–13, 118, 124–25, 129–31, 135, 194
creative writing programmes (MFA) 41, 209–12

Dingane 84
disconsolation 29, 88
District Six School 32, 113
Doulton Fountain 127–32
Driver, Dorothy 34n96, 50, 51, 104, 105, 122, 123, 134
Drum 30, 32–35, 37, 208

ellipsis 10, 27, 38, 43, 68, 88, 103, 104, 107, 114, 118–23, 135
Encyclopaedia Britannica 126
Eyers, Tom 20–25

form
    architecture 83
    difficulties of definition 16–17
    as a heuristic device 4–8, 15, 16–29, 27, 44, 60, 66–67, 102, 113–14, 122–23, 130–32, 135–36, 137, 138–39, 144–47, 151, 158–60, 164–70, 184–85, 192, 200–05
    new formalism and postcolonial studies 19–29
    postcolonial studies 9–10, 17–19, 203
    recalcitrance 28–29
    short story criticism 15
Fourie, Abrie 79, 93–94, 97
Frank, Joseph 44, 161–62, 164–69, 177, 185
Frow, John 204

Glasgow 118–20, 124, 125, 127–29, 133–34, 209
Gordimer, Nadine 4, 14, 33, 42, 47–74, 82, 84, 86, 98, 106, 107, 120, 123, 137, 151, 155, 161, 166, 168, 173
    career and influences 51–52
    censorship 35
    form 50–53
    liberalism 34, 36
    publishing 207, 53
    on the short story 47–50, 52
    style 38, 48n7, 53, 61
    time 48, 53–54, 57–60, 205
    works
        'Alternative Endings' 67, 71–73
        Beethoven Was One-Sixteenth Black 48, 49, 67–74
        Burger's Daughter 49, 63
        The Conservationist 1, 49, 62
        Face to Face 49, 51
        'The Flash of Fireflies' 47, 66, 169, 206
        The House Gun 61
        'Is There Nowhere Else We Can Meet?' 34, 132n80
        July's People 49, 54, 63
        Jump 48, 52, 53–60, 62, 67, 83
        'Jump' 53–60, 64, 69, 86, 155
        'Karma' 66–67, 151
        Loot 48, 52, 53, 60–67, 70, 71, 73
        'Loot' 60–67, 69, 82
        No Time Like the Present 49
        Something Out There 39

Head, Bessie 35, 37, 108, 138
Head, Dominic 49, 122
Hemingway, Ernest 26, 52

Jameson, Fredric 62, 72, 85, 172, 184, 185, 187, 190–91
    on Third-World literature 9–10
Jankowski, Christian 100–02
Johannesburg 31, 96n56, 100n65, 139, 151, 155, 157

Kaufman, Robert 6–7, 72
Kornbluh, Anna 20–24
Kruger, Paul 96

La Guma, Alex 32, 35, 108
Laroche, Léon 97
Levine, Caroline 6, 20–24
liberalism 34, 36, 37, 52, 73, 173
Loesberg, Jonathon 5, 204
Lohafer, Susan 143, 162, 169–70, 177
lyric 6, 79, 86–87, 89, 92, 95, 98–99, 179, 180, 184, 206

MacKenzie, Craig 1, 12–13, 32, 67n61, 207
Magritte, René 97
Malan, D.F. 82
Mandela, Nelson 2, 96, 209
Matshoba, Mtutuzeli 37, 138
Mbeki, Thabo 60, 62
memory 43, 5, 76, 78, 90–91, 98–101, 121, 146, 174, 185–86
   see also monuments
MFA *see* creative writing programmes
Mhlongo, Niq 162, 208, 210, 13n31
Mitchell, W.J.T. 164, 166–68, 177, 182
Modisane, Bloke 32, 35, 137, 138
monuments 109
   counter- 78
   in Vladislavić, Ivan 42–43, 75–102, 212
   Voortrekker Monument 78
   in Wicomb, Zoë 127–33
Mpe, Phaswane 1, 43–44, 136, 137–60
   Brooding Clouds 43, 137–60, 207
   career and works 139–41
   orality 153–54
   Welcome to our Hillbrow 1, 140–44, 148, 152n44, 158
Mphahlele, Es'kia 34, 35, 203
Mutloatse, Mothobi 37, 138

National Party 51, 82, 111
Naudé, S.J. 41, 88, 212
Ndebele, Njabulo 13n30, 14, 38, 39, 132, 159
The New Yorker 62

Nkosi, Lewis 34, 25, 38–39, 105
nostalgia 36, 94, 98–99
novel, the 5, 140, 171, 204
   centrality to South African literary history 1
   new formalism 20, 23
   publishing in South Africa 40, 208, 210
   relation to the short story 47, 49–50, 63, 100, 102, 107n16, 114, 142–43, 168, 184, 196–97
   role in postcolonial literary studies 9–11, 19
   time 165, 171

O'Connor, Frank 102, 106
Oliveira, Paolo 55–56
Olszański, Michał 100–01
orality 12–13, 30–31, 40, 154
Oxford Brookes University 140

Paton, Alan 1
People's Palace 127, 129
Peterson Bhekizizwe 148–49
Poe, Edgar Allan 89
poetry 20, 35–37, 87, 140, 166, 184, 204
post-apartheid 65, 108, 137, 141, 144, 203, 212
   apartheid past 48, 50, 76–77, 90, 206
   characteristics of its literature 154, 158, 179n54, 205
   difficulties of definition 2–4
   literary experimentalism 38–39, 45, 57, 63, 73, 135
   nationhood 66, 73, 74, 162
   space 164, 192
Pretoria 78, 82–83, 96, 209
publishing concerns 29–42, 207–12
   in Mpe, Phaswane 140–41, 153
   in Rose-Innes, Henrietta 174n40, 193n73
   in Vladislavić, Ivan 79, 80, 92–94
   in Wicomb, Zoë 106, 107, 114–18

race 43, 68–69, 104, 109–14, 125, 129, 131
Reagan, Ronald 101
realism 35–37, 172, 188
    in Gordimer, Nadine 50, 52, 60, 62, 64–65, 72–74, 84, 137
    in Rose-Innes, Henrietta 188, 189, 198
    in Vladislavić, Ivan 79, 80, 87, 93
Renamo 55–56
Rhodes, Cecil 75, 76, 95
Rhodes Must Fall 43, 75, 78, 95
Richards, I.A. 6, 25n71, 204
Rive, Richard 32, 34, 108, 111
Robben Island 183–84
Rose-Innes, Henrietta
    career and works 161–62
    engaged writing 161–62
    works
        'Bad Places' 162, 171, 172, 176n46, 193–201
        'Falling' 132n80, 162, 171, 174–85, 186, 195, 198, 200, 201
        Green Lion 161n1, 171, 174
        Homing 44, 161, 162, 168
        'Homing' 162, 171, 172, 176n46, 185–92, 195, 199, 201
        Nineveh 161, 176n46
        'Poison' 161
        The Rock Alphabet 161n1, 176n46
        Shark's Egg 161, 162, 172, 176n46

Sartre, Jean-Paul 191
Schreiner, Olive 32, 37
Scotland 109, 115–16, 118–35, 209
Sharpe, Christina 142, 146–49, 158
Sharpeville Massacre 36, 121
Shattuck, Roger 165, 167, 174
short story
    anthologies 4, 13, 40–42

commercial viability 207–08
cycles *see* short story sequences
history of in South Africa 29–42
sequences 12, 14, 39, 43, 66, 77, 107n16, 113, 114, 145
shortness 17, 26–29, 43, 50, 58, 114, 158, 168, 196, 206, 212
Sophiatown Renaissance 32
South African literature 1, 8, 15, 23, 29, 30, 35, 44, 130, 162
spatial form 162, 164–69
Staffrider 37, 38n112, 77n7, 79n12, 208

Taylor, Charmaine 183–84
Templeton carpet factory 133–35
temporality *see* time
Themba, Can 32, 35, 138
thresholds 59, 189, 195, 197
time 4, 7, 57, 68, 102, 206–07
    finitude 25, 61, 97, 141, 144, 148, 155, 206
    formalism 165–67, 178–79, 190, 206
    lyric 86, 87, 92, 95, 180, 206
    monuments 79, 98
    narrative 58–59, 144
    operation in short story 23, 48, 67, 69, 84, 93, 154, 178, 189, 205
    post-apartheid period 50, 53, 60, 77, 89, 154, 164
transition 2, 10, 48, 53, 54, 73, 77, 110, 154
Twidle, Hedley 31, 75, 76

Ullman, Micha 78, 91, 93–94
University of Cape Town (UCT) 75, 95, 209
University of the Witwatersrand (Wits) 139, 140, 209

van der Vlies, Andrew 14, 89, 98, 104, 107, 144, 154, 158
Verwoerd, Hendrik 32

Vladislavić, Ivan 3–4, 43, 74, 75–102
　career and influences 76–78
　intermediality 79–80, 81–85, 91–95, 98, 100–02
　lyricism 87, 89, 92, 95, 98–99
　style 77–80, 85–87, 88–90, 92, 99–100
　works
　　101 Detectives 80n13
　　'Cold Storage' 88–95
　　Double Negative 92n47, 98
　　The Loss Library and Other Stories 41, 79, 88–95
　　Missing Persons 39, 76, 77, 80, 90, 99, 100
　　Propaganda by Monuments 88, 90, 99
　　'Propaganda by Monuments' 91, 96n56, 99n61
　　'Save the Pedestals' 95–102
　　'We Came to the Monument' 80–88

Wicomb, Zoë
　career and works 108–09
　intermediality in 103
　as 'minor writer' 107–09
　works
　　David's Story 106n12
　　'In the Botanic Gardens' 103, 114–24, 126, 127, 128, 133, 135, 207
　　October 106n12
　　The One That Got Away 14, 41, 43, 103–36
　　Still Life 106n12
　　'There's the Bird that Never Flew' 103, 124–36
　　You Can't Get Lost in Cape Town 39, 107, 108
Windham-Campbell Prize for Fiction 107–08

Printed and bound by CPI Group (UK) Ltd, Croydon, CR0 4YY
21/07/2024
14530776-0003